THE WORLD OF THE HORSE

A Ridge Press Book ⬤ octopus Octopus Books

by Judith Campbell

THE WORLD OF THE HORSE

Special
photography
by
George
Rodger

Editor-in-Chief: *Jerry Mason*

Editorial Director: *Adolph Suehsdorf*

Art Director: *Albert Squillace*

Managing Editor: *Moira Duggan*

Art Production: *Doris Mullane*

Picture Research: *Marion Geisinger*

This edition published 1975 by
OCTOPUS BOOKS LIMITED
59 Grosvenor Street, London W1

Prepared and produced by The Ridge Press.

© Copyright 1975 by The Ridge Press.
ISBN 0 7064 0464 5

Acknowledgements

*I am most grateful to the Duke of Edinburgh for his
kindness in allowing me to reproduce the photographs
on pages 17 and 222. I would like to thank in
particular George Rodger for his happy collaboration;
my publisher and editor for their help and confidence;
the members of the Twala Club; Leslie Bower Cawein;
Mrs. A. B. Green, Green Pastures, Oklahoma; Lynne
Krug; Michael Kaye of Rokeby Stable; Ray Reed;
Neal Shapiro; and Walt Wiggins. J.C.*

Designed by Norman Snyder.

Printed and bound in Italy by Mondadori Editore, Verona.

To all those good friends—

two-legged and four—throughout the world,

who made this book possible.

Contents

Introduction

The sky lies leaden, a lowering gray that threatens sheets of rain or maybe snow. And for all the warmth of the morning's sunshine, which brought crocuses and daffodils from bud to blossom and tempted me to remove the cob's New Zealand rug, there is now a bite to the wind that means she will be regretting my decision.

Abandoning the seduction of a log fire, I huddle into parka and boots and whistle up Lara, the Spitz. Outside, the remaining daylight is being overtaken by the sky's steely murk, the wind moans through branches still winter-naked. By the time we reach the field, rain and sleet are hissing on the lane, Lara is as wet as I am, and the gateway has once more become a morass. Both ponies have sought the refuge of their open shed, but Jobiska is obviously thankful to be restrapped into her rug, and Spot, the Welshman, appreciates a hand-rub for his chilly ears.

I unhitch their empty haynets, collect those from the other paddock where Twala and Paint are peering from their shelter to watch my coming, and set off to the hay store to refill them. The wind is bellowing and the sleet has changed to snow that stings my face. I refill the nets—ten to twelve pounds of hay to each—tie them in pairs and trudge off back to the fields with them slung across my shoulders. My hands are frozen and thistle-pricked, rivulets trickle down my neck, and I wonder, as I have before and will again, why one does it. Why bother—in an age when there seems so little time to spare—with animals that even when kept under the most labor-saving conditions still demand considerable work?

For me there is always an answer. It comes to me on mornings when a hazy sun lights hedgerows frothing with blackthorn blos-

som, and Paint spooks playfully at the sere and rustling heads of last year's reeds. His hooves spurt the earth as we ride the edges of newly tilled fields, a heron flaps heavily from the water, and Lara, in optimistic pursuit, bellyflops through the duckweed she mistook for grass. Paint snorts and, sensitive to the lightest aids, he canters on until the stench of sweat, streaking the remnants of his winter coat, mingles with the sweet smell of the morning. In such a moment as this, the world belongs to horse, to dog, and to me, and I do not ask myself "why?"

Perhaps down the ages the horse entrenched himself in the subconscious of most of us. After all, only three human generations have passed since technology relieved the horse of his key role in the progress of civilization. It may be that some imperishable relationship was forged in those thousands of years since man first learned to use thigh and heel to control the pent-up forces of the horse he bestrode; that some dependency was created during the centuries of recorded history when war, trade, and tillage all were powered by the horse.

The coming of cars, airplanes, and rockets appeared to sever that relationship, although there were groups which never for a moment considered the possibility of a world without horses. The hunting fraternity, the lovers of the turf, the haute école specialists, the show jumpers and marathon riders all went their way knowing better than to accept the "enlightened" machine-age view of the horse as obsolete, as a class symbol of snob value only.

Then World War II came to demonstrate both the curses and

.the blessings of technology, and when it was over civilization had forgotten its disenchantment with the horse. In the years since the war, people all over the world have been rediscovering that life is enriched when horses and ponies are part of it. In ever greater numbers they are enjoying the partnership of horses in sports and pleasure riding, even—surprisingly—in work.

Whatever form the alliance takes, so long as it is based on mutual trust and on understanding by the human element, the result is an embellishment to the art of living. Horses are one means by which we can return to the basics we need, to solitude and silence and self-reliance in a world that appears to be out of our control.

There are snags. There are opportunists who exploit both horses and unsuspecting would-be horsemen. Comparatively few families today have a tradition of know-how when it comes to horses, and sometimes there is an awkward, even painful, period of education in horse sense to be gotten through.

Still, the possibilities of the horseman's world are innumerable. There is something for everyone, at all levels: the tough challenge of competition; a means for savoring some of the remaining solitudes of the earth; the fierce excitement of racing; the rough and tumble of rodeo, polo, and polocrosse; the almost mystical comradeship between a child and his pony, a man and his horse. Learning to ride a horse is a most worthwhile achievement. Being able to coordinate your own skill with a horse's strength and innate wish to comply can well be the pinnacle of ambition. —J.C.

1.

The Make-up of the Horseman

There are not many shortcuts to learning how to handle and ride horses and ponies to mutual advantage, although many people think there are. There is the occasional lucky mortal who is a "natural," who has an instinctive way with a horse, but otherwise it is normally only those for whom horses remain a part of the workaday world who seem to imbibe horse sense and horsemanship with their mother's milk. These are the people to whom riding comes as naturally as it does, for instance, to the Afghans, the herdsmen of Outer Mongolia, and the Turkomans, the traditional horse raisers turned farmers who live on either side of Iran's northeast border with Russia.

My own first exposure to the expert horsemanship of the Turkoman tribesmen began one evening on the high steppes southeast of the Caspian Sea. The sky, shading from deep blue to the translucence of a green pearl, was still slashed with orange and carmine along the rim of the horizon, where the sun itself had disappeared and a string of camels was grotesquely silhouetted in the afterlight. Unseen fires threw a strange glow over the landscape, softening the outline of the beehive yurts with their silent, watching inhabitants and enveloping the advancing bunch of galloping horses in a haze of pinkish dust. It was difficult to pick out the three or four riders who were bringing in the mob, and not until they leaped from their saddleless, bridleless mares could it be seen that they were young boys.

The Turkoman boys have their counterparts in different countries throughout the world, innate horsemen riding as their ancestors rode for centuries before them. Their common factor —that which makes them all "horsemen"—is their ability to inspire trust between themselves and their mounts. And it is the exercise of this ability under different conditions that explains the great variety of riding styles and tack.

The Hungarian herdsman who uses a saddle but dispenses with a girth has a different approach and seat from those of the Australian stockman. The former Olympic show jumper I watched schooling his horses in a paddock not far from New York City was proceeding differently from his wife, whose horses are destined for showing in hunter classes. When fifteen Bedouin grooms from King Hussein's Royal Stud

accompanied me into the mountains that lie between the Dead Sea and Amman, some were riding with legs thrust forward in the style of their tribal ancestors. Others, taught by the Royal Horsemaster, employed the English seat. On the stony approaches to the mountains—where a donkey rolled in gay abandon in the sun and an Arab girl glided past with only her eyes visible to betray awareness of the men's irrepressible remarks—riding style made little difference. But when Rahdi the stud groom put his mare down a one-in-two incline covered in loose shale and there was no option about following, I felt the local method came out best.

This is, of course, the answer. The "right" seat, hands, aids, and equipment are determined by what is right for the terrain, the horses, and the sport or way of life involved. Each method is correct in its own context and they are all linked by that mysterious something called "horse sense."

For me, riding western was an unknown quantity until I rode an American Quarter Horse in Oklahoma. She was a lovely mare of top show standard, with beautifully ornamented and tooled tack on a par with her quality. The required seat, with the stirrup on the ball of the foot, was more elegant than the utility style used with purely working horses.

It was one of these, a functional cow pony named George, whose cow sense compensated for a certain lack of looks, who furthered my education a few days later on a feed lot. But the stiffest test of my ability to "ride western" came later yet at Ruidoso in the high mountains of New Mexico.

Up there my guide was Ray, an old-time cowboy whose years sat lightly, who knows every prairie trail and canyon, mountainside and forest track as well as he knows the history of the region and the people who go with it—and whose autobiography would be a best-seller if he would tell it. The real cowboy of old, he said, little resembled the popular depictions of him. He was something of a dandy, always freshly shaved, proud of his clothes, and if you saw his camp, the bed made, the wood stacked, his saddle put up, and everything in place, you rode in confidence of finding a worthwhile personality to match.

The day of my initiation we drove a short way out of town trailering two of Ray's own Quarter

This fledgling
vaquero's Spanish dress,
heavy saddle, spade
or half-breed bit are
legacy of the conquistadors
and originated with
"cowboys" herding cattle
in southwestern Spain.

Opposite: Charro horse
is Mexico's most prized,
trained for range work,
parade, and specialized
roping and horsemanship
exhibitions of the
charreada.

wooden stirrups rested against the heels of my calf-high Mexican boots—the position I was taught many years ago by an Irish ex-Army captain who was a great hunting man.

This is the seat adopted by men who spend most of their lives in the saddle, and who would find it an unnecessary strain to remain with weight poised on the ball of the foot for hours on end. Everything about a cowboy—the clothes he wears, the equipment he uses, the way he rides—has been evolved with a purpose, and with safety and comfort as priorities. The high heel and pointed toe of his boots are primarily safety measures, although not without some concessions to vanity.

Cowboy country is big country, and the cowboy worked usually on his own, the boss dropping off a man and his horse at one-mile intervals. If you got in trouble there was no one to hear you holler, or if they did, help might come too late. In the old days—the late nineteenth century—the horses they rode were not too well broken, and if your animal started pitching or got spooked and set off bucking and you got tangled in a stirrup as you fell, that could be trouble.

So the boots were made with heels that gave purchase for roping, and that could not possibly slip through the stirrup whatever happened, and with toes that would pull out sharp. And if there was some unlooked-for accident, or if the worst happened and your horse fell on you, you still had your six-shooter as a last resort and you drew and killed him, quickly, before he killed you. Those six-shooters were handy too for coping with rattlers—not quite so peaceful as the one we saw weaving across a track in the Apache reservation—but contrary to the moviemakers, and despite the fixed belief of the cowboy film and novel addicts, the hand guns were seldom used against people.

There were exceptions, of course, and after Ray and I had moved off in the heat and dust, and begun scrambling up and down and around boulders and shale and the smooth, flat rocks, riding past miniature cedar trees, the brush and prickly pears, and so at last reached the trail we sought, I heard something of a legendary man who was "an artist with a gun." His name was Billy Bonney, Billy the Kid, and he had the misfortune to possess a split personality that made him uncommonly quick on the draw and capa-

Horses, a dun for himself, a black mare for me. There was no padded comfort about these horses' accommodation! They stood one behind the other, ready tacked and without so much as a bar between them, the bare floor beneath their hooves. They appeared unconcerned about the surrounding space and kept their balance without effort, even when Ray swung truck and trailer off the road and bumped into the yard behind a service station.

No one appeared to ask our business, no one appeared at all, but when the dun's shoes clacked as he was disembarking, his owner handed me the black's lines and disappeared with his gelding behind a shed. Ten minutes and a lot of hammering later they came back, Ray announcing laconically that someone had given him six nails (losing a shoe in the mountains can amount to more than an annoyance) and swung himself into the saddle.

I was already mounted on Begum, sitting deep and comfortable in a stock saddle—a derivation from the war saddles of the conquistadors —double-rigged with two cinches and a breast-strap that was to prove its worth anchoring the front end. This was a type of what is called a "balanced ride" saddle, without the older fashion of a sharp slope back to the cantle, and the fenders, the broad leathers that protect the rider's legs, were hung English-style. I was encouraged to thrust my feet home so that the wide

ble of repeated and remorseless killings. His story is inextricably linked with the Lincoln County range war that began in 1875 and ended in 1881 around and about the little town of Lincoln, New Mexico.

The trail we were seeking still bears the wheel ruts of the wagons that bounced along it over the mountains from Ruidoso to Lincoln. And in that last turbulent center of the Lincoln County war I saw the grave of John H. Tunstall, Billy's employer, whose murder set off the hostilities, and his store, near where a group of men that included Billy took shelter to shoot and kill Sheriff Bill Brady, who took his orders from Tunstall's enemies. It is a complicated tale, with many bloody, dusty interludes, ending with Billy's death at Pat Garrett's hands.

In the first hour or so of our ride there had been little time for Billy the Kid. The black mare twisted and turned and zigzagged up and down precipitous slopes, following her dun companion and sure-footed as a goat, while I thanked heaven for the raised cantle and pommel of a western saddle, for the chaps and boots that warded off brush and thorns and the tortured forms of cacti, living grotesquely through the desert's persistent drought.

The mare carried her head low, the split-ear bridle, without throat latch or noseband (the usual pattern from Oklahoma to New Mexico) somehow giving her a coquettish air. I had taken the precaution of knotting the long, divided reins, and did my best to neck-rein and leave her mouth alone. When she slipped her front feet confidently over the edge of a sheer, fifteen-foot drop to sit back on her haunches and slide to the rocky bottom of a gully, I found the horn of my saddle to have excellent uses other than for holding a roped steer.

As we wound through ravines the heat beat back off the rocks and mountainsides and the dust came up in clouds. Far overhead buzzards planed on stiffened wings, gliding the thermals, their telescopic eyes alert for the dead and the dying. In those parched regions there were few wild creatures that were not suffering from lack of food. There was a big jack rabbit, his stiffly held ears as large as himself, that galloped off over the scree, and when we hit the heights where the wind blew hot and gusty, and the distance held a dust storm, a small herd of

whitetail deer bounded away. Otherwise, in a season when the canyons should have been rushing riverbeds, the cactus studded with purple or yellow flowers, and the lush prairies stirrup-high with grass, drought had sent the game questing food far from their usual haunts.

After we hit the trail and the going eased, Billy the Kid returned in force. The years slipped away. It was easy to expect a posse around the next bend, or a wagon lurching in those still-visible ruts. We surprised a herd of cattle drinking and they began to drive up the valley before us. Ray spurred his horse and galloped along the rock-strewn slope of the mountain to pass and head the animals back, and despite the terrain I could not resist the challenge. Begum was eager

All aspects of western riding stem from cowboy work. Now western pleasure riders learn mostly from instructors, but the best way is still the old-time way—doing the work of the range, like this rancher cutting out Santa Gertrudis cattle. It means learning to neck-rein, to go in balance and mutual confidence with your quick-turning horse.

and Ray out of sight, so I let her go off on the kind of work she had been doing for the past sixteen years.

We came off the mountains with fir trees and a deep canyon to one hand, the heat of the sun pulsating off a white wall of chalk or limestone to the other, the horses slipping and sliding down rocks and slabs normally forming the bed of a stream. Ahead, as far as the eye could see, fold after fold of mountains gave back the vision of space and room to live and breathe, until they fetched up against the solid rock wall of a range that seemed to hit the sky. It was a jolt to ride down to reality and the verges of a modern road.

For all his aura Billy the Kid was not in Lincoln town that day, and neither was there a truck and

trailer for the horses, so we led them to an unused lot beside the road, hitched them by their reins and left them—still not sweating after fifteen miles of tough going—to await collection later in the day. In addition to the history of Billy the Kid, I learned that day just how "right" are western gear and western tack on a western-schooled horse for a rough, glorious ride in the mountains. I learned also just how good iced beer can taste, after three-and-a-half hours on horseback when the temperature is hitting ninety degrees F.

Those efforts at riding western were a very rough-and-ready adaptation for a particular situation, but as with any other form of riding even more enjoyment would have come with

21

the time and opportunity to learn the finer points of technique. Despite mechanization, a number of ranches still use cow ponies, and in Australia and New Zealand the stock horse is a familiar necessity in the cattleman's or grazier's life, but for the majority western riding and western horses are for pleasure. In America you can ride Texan or you can ride California, but both are part of the tradition of the Old West, both having evolved from the working skills of authentic cowboys.

The Texan adopted his ranching ideas from the Mexicans, working the vast plains with half-wild cattle taken from Mexican ranches abandoned after the 1836 Texas revolt. Within a few years these cattlemen were driving their wares to markets many hundreds of miles away, and the stock horses on which their livelihood depended were often bred from captured mustang mares, and valued more for endurance and cow sense than for beauty.

Today the Texan-style horse is still rated for his free movement and steady working ability, the saddle often double-rigged and heavier than that used with California style, the bit a snaffle or light curb "grazing bit." Many Texan horses are still taught to ground tie, so the rider uses the long split reins, bringing them up through the hand between the thumb and base of the first

finger, and divided by one finger if he pleases. The horse's free, natural head carriage must be unimpeded, but an exaggerated length of rein is no longer required.

The California style grew from that of the old Far West, where horses and horse training, accoutrements, and outlook were strongly influenced by the Spanish-Mexican tradition which in turn goes back to the Moors who conquered Spain in the eighth century. The invaders from North Africa rode fiery Barb horses that were instantly responsive to one-handed neck-reining and able to run rings around the cold-blooded Iberian chargers.

If you ride California you need a more eye-catching kind of a horse—"flashy" can be the word—a high-stepping reining horse that has been trained for years in a bitless hackamore before progressing to the heavy spade bit that, correctly used, gives higher head carriage but more collection. This bit, the beautifully worked silver ornamentation on the bridle, and the skillfully tooled leather of the saddle are some of the hallmarks of this form of riding.

Both the Texan and California styles now encourage a balanced seat. California requires closed reins, and there is a steady, light contact with the horse's mouth, but although there are exceptions "impulsion" is often a term absent

Ride all day on the range with the stirrup on the ball of the foot— elegant position required for show ring and dressage—and leg muscles would die on you. But with feet thrust home, so stirrups rest against heels of his boots, cowboy works in comfort.

Above: Western saddles are built on frame of heavy pine sewed into rawhide, providing "give" and strength needed for roping a 1,000-pound steer.

23

from western riding, and riders tend to concentrate on the front end of the horse, rather than the source of forward movement, which lies in the quarters.

Western riding is not confined to the United States. A few years ago one of our daughters, who was working her way round the world, arrived at an Australian sheep station in answer to an advertisement for a "jilleroo." Her boss appeared unimpressed by his new hand's youthful looks and pocket size. He doubted both her physical strength and her riding ability, and if only shearing time could prove her muscles when it came to heaving around the greasy, heavy clips of wool, he took steps to "take her for a ride" on her very first day.

It was not the easiest of tests, but the new hand gritted her teeth and followed without complaint, regardless of gradient, terrain, and speed, and of the fact that this was her first time in a stock saddle and with a neck-reining horse.

Within a week this form of riding—indispensable through Australia's famous overlanding and droving era of former times—had become almost as familiar and comfortable to her as it was to the modern stockman. And in the happy months to come, mustering 1,000 sheep by herself for hours on end with only her horse and trusty kelpie dog to show her how, the new jilleroo was frequently thankful for a way of riding so exactly suited to the job at hand.

"Western" was officially introduced into Britain in 1968 with the formation of the Western Horseman's Association. It is a growing cult providing a lot of interest and enjoyment among young and old alike, and where taught and practiced at the high level aimed at by the Association, it results in good riders and well-balanced, highly schooled horses.

If western riding is a relatively new British import, we can scarcely claim that riding English is one of the more recent exports to the eastern states of America. This manner of horsemanship came in with the early settlers as part of their heritage. Only in the West is English riding a comparatively new but up-and-coming sport. Most shows now have English Pleasure classes, and many versatile Quarter Horses, Appaloosas, and Arabians, the traditional animals of the West, are proving themselves as adaptable as their riders to postage-stamp saddles and the English seat.

English riding, yes, but *sidesaddle?*

It is a long time since our second daughter was seven years old and the proud possessor of a pretty, miniature Exmoor pony of devilish intent, but we do not forget the day she entered for a Fancy Dress class, riding sidesaddle.

Her Robin was of the shape that demands a crupper, and owing to the lack of both funds and expertise her saddle was a child's ordinary felt pad, astride version. The rider wore her uncle's opera hat decorated with a veil, and a long-skirted riding jacket of ancient vintage sporting a bunch of violets in the buttonhole. An ex-maternity skirt of hairy material did duty as a "habit" and was sufficiently voluminous to conceal the lack of a pommel. It also adhered the

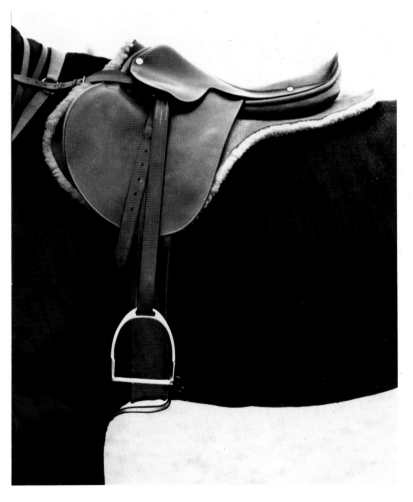

Opposite: Horses have different ways of expressing their exuberance. Invitation to ride this Persian Arab stallion at Imperial Stud, Farahabad, came with assurance, gratefully received, that the majority are "quieter under saddle."

Above: Modern saddles offer comfort and safety. This French-made "all-purpose" type has panels cut for modified forward seat, raised cantle, knee and thigh rolls.

rider to the felt saddle as though glued, keeping her there in the correct position even when Robin indulged her normal routine of kicking out at another pony and then bucking. In fact, the overall effect was so good that a first prize came our way, plus the judge's treasured comment: "How nice in this day and age to see a little lady who obviously always rides sidesaddle!"

That episode happened years ago, but the point is that even in a country where tradition is a recognized part of life, sidesaddle riding was then a rarity. Today Queen Elizabeth always rides sidesaddle for the ceremony of Trooping the Color. At a few of the larger British shows there are still a few elegant ladies, elegantly turned out, who show equally elegant hacks in sidesaddle

classes. And there is even a tiny, diminishing number who still ride to hounds in this manner, showing the way over fences both in England and Ireland, and to the hunting fraternity in Virginia. The method, done well, is undeniably attractive and, so they say, very safe, but in the hustle and bustle of modern life the disadvantages—such as the problem of mounting, not to mention the considerable extra cost of the saddle, and of a suitably schooled horse to carry it—would seem to make sidesaddle riding fairly dead. Yet California boasts sidesaddle classes with thirty or more entries. There are at least fifty lady addicts in New Jersey, and the Ladies' Hunter Side Saddle class at the International Horse Show in Washington, D.C., is a really big

event that includes jumping.

Whether you ride English or Western, bareback or sidesaddle, or aspire to the quintessence, the art of haute école as practiced in the Spanish Riding School in Vienna, if you want to get the most out of your chosen style you will have to learn the correct way. Maybe the boy, in South Africa or anywhere else, who just gets astride a horse and rides, gets no less pleasure than the rider who uses a thought-out and proven style. But for most riders, the more one learns about horses and riding the more there is to learn, and the sport becomes progressively more enjoyable. We cannot all be like the American, Rodney Jenkins, in 1974 the world's most successful professional show jumper, who says that he has always followed his father's advice just to ride as he feels. For most of us correct tuition is a must, with the emphasis on "correct." And that is something it not always easy to find or to assess. The difficulty for the would-be rider is to know what to look for and what to avoid.

So-called schools where cut prices prevail should always be suspect. Unfortunately, inflation is not bypassing the horseman's world: shoeing, food, veterinary fees, tack, and such items as fencing materials have all doubled or trebled in price. And if horses and ponies are to be even adequately looked after, if the saddles and bridles they wear are to be at least safe, the fees charged have to be in relation to rising costs. And though teaching equitation is not one of the better-paid professions, anyone with even minimum qualifications is unlikely to work for less than standard rate. So learning to ride correctly is not something that can normally be done on the cheap. Apart from prices, there are things about a riding school that will reveal even the complete novice something of the standard that prevails there.

Other people's children are twice the responsibility of one's own, so before I undertook to start up the Twala Club for novice riders, intended for members who can look after and ride ponies more or less on their own, it was essential that they should all know at least the basics of horsemanship. Their lessons were sponsored, and the riding school to which I toted them one evening per week was chosen for a variety of reasons.

To begin with all the horses and ponies there looked happy and well. They were clean and their coats had a bloom on them, the overall outline of each animal was round and not angular, and their manes and tails were neatly pulled. Their feet were obviously looked after; they did not have loose shoes or feet so overgrown that the shoe was almost invisible, and the nail heads (clenches) were not sticking up out of the hoof. Several of the inmates were distinctly elderly and had been donated or loaned by their owners—a sign anyway that they were likely to be well cared for—and these old horses and ponies were as sprightly and happy as the others, and that was the proof. The stabling was not classy, but the boxes were roomy and the bedding clean and

Cowboy riding the prairie, child and pony galloping the downs, Turkoman traversing his steppeland—each to his own style of riding, each a horseman linked by "horse sense," each a king of the faraway places.

Overleaf: Many top horsemen and competitors receive their grounding at Pony Club camps like this in South Devon.

Horsemanship is not just riding your horse or pony. It means a rounded understanding of animals' needs, competence in matters like feeding, grooming, care of feet.

plentiful. The tack room was kept tidy, each saddle and bridle hung up under its owner's name; bits were clean and leather supple.

These are details, easy to look for, that denote a well-run establishment, and if people know how to look after horses and take care of tack, the teaching will probably match up, and the horses and ponies be properly schooled for different grades of rider.

Facilities are a variable quantity. Sitting in the gallery in the early days watching the incredible knots into which my class of Twala Clubbers managed to tie themselves; having to endure the third time in one lesson when someone else's son, for whom I am responsible, hits the dust while his horse takes off; seeing some dear but inadequate little girl being carted at speed back to her position in the ride when she should have been trotting calmly in the opposite direction—many is the time I have been more than thankful for the four walls of the covered school that contained us.

A safe, enclosed school is an essential for any teaching establishment that operates in a variable climate or conducts evening classes. There must be a suitable area for jumping, although as long as the poles are reasonably heavy,

adequate fences can be built from a variety of objects ranging from hay bales to oil drums. After that, as far as facilities are concerned, the sky is the limit. It is the quality of the teaching that counts.

Just after the war, when in England we were trying to give ourselves a shake and start up some form of normal life once more, I had the opportunity of watching an Irish riding master, not then in his first youth, prove the point. In this district a group of mothers with young children who were all pony mad were striving to get their offspring some sort of proper riding instruction. Most of us seemed to have acquired a rough —and rough is the operative word—pony or even two during the war. But with time and sometimes knowledge in short supply, the pony had in most cases taken charge. So we acquired this instructor—he had taught the majority of us when we were young—and with the aid of friendly farmers willing to lend a corner of a field, started up a weekly riding class. The locality was changed most weeks so that the dedicated mothers who walked, bicycled, or even ran beside offspring and pony, often for miles, could vary the distance they had to travel. The overall fee was divided among those who came, and with the aid of a stake or two balanced on boxes for jumps, a number of very inadequate children with formerly nappy and uncontrollable ponies, were turned into a nucleus of riders who were a credit to their instructor.

The ideal, attained by very few riding schools, is to have the room and sufficient staff for an instructor to be able to ride beside each beginner, so that working without stirrups he can become confident in balance before having to worry about maneuvering a horse. This is a state of affairs certainly impossible in the last remaining riding establishment in New York City. It functions in Manhattan, in a district distinctly unfashionable, yet is fulfilling a need in an environment where its presence seems as unlikely as it is heartening.

And just what is a place like this doing in a city that epitomizes modernity and the technological age? What place have horses on those miles of dead straight, intersecting streets and avenues where the traffic crawls nose to tail?

The answer lies with the fact, not always comprehended, that we cannot live by machines and inanimate objects alone. That to remain truly human we need contact, not only with other humans but with flesh-and-blood creatures of the animal kingdom. This is the most important aspect of the horseman's world, and the occupants of those antiquated buildings, a couple of hundred horses that with only a slap on the rump clatter obligingly upstairs or downstairs to their respective stalls, fulfill the riding aspirations of hundreds of students and the hundred or so New Yorkers who keep their own animals there at livery.

Most of the horses stabled there are school animals, which the instructors use in coping with all and sundry who come in off the streets wanting to rent a horse. There is no picking and choosing of clients. It someone wishes to try out a sport that he has seen on TV, then, regardless of whether he has ever seen a horse off the screen, ride he must. The only condition is that if this is a genuine first time on horseback, he must stay in the school.

The hack string rides the streets to Central Park, where there are six miles of tracks and the landscape is both pretty and pleasant. The horses may be a motley crowd but they are mannered, with an admirable willingness to strike off into a lope from a slow trot, and to brake as requested. The big, razor-backed Appaloosa that partnered me, not much of a looker but with a good head carriage and an equable interest in life, showed the same unruffled indifference to barking dogs and stone-throwing children as to the low bridges, where his hooves echoed like muffled drums.

The instructor taught as the string moved along. A more intensive kind of teaching is done in an indoor school on the premises, where defects serve to highlight the good standard of the instruction. The school is very old and far too small, with supporting pillars that are a hazard well appreciated by the horses. The dimensions allow only two fences in a straight line as obstacles for a jumping lesson. The different grades seldom if ever materialize at the same moment, so that a class all at roughly the same standard comes in the category of a longed-for dream.

The day I was there I could only admire the three instructors who were at work at the same time. One was teaching second-grade dressage to a girl riding her own American Saddle Horse,

one encouraging a nervous novice to trot and canter, and the other dealing competently with a typical "try anything once, first time on a horse and likely to make it the last" customer. The instructors sat in a tiny alcove at one end of the school, of just sufficient depth to prevent their being trampled on, and each criticized and taught a particular pupil as he or she came by. It should have been an impossible situation; it could so easily have been bedlam or both, but it was not. Those riders were really getting their money's worth, and instruction that can get the message home under such circumstances must be of the very highest quality.

For every style of riding the basic principles are taught in much the same way, and the instilling of elementary horse sense is mostly copy book. Otherwise different teachers often use different ways of putting it all across, and what is successful with one novice may fail with the next.

It was most interesting to watch the diverging reactions of members of the Twala Club to the professional instruction they were given, and to follow their development during some two dozen school lessons into horsemen of some form or another. Unlike my own, or any other horse-minded family with a horse background,

31

these young people had not only to learn to ride. They had to learn to touch, trust, and handle a horse or pony as a large, overpowering and sometimes frightening creature of flesh and blood rather than as something from which dreams, and occasionally nightmares are concocted.

One such dreamer, so terrified by an actual pony that for weeks she screamed and clutched it round the ears if it so much as sneezed, was equally likely to dissolve into tears if her instructor raised his voice. Since horses can move briskly and novices make mistakes, shouted commands are more often necessary when teaching riding than any other mode of address, and so this pupil was a problem. Yet somehow her years of longing to ride overcame her fears, and without realizing it she absorbed some of the basic principles. When the lessons were finished Aunt Jobiska took a hand, patiently, willingly interpreting her rider's hesitant aids, never shying, never changing gear without being asked. And today that particular member of the Twala Club will confidently take any of the ponies round a small show-jumping or cross-country course, ride out alone or in company on every possible occasion, and happily, safely take charge of new members.

A big hurdle for many novices is acquiring the right attitude of mind toward falls and falling. Except for very young children, it is to my mind an essential to good instruction and eventual riding ability, to instill an awareness of the fact that falling off now and again is an inevitable and normal part of learning to ride. This is one of the many good reasons why ponies, which may be quicker in their reactions than horses but are much nearer the ground, are more suitable for children to learn on than the larger animals.

No one likes falling off, and the fear of doing so is the natural reaction with most beginners, but it is counter to relaxing and can impede learning. It was interesting to see how quickly the Twala Club members improved once they had had a harmless tumble or two and realized that to fall off was not such a dreadful thing after all. One boy even found it an amusing pastime, and with small excuse took to dropping off and rolling across the soft tanbark of the indoor school where they were being instructed. The same thing, done in the paddock and achieved inad-

vertently when Slingsby turned right and his rider went on left, proved less painless and not quite so funny.

Unfortunately, no one can guarantee that any fall will be harmless, but the majority are, and a spice of danger is an added attraction to many popular sports. We have always insisted on the common sense safeguard of a hard cap secured by a chin elastic even for everyday riding. And we try to teach members how to fall, by letting themselves go and, if possible, rolling out of the way with head tucked in, in the style of a steeplechase jockey.

Beginners' falls can be more nerve-racking for the instructor than for the pupil. A matter-of-fact calmness is essential, but you have to try to assess the nature of the fall as it is happening, and then make a speedy decision about possible damage. Unless there is a cogent reason against, the rider must be got back onto his horse as quickly as possible, even if only to walk around, or the happening becomes blown up out of proportion. Be too unperturbed and tough once too often and you may find later that the tearful child put back into the saddle has in fact been injured.

Some instructors consider that a hard fall can be the factor that tips a learner onto the next highest level. With the dedicated, intrinsically tough type of novice determined to get to grips with riding come what may, this can well be true, but it is dangerous to generalize. Handled the right way by the instructor, such a fall could also materially help a more nervous rider. Handled wrongly, particularly with a young rider, whose love of horses only just outweighs his or her fears, it can be the end of riding.

When it comes to competing on horseback —to a lesser or greater degree, according to what you are doing—falls are an accepted hazard of the sport. Steeplechase jockeys acknowledge injury as part of their trade, and few would survive if horses did not instinctively try to avoid treading on bodies. Eventing, at the top levels, produces numerous falls, many of them spectacular but with comparatively few injuries, and the top eventers will tell you that they and their horses learn a great deal from falling about how, and how not to ride across country. Women were for long excluded from the equestrian Olympics, partly because it was felt that females would not

be sufficiently tough to pick themselves up and continue if they fell and were injured. This theory was finally disproved by the two girls included in Britain's team for the European Championships of 1973, held at Kiev, who both finished that notorious course with honor after bad falls and unpleasant injuries. Show jumpers expect their quota of tosses, but the sport is less hazardous than eventing because the fences are not fixed, and the horse has only the one short course to complete, however high it may be and even if it does entail several rounds.

A fall on the flat is the most dangerous because of the speed involved. Smith II, being galloped happily along a grass track, put his foot in a rabbit hole. This stopped him dead, and then projected him and his rider into a crashing fall and, for her, the first serious injury in thirty-two years of riding and falling. Getting well was a matter of many weeks, but as she maintained, this is the kind of unpredictable accident that can happen to anyone, at any time, and under any circumstances.

Instruction does not only concern the novice rider. One of the chief attractions of riding, or driving as a sport, is that there is always something more to learn. And this is something that I hope the young man, who announced after six lessons that now he could ride he thought he would go on to figure skating, will yet have the opportunity of realizing.

2.

Horse Sense

The shout to "Bring out the chestnut!" produced no immediate result, but it did give me breathing space after being led flat-out the length of one of the horse dealer's more strenuous fences. Then a saddle flew through the stable doorway, followed by a wild-eyed horse that disappeared full gallop up the yard with a small boy in pursuit. The dealer shrugged. "Oh, well, don't expect he'd have done you anyway."

That happened long ago, on a day when a horse-minded friend and I had been experiencing the frustration of trying to buy the kind of animal that was just not to be had for the money I had allotted to the purchase. Yet it was to be the day that culminated in a stroke of four-legged luck called Twala who, twenty-five years later and now retired, remains a beloved part of the family.

It was one of many experiences, over many years, in acquiring horses. In themselves, the incidents are personal and small-scale—I have so far restrained myself from spending lavishly on Irish hunters or Thoroughbred yearlings. But in their variety—in the range of equine temperaments and abilities they reveal, in the catalogue of equine faults and deficiencies they suggest, not to mention the equivalent qualities in horse seller and horse buyer—they make some valid points. I think they apply at all levels of horse trading.

The morning I found Twala had been spent in riding a number of animals, a few that might have suited certain riders but were unsuitable for us, and some possibles that were far too expensive. We were tired and despondent when the dealer led us to our last hope, a remote field where his latest shipment over from Ireland were indulging in what horse dealers ambiguously term the "Irish cough." And there, leaning over the gate and watching our arrival with benign interest, was a big, black, woolly-coated pony, 14.2 without his shoes, with a white blaze running the length of his face to end in a shovel-shaped, pink muzzle. The eye on our side was pale blue and of that zany expression sometimes imparted by a "wall eye." It was the look—friendly, inquiring, and kind—in the brown one on his off side that prompted me to suggest trying the pony out.

Because of his cough there was little to do but walk and slow-trot him in a few circles, and it was

quickly apparent that this fellow knew nothing of aids and possibly had made a first acquaintance with the saddle only a few days before, but he did his best to please. His braking system seemed in good order and he was so amiable, so confidence-inspiring that after we had watched him clop happily up and down the road in traffic with a couple of small boys perched bareback one behind the other, I dared to make an offer for him of all there was to be had.

The dealer laughed. That horse might be a cobby as opposed to a breedy type—his parentage could be Connemara crossed with good old Irish draft—and his head might be described as plain Irish. But his legs carried only a silky tuft of hair at the heels. His general conformation was good. He moved well and was full of that indefinable asset known as "quality." For all his greenness, his temperament as a family pony appeared to leave little or nothing to be desired, and for what he was the price asked was a fair one. It just happened to be about double what I had in mind.

Sadly I bid goodbye to that particular dream at the gateway to his field. On returning to the dealer, who was waiting with my friend, I heard him mutter something about "not wanting too many coughers on m' hands." He accepted my offer, forthwith and without demur.

It was unbelievable and, too elated and surprised to question his change of heart, we straightway incorporated our find into the family, christened him Twala after H. Rider Haggard's one-eyed Zulu king, and with joy set about coping with his cough, his inexperience, and the revelation that he might be considerably younger than supposed.

As the years of happy hunting, eventing, pony clubbing, show jumping, and just riding rolled by, we came to bless our fantastic luck ever more wholeheartedly. But it was ten years before it came to light that the good friend who accompanied me on that far-off day had seized the opportunity of being alone with the dealer to purchase two of Twala's legs to make up the asking price, and had then sworn the dealer to secrecy.

That kind of miracle happens seldom. The dealer, after all, makes his living from buying and selling horses at a profit. But even if buying from a dealer isn't likely to produce a bargain, when

Most owners do their own grooming these days, and it helps when extra hands share the work. Like other routines of horsemastership it has to be done regularly and thoroughly. Long and ample tail of pony opposite will look its best thanks to owner's careful attention.

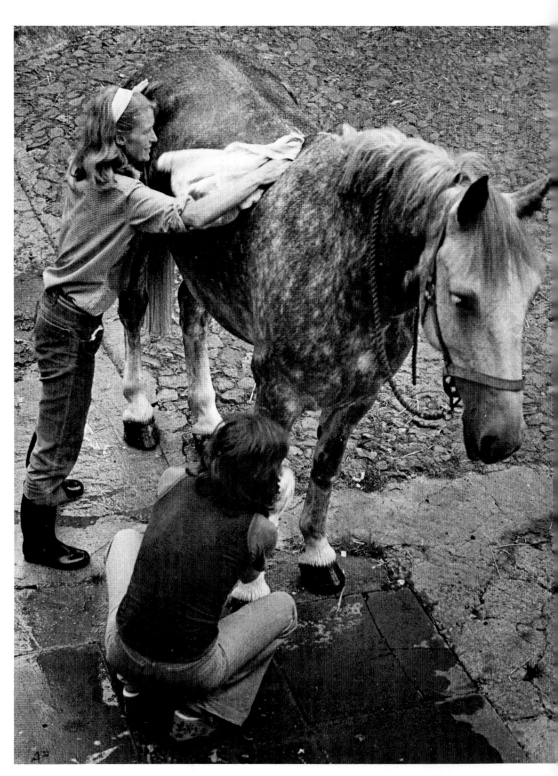

you are in the market for a horse it makes good sense to see what a reputable man has to offer. While the horse of one's dreams may not exist anywhere, a good dealer will do his best to suit. Also, once he has a reputation to uphold, he will usually try to make an exchange, with the appropriate price adjustments, for an animal that proves unfitted for the job. Occasionally the less reputable dealer can be prevailed upon to do the same.

Not too long ago, I was looking for a well-schooled, outgrown 14.2, one of the many animals of that type advertised each week in the horse magazines. It had been a while since we had followed up any of these ads, and it came as a surprise to discover that anything of the sort had come to be worth its weight in gold.

Eventually, among the offerings of a dealer, we found Spiridion. He was a good-looking gray of unremarkable antecedants, the right size and age, seemed impervious to traffic—an essential in this day—and did what was required of him within the confines of the dealer's field. He was not exactly enthusiastic about the obstacles he was asked to jump by the dealer's daughter, but it mattered little since I did not expect to be doing much jumping with him.

Spiridion came home, and every day for the next two months we joined battle. I have ridden all my life, but never before had I met a horse or pony on whom the rider's legs, however applied, made no impression whatever. If Spiridion was hit, his only reaction was to become more mulish, and the aid of spurs made him worse. If he should feel inclined to go forward he could be a delightful ride, maybe for a mile, then the sight of a cow, or a tree trunk, or a hazard apparent to no eyes but his own, brought us to a full stop for as long as he chose. The only direction in which Spiridion would willingly set off, of his own choice and at speed, was backward.

After trying everything in and out of the book, including pulling him in circles until he must have been as giddy as his rider, and making him go backward until any normal horse would have been thankful to proceed forward, the services of a professional trainer were called upon. He returned after an hour, most of it spent in contemplation of the sun shining on a dock leaf, with his patience, skill, and vocabulary equally exhausted.

The horse dealer had been kept informed of the situation, and after expressing incredulity had made one or two suggestions that proved abortive. Naturally he was no more eager to take the horse back than I was to concede defeat, but after being toted along a track uncontrollably in reverse to erupt into a busy road, life seemed too sweet to me to jeopardize it further and an exchange of horses was agreed upon.

They came to fetch Spiridion and just to prove a point the dealer's daughter first rode him, bareback and in a halter, full tilt and without

Overleaf: Gregarious behavior may be for mutual grooming, for use of each other's tails as fly switches, for simple companionship. Occasionally two horses will form a special friendship and object to being separated.

39

trouble, through the village. But since riding with flailing legs, whirling a halter rope like a lariat, and emitting Indian screeches is not my idea of a quiet hack, the exhibition failed to affect my decision.

At first glance the proffered exchange did not look very promising. She was a cobby mare, thin-necked, goose-rumped, out of condition. But when I climbed into the saddle she arched her neck and pricked her ears and did everything within her capacity to cooperate. Although there was a rebate on Spiridion, the price asked for this exchange was not a low one. Still, it was impossible to resist her kind, almost pleading expression. And if time and subsequent veterinary bills have proved the truth of the maxim that buying a case of debility is seldom sound economy, the Twala Club knows she was one of the best bargains ever made. Her name is Aunt Jobiska.

There had been another horse in my life bought partly for her expression. She was the end product of a check I received as an eighteenth-birthday present with which I had set out to obtain the handsome horse of my imagination. It was not surprising that with the sum I had in hand—eighteen guineas, equivalent at the time to about a hundred dollars—my choice narrowed to this odd-appearing, little rusty black mare of quizzical mien, later to become notorious in East Kent as Smith I. Now, much can be gleaned from a horse's eye but that is no sensible way to buy a horse. It was only by luck that Smith gladdened my heart for the next eighteen years.

In buying a horse, one needs the benefit of experience—one's own or that of a professional. And even if one is experienced, a second opinion can prevent a wrong decision being made on the basis of an emotional response to the particular animal. This is sound advice that I always preach and usually apply. In Aunt Jobiska's case it was omitted because the mare certainly would have been turned down, as would Smith. Not that the verdict would have affected my decision in either case, but for my money's worth at least, it could have been helpful to suspect that nothing was ever going to induce Smith to jump in cold blood, and that nothing on God's earth was ever going to prevent her from having a go, often unsuccessfully, at the most horrifying obstacles when hunting.

We have bought and sold horses and ponies

through advertisements in weekly horse magazines, and it never ceases to amaze how many people will ignore such vital scraps of information as "not a novice ride." Admittedly the definition and capabilities of a novice vary, but no would-be seller is going to suggest his animal is less than suitable for any rider unless it is. When one of the family's ponies was advertised—an excellent Welsh Mountain, sold because his rider did not share his views on galloping at speed over cross-country fences—he was truthfully described as a "super *second* pony." Yet there was real difficulty in warding off the numerous parents who turned up, bent on acquiring him for some microscopic child with perhaps half a dozen riding lessons to its credit.

Even when buying through impeccable "friend of a friend" channels, it still pays to be wary, as Justin was to teach us. We knew when we went to see him that he was both young and green, and we found him undeniably handsome, but when we saw him to be shoeless we should have questioned the explanation that his owners' smith had been unobtainable but that he would be delivered shod.

On arrival, Justin was still shoeless but his feet were iron-hard and it seemed to matter little that our own smith could not come at once. By the time four successive attempts to shoe our new acquisition had failed, we were fully occupied with other and worse manifestations of the horse's temper, such as a tendency to rear, and real battles if we attempted to tie him up.

Since Justin was obviously a horse of high quality and breeding, we were inclined to blame ourselves for his bad behavior. Perhaps the fault lay with our methods of training. We decided to do some lungeing work with him—moving him

in circles at the end of a line—normally an excellent method of instilling obedience. Justin was singularly uncooperative at the first attempt, at the second he suddenly swung in, bared his teeth, and came for me, striking out with his forefeet.

Fortunately, a slap across the nose with the butt of the lungeing whip deterred him, but it was a frightening moment and confirmed what we already suspected—that this was no horse for us. The incident also suggested that he might be a "rig."

Rigs are imperfectly castrated males that often possess the characteristic masculine good looks and courage of the stallion, but as "half" horses are often very tricky customers. In the hands of the experienced, a rig can make a highly successful show jumper or event horse, but such an animal has no place in a family stable.

Evidence was now forthcoming from hitherto prudishly silent sources that Justin had been "going on something awful" with their pony mare! Some geldings "go on" in the same way, but in this case it seemed to confirm our theory and the vet was summoned. Although he could find no visible signs of the condition, he did offer a wise comment, that "if the animal behaved like a rig, it really didn't matter whether it looked like one or not!"

Justin behaved in character to the end, by defying for three hours all efforts of a team headed by an experienced groom to get him into the horse box for the return journey to his previous home. He capitulated eventually, and from our point of view the story concluded satisfactorily. With much reluctance and professed disbelief in our "rig" story, his owners took him back and the price was refunded in full.

Famed Appleby Fair brings horse dealers together yearly in Cumberland town to buy, sell, celebrate, and— for younger members of gypsy clans—romp in River Eden with their four-footed wares. Saddlery and other equipment tempt the buyer, and the atmosphere is that of an earlier age when horsepower really *was* horsepower.

Piers is not quite ready for a hunter the size of Sir Harold. Perhaps something more on the order of the pony opposite, whose diminutive rider is putting himself up with proper determination. Where horses and ponies are part of family life, children's education in horsemanship comes naturally.

Horse fairs and smaller sales are a worthwhile experience, guaranteed to produce the maximum fun if nothing else. It used to take the gypsy folk a week or more to get to Appleby Fair, which lasts for several days each June in this market town in Cumberland. The length of time spent traveling was not only because the traditionally decorated Romany caravans and bow-topped *vardos* were horse-drawn, but because the hundreds of horses the gypsies brought with them to sell had to arrive fresh and in good trim,

so the pace was deliberately leisurely.

Despite modern innovations, gypsies still barter horses at Appleby Fair, buying—and principally selling—the animals that remain part of the Romany way of life. For all the stench of fuel exhausts in the main street, there's still a good, old-fashioned aroma of horse dung about. For all the background blare of pop music, the core of the din still has to do with the harness horses and vanners, the cart mares and new arrivals from Ireland brought over especially, the local ponies from the dales and fells, the would-be hunters, the Shetlands, and the posses of little donkeys tied up in every convenient corner. The shouts and yells and tumult concerns them, and the overall noise is punctuated by the shrill neighing of stallions, the anxious whinnying of mares separated from their foals, the doleful braying of the donkeys.

Each day the doings of the Fair start early with the youngsters, boys and girls alike, riding the piebalds and skewbalds, the grays and duns and spotted cobs and ponies—all the colors dear to a gypsy's heart—down the river bank into the waters of the Eden, to soap and rinse, swim, flounder and fall off, until animals and riders alike are well laundered to meet the customers.

Later the crowds swell ever more, choking the downhill road where the wares are shown off, eddying and swaying back just in time as the whips crack, the shouts of "Hi! Hi! Hi!" rise to a crescendo, and a trotter drawing a sulky storms by. There's a thickset cob hard on its heels, urged on at the requisite flat-out trot by a small boy with legs thrust forward, and always perched bareback, since the presence of a saddle would denote its inclusion in the sale. Behind him clatter a trio of wild-eyed colts, haltered together and run out in hand, as tradition demands, by "t'boy," the dealer's assistant who may be anything from sixteen to sixty.

There's something to suit many tastes, but at a price, for if book learning is in short supply here, canny bargaining and know-how are not. The sales are made without the aid of officialdom, in the thick of the crowds with a hundred vociferous voices to proffer advice, to comment on the virtues or otherwise and the antecedents of each animal concerned. Bare palms are struck to conclude the sale, and if in old times there was the occasional ill-tempered horse miraculously

sweetened by age-old remedies for the requisite hours, if some old wreck were given a physic to keep it on its feet long enough to make its new home, if that rare phenomenon, a spotted mule, were sold only to lose its attractions in the first rain storm, nevertheless these days most of the dealing is straight.

The Appleby Fairs of the world can hardly offer greater contrast to the sophisticated surroundings in which Thoroughbred racehorses change hands. This thought struck me during a visit to Lexington, Kentucky. I was standing in the middle of a huge auditorium. It was empty at the time, but I could easily imagine it during the sales, with buyers and onlookers crowding the nearly one thousand red-plush seats, the press writers and sales officials surveying the scene from their raised boxes. Eight closed-circuit television screens would be relaying the proceedings to every part of the pavilion. The raised stage, two-thirds of a circle with entrance and exit to either side, was relatively small and lacked an orchestra pit, otherwise the only clues to this arena not being the opera house or theater it looked like were the ornamental horses' heads on the iron supports of the rope barrier in front of the stage, and the thick, antiseptic-smelling covering of tanbark over the boards.

This was the famous Keeneland Sales pavilion, part of the nonprofit-making complex that includes training facilities and a covered circuit for winter use by local breeders, and the Keeneland track, where they can test their hopes. This track is second only to Churchill Downs as the best patronized and most attractive in Kentucky.

At those four annual bloodstock sales in the Keeneland pavilion, yearlings, breeding stock, and horses of all ages hold the stage on the appropriate sales days. As with similar sales—at the Tattersalls that adjoins the Lexington Trots and nowadays deals in equally valuable Standardbreds, at Tattersalls in Britain's Newmarket, at Dublin, or any of the other famous bloodstock auctions—it is well not to catch the auctioneer's eye unless your pockets are exceptionally well lined.

Bloodstock generally is acquired only for breeding and racing, and the horses bought at these sales are normally installed in new homes with facilities approaching the luxurious. Thoroughbred and part-bred hunters and show

hacks are generally not far lower in the scale of comfort.

The Thoroughbred horse, as a fairly recently evolved breed, is about as far removed from the truly wild Przewalski's horse as you can get. Thoroughbreds are comparatively delicate. Like their Arabian ancestors and all oriental horses, they have fine coats and—usually—sensitive skins. They must live in stable or barn if they are to thrive—even sometimes to survive—and be in fit condition to work. They cannot be expected to hunt two days a week unless in the hard condition made possible by clipping out and being kept stabled. There are many advantages to keeping your horse stabled, but he needs much more care and attention, and this method spells a constant tie and a lot of hard work.

Whatever the difficulties, the keeping of horses is the aspect of the horseman's world that brings the most intimate knowledge and appreciation of the individuality and needs of each animal. Soon after leaving school I acquired some grounding in stable management by working for a while at a local riding school. These were school horses and hunters, not exactly "blood" animals, but they were kept in for the sake of convenience and—in days when grooms were plentiful and wages very low—as a matter of course. In winter all the horses were clipped right out except for a saddle mark, but despite the grooms' love of an overwarm stable because

Young riders are getting benefit of group instruction at Pony Club camp in Devon. Students' natural urge to measure up well against each other makes for quick progress.

Overleaf: Winter in the American West does not favor pleasant days in the saddle, but this owner is faithful to exercise routine, and her horse will be the better for it.

49

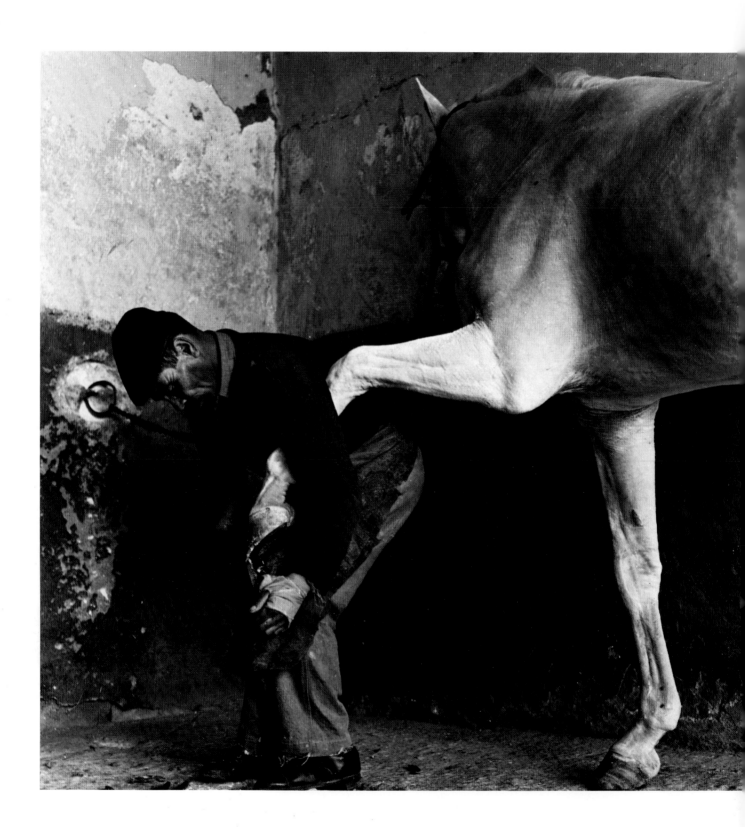

it keeps a bloom on the coat, the tops of the half-doors were never shut, and the inmates remained healthy and hard, their warmth and comfort ensured by stable rugs, extra underblankets at night, and deep beds.

Mucking out thoroughly once a day, with removal of soiled top bedding and dung at intervals, are inescapable chores with a stabled horse. In those days bedding was always the long wheat straw that became a costly rarity with the advent of combine harvesters, or the innovation of a peat bed for those greedies that persisted in hoovering up their bedding to the detriment of their wind and figures. Oat straw is very palatable and therefore useless for the purpose, but nowadays combine harvesting mashes up most of the bristles that used to preclude the use of barley straw. All straw now tends to fetch high prices unimaginable not long ago. Peat is still considered a good material but it, too, is very expensive. For anyone who lives where they are obtainable, wood shavings are clean, aromatic, inedible, and cheap. Sawdust possesses similar virtues, but clogs and becomes heavy to handle when soiled. Some people swear by deep-litter straw, where only very soiled material is removed, clean straw added daily on top. It generates heat to dry out and is totally removed every four to six months.

I found grooming a stabled, clipped-out horse a welcome change from trying to cope with the wet, greasy, mud-encrusted and hairy winter coat of a pony at grass, but it has to be considerably more thorough. Animals living out need the grease in their coats to keep them "waterproof" and warm, and grooming is a minimal tidying up. The stabled horse has to receive a daily and lengthy grooming, with a short-bristled body brush and plenty of elbow grease to keep its skin in condition and to help with muscling-up. The stud groom was meticulous about the state of his horses' feet and woe betide anyone who skimped picking out her charges' hooves. Animals living out need hooves cleaned of stones and other foreign bodies, but seldom do they develop thrush, that stinking rot of the frog usually due to neglecting to remove the residue of manure from the feet of horses that have been standing in dirty bedding. If this occurred to horses in your charge you were likely to be sacked.

It is a joy to have the horse you want there, clean and ready to go, instead of in a muddy field, maybe in a mood to evade capture. He is fit because his food and exercise have been controlled, and if you ask the difficult from him he is ready to deliver. Since he is clipped, there is no problem about drying off on return home.

On the other hand the routines have to be observed religiously. The stabled horse has to receive a minimum of three feeds a day—the largest with the bulk of his hay at night—and because he and his digestion are creatures of habit, the meals have to arrive at the same times each day, week in and week out. All working horses should have a day off per week, and after hunting or other strenuous events they are the better for little or no work. Apart from this you have to give your horse approximately, in a more concentrated form and according to the work expected of him, the same amount of exercise he would give himself throughout a day in a paddock—and that means in the region of two hours' steady work per twenty-four hours.

Undoubtedly for the dedicated horseman with no other commitments, for someone who intends doing the maximum competing, for the hunting man whose riding interests center on that sport and cease with the end of the season, a

The craft of the farrier is one of the world's oldest, differing little in its methods whether practiced, as opposite, on a splendid "charger" in barracks of Jordanian Royal Guard, or by village blacksmith on clients of less exalted station.

horse stabled during these periods of activity is the only answer. But in an age when the majority of owners are also their own grooms, there are now modifications to the system. Hunters and most horses other than show animals (which generally work in the summer anyway) seldom have their legs clipped right out. This means that even a clipped Thoroughbred, wearing a New Zealand rug, can spend an hour or so in his paddock on a fine day—and will be the better for this occasional substitute for part of his daily exercise.

Those of us who love to ride and/or hunt but whose equine activities, either from inclination or necessity, have to fit in with family or business life, are likely to have a part-bred hunter type—much hardier in constitution than a Thoroughbred—or a horse with no pretensions to being anything in particular. An animal like this, clipped, but with the hair left on its legs, and rugged-up for warmth, will be happy living out by day in a paddock where there is some form of shelter, and stabled by night. Feeding, adjusted according to any pickings in the paddock (in winter of bulk value only), is much the same. This approach solves much of the exercise problem, and is a boon to weekend riders. If you are content to compromise further and trace-clip your horse—which removes the coat only from the chief sweating areas (lower chest, neck, and belly)—with the rug and a good open shelter to be used at will, a stable can be dispensed with. He will be less hard than a fully stabled animal, but without many of the disadvantages of an unclipped one. As always, good feeding is essential to health and warmth, and although New Zealand rugs are fitted with self-adjusting leg straps, they are not infallible and need to be removed and replaced at least once a day.

After I married, my husband and I settled down some miles from my family's farm on property that does not include a barn structure. The simple solution for owning horses has been to stay with ponies and part-breds that require no more than a shelter. They graze on a series of small fields.

There are times in winter when the fields churn to liquid mud and gateways are bogs that suck the rubber boots off of the unwary, when it is difficult to differentiate between the ponies and their surroundings, and saddles have, perforce, to go straight onto sodden backs. At such times I think with envy of those Australians who can keep their horses out all year in a climate both warm and dry. Or of that stabling in Devon, adapted from old farm buildings and within view of the kitchen windows, where Sir Harold and Mr. Smith, clipped-out and rugged-up, spend each winter's night. But for ponies, living out is much closer to the way nature intended, and it enables them to exercise themselves. They seldom ail and never experience the boredom that can lead to crib-biting, or weaving, or similar vices not uncommon among animals stabled for the greater part of their lives.

We find that with correct management and supplementary feeding in winter, four ponies can thrive on a total of about eight acres. The fields vary in size and are grazed in rotation. Fertilizing and selective weed spraying, which are essential, are done seasonally. The unromantic chore of dung collecting, especially necessary on small areas to prevent the ground from becoming horse-sick, is helped out by a queue of appreciative local gardeners.

Through the years we have decided, after trial and error, that our ponies do best in winter on almost unlimited good hay supplemented with a pound or two of boiled barley and sliced carrots, a good warming ration for an animal living out and not required to do fast work. In addition, they get a ration of the feeding cubes specially compounded for ponies, taking into account the amount of work they are expected to do and the capabilities of their riders. We are always wary of feeding small ponies the concentrates that inevitably seem to go to their heads, but otherwise this is the kind of diet for ponies at grass that seems to keep them in good physical trim and a sensible frame of mind. For summer, grass can substitute for hay, and cubes—according to work—replace the barley and carrots. Obviously horses eat more than ponies and need more in the way of hard tack, but again each animal's physical requirements and mental reactions to the stimulus of concentrates differs, and the art of good feeding is based on taking these factors into account, as well as the vital matter of what role the horse is required to play.

It should not be thought that ponies are the answer for people with little time or attention to give. Too often one sees this idea in operation, generally on the part of parents who have decided to "buy a pony for the kids for Christmas." They probably will not expect—or they may refuse to accept—that until a pony is three years old it is not sufficiently mature, either physically or mentally, for riding, and that even then it should be ridden for a while only by the experienced. These are the people who just do not know that a pony needs space to gallop about or graze at will; that weed-infested yards or the front lawn are totally inadequate facilities; that pony foals and yearlings cannot thrive and quickly become impossible to handle if they are stabled in shed or garage, their only exercise a walk out in hand. They cannot visualize the bewildered young creature they buy so gaily quickly becoming a strong, potentially dangerous animal, unless it has the right facilities and receives firm, experienced handling and training. Or that to feed and look after it correctly will be a considerable annual expense. They cannot realize that a sentimental "love" of a pony "as a pet" is no substitute for essential knowledge and horse sense. Where, as often happens, the ponies are soon half starved, or spoiled through ignorance, or neglected through boredom, it would have been more humane if they had been expertly slaughtered in the first place.

Fencing is a problem that almost every horse owner has to deal with. Ponies are born escapees, with a genius for causing damage to any surrounding barriers. Time and again some stout post, supposedly entrenched well enough to withstand an elephant, has been angled over by Twala, a sufferer from mild sweet itch, while using it as a convenient rump scratcher.

Oddly enough, horses, as opposed to ponies, seem less often possessed of the urge to escape. Something built on the massive lines of Sir Harold, our son-in-law's heavyweight hunter, can often, metaphorically speaking, be contained with a length of string. But there are too many ponies like Spotty the Welshman, who is practiced in the art of climbing out between strands of plain wire.

These are among the reasons for the regretted and regrettable fact that most of our fencing is composed of barbed wire.

I hate barbed wire.

There was that fraught moment when Slingsby, always liable to paw the ground in excitement, struck out on seeing his evening's ration of hay coming and caught the heel of a fore shoe under the strand of barbed wire alongside the gate. This left him with his front leg outstretched at elbow height while Twala, often one to indulge a misplaced sense of humor, chose that second to bite his companion's bottom. It appeared that if Slingsby struggled—and he was never one to take misadventure calmly—he must at least dislocate his shoulder. To this day it seems inconceivable that he should have stood like a rock while I approached quietly, talking him down, and that eventually he allowed his leg to be pulled forward so that the shoe could be unhitched, instead of obeying the natural instinct to leap back.

If feasible, all our fields would be enclosed with wooden palings of the sort that surround Thoroughbred studs and comparable places. As it is, not having the young stock, blood horses or "scatty" characters that would make the use of barbed wire criminal, we have found that, with each strand stretched taut and none lower than eighteen inches from the ground, it is a relatively cheap form of fencing that is effective and easy to erect. Barring two instances of danger, our ponies have lived with it without mishap and seem to understand the dangers. In twenty-five years Twala has not received a scratch, although he appears to be able to lean on the barbs with impunity when trying to graze on the other side.

An alternative to barbed wire is electrified wire. The mild shock it delivers on being touched is an inducement to horses to observe the boundaries of their enclosures. It is safe, economical, and—barring power failures—effective.

We recently installed a length of it as a supplement to a long stretch of fencing that is inadequate on its own. For "strip grazing" it has no equal. I am not sure I would trust ponies not to find some method of circumventing the electric wire enclosing an entire field. Again, horses are likely to be much more respectful than ponies. When Spot, for instance, first investigated our fence and received a shock, he was so incensed that he turned and let fly with both heels, hit something vital, and fused the entire caboodle. Once Jobiska and Paint had discovered what happened when the wire was touched, they grazed no nearer than five yards, but although Twala has not been tried out, since he has been taught to jump wire, he would be more than likely merely to canter up and jump it if he wished. But this cuts two ways. The hunter that, like Twala, has been taught to jump wire and then is touched by the electric variety, may thereafter refuse to approach the stuff in any form.

There is no substitute for in-the-field instruction in matters of horse keeping and training. For advice on the finer techniques of bringing a horse up to competition form, we drew on the expertise of the Pony Club. There must be thousands of people all over the world who could similarly acknowledge their debt to that admirable institution.

The Pony Club was begun in England in 1928 and was revived after the war. Today there are more than 300 branches with a growing membership of more than 40,000 in the United Kingdom, and a further 600 affiliated Pony Clubs with a large membership in other countries. In addition to the more obvious aims of furthering an interest in horses and ponies, in their welfare, and in all aspects of riding, the Club endeavors to cherish ideals of good sportsmanship and to cultivate strength of character and self-discipline within an age group that in this day does not always give evidence of these virtues. Since the Pony Club is an international voluntary youth organization, those of its competitions that are on an international level provide a number of young people with opportunities to travel and to meet their counterparts in other countries.

The majority of Britain's foreign contests are with European Pony Clubs. Australia, where the organization is particularly strong, participates every two years in the Inter-Pacific Exchange involving Canada, New Zealand, and the United States.

The United States Pony Club Inc. was founded in 1954, and although the present figures of around 250 clubs with about 10,000 members are not large in relation to the size of the country, the movement is growing steadily. This American version is not officially associated with the parent club, but its program, standards, and training are all based on much the same British concepts.

The Pony Club is sometimes criticized for concentrating on the competitive side, with consequent emphasis on good riders with better ponies at the expense of average riders with average ponies, which are the young people for whom the Club was originally intended. There is some truth in this. Yet we live in a competitive age—the majority of Britain's top show jumpers and eventers started their competitive life in the ranks of the Pony Club—and branches of the Club do try to be flexible. The aim is to keep the instruction at the working rallies—the backbone of the organization—at more or less the same standard, but to make it fit the needs of the local conditions.

When eventing became the "in" thing with our local branch, Twala started a new career. Note had been taken of his stately but unruffled progress over cross-country fences, and of his obedient attitude toward elementary dressage, and we were pleased when he and his rider found themselves being considered for the horse-trials team.

Until this time we had been enjoying Twala as a delightful hack and a reliable performer. He hunted with verve, straight off grass and therefore for short periods. Now, with his inclusion in the horse-trials team, it was necessary for him to be in really fit, hard condition in order to be physically capable of what was to be required of him. Twala has always been a "good doer," and after the Club's District Commissioner had contemplated his ample figure someone offered us the loan of a stable.

(Confinement alone is not proof against over-consumption. Once, while Smith was being kept "in," we had to summon the vet to look at a number of bumps on the mare's neck. Too rich a diet, he said. The diagnosis remained inexplicable, until it was discovered that each day Smith ate the offering of an egg, deposited in her manger by an obliging hen.)

In Twala's case, time was short, but it was imperative he should be sufficiently fit to cope within the time limit with the cross-country phase of the horse trial, a gallop of about two miles with a considerable number of fences. There is an art to such preparation, and for those doing it for the first time, guidance of the sort the Pony Club offers is important if mistakes are to be avoided. To condition a grass-fat hunter there should be a gradual build-up of concentrates over several weeks, combined with the two or more hours of slow road work each day. Failure to combine

Conversano Caprice, now retired, enjoys the freedom of a paddock when weather permits. Otherwise, snugly stabled as befits his years, this famous Lipizzaner is kept well and healthy with the knowledgeable stable management essential for bred horses.

added exercise with the richer diet is to risk an attack of colic.

A fitter, handsomer Twala was the outcome of our efforts, and to our surprise we found ourselves the owners of a creditable event horse.

There is a subtle difference between imbibing horse sense almost unconsciously, as do the younger factions of a horse-keeping family, and having actually to learn it in the same way as having to learn to ride. As a baby our grandson Piers was accustomed to sitting in his carriage in the yard watching the horseman's world revolve around him. By the age of three he accepted as a normal part of life that, since horses and ponies are entirely dependent on their owners for health and happiness, within reason the needs of the family animals are attended to before those of their riders; that horses are watered and fed, put in or out, groomed and exercised, and, if they are at grass, at least looked at.

If these routines aren't learned unconsciously then they have to be taught, which is one of the objectives of the Twala Club. Members are encouraged to acquire that sixth sense of the horseman, the something that tells them at a glance whether Jobiska's stance in the field is

that of an old lady having a quiet snooze, or that of an animal feeling under the weather. They have to learn not to take Spotty's furry rotundity in winter for granted, but to check with fingers under the hair for a hint of ''ribbiness,'' or that telltale groove down the quarters rightly called the poverty mark. They have to acquire the horseman's ear, which automatically notes the irregular beat of Jobiska's hooves on the road, meaning that she has wrenched off a shoe during that last canter through the mud and must be walked home.

From the age of four until boarding school at fourteen, my mecca was the blacksmith's forge just down the road from home. I spent hours there watching farm horses having their worn-out shoes removed—first with the buffer to cut the clenches, then with the pincers to wrench them off. My ears were tuned to the rasping off of the excess growth of new horn, and to the gasp and suck of the hand bellows, and the following roar of the flames as the smith scooped on fuel with a practiced art to bring his furnace to life once more. It was enthralling to watch him plunge the correct length of heavy, straight iron bar into the heart of the fire, then draw out the

red-hot metal and shape it on his anvil into the flat shoes the heavy horses wear, while the sparks flew and the hammer rang and stuttered in between the strokes. I liked the clouds of smoke, the sizzle and acrid smell of seared hoof as each shoe was tried for size, and the final hissing and steam as the set was plunged into water to cool before being nailed onto the customer.

Not many of today's horse owners know these sights and sounds. Having a horse shod nowadays does not normally entail leading it down to the forge. The modern smith more often comes to his clients, and he is an excessively busy man who travels a wide area.

A few smiths transport a small furnace and shoe "hot," but most make individual sets of shoes for each of their clientele back in their own shop, and then bring them along to fit on "cold." This can lead to the undesirable practice of fitting the hoof to the shoe instead of the other way about, but a good smith is a craftsman, whichever method he uses. And good smiths, like ours, are worth their weight in gold.

We try to give our smith maximum notice, and the horses have been taught to pick up their feet

as required and stand still until the job is finished. The smith is a man with the right to consideration and the right to refuse to shoe an awkward, time-consuming customer whose behavior is mostly due to an owner too idle to teach his horse basic good manners.

Horse sense is an essential of good horsemastership, and no less important to the rider. That girl who slipped off Spot's bridle and told him to "stand still, darling!" while she hung it in the tack room, was astounded to find on her return that pony and saddle had vanished. The boy who took it for granted that the normally imperturbable Jobiska would ignore a reed-cutting boat chugging up the canal with rotary blades whirling in a cloud of spray, discovered his mistake as he was being carted full tilt through a growing crop of wheat.

Obviously, horses react in direct ratio to the capabilities of their riders. The good horseman can get unexpectedly good results from a mediocre horse, and the converse is equally true. The mannered Paint reacted to a daydreaming rider who had no contact and little impulsion by turning around and making for home. Spotty came to the Twala Club from an experienced family where he and his young rider had built up their mutual confidence and ability to a high level. It took him just about a week to get the measure of his novice riders and exploit the situation to the full. If he did not wish to pass the gateway in the schooling field, he stayed put. If he had no wish to pop over a foot-high pole he scuttered round the end. The problem, of course, was not with Spotty but with the way he was being ridden. Once his riders began to sharpen their horsemanship, Spotty immediately recovered his normal good manners to become the delight of all who know him.

Apart from the riding aspect, horses do react to people and will do more, or less, for some than for others. This is an equine trait that the mounted police well understand. Whether it concerns the officer who is fully operational or the trainee learning the ropes at school, care is taken to ensure that the temperament of the rider equates with that of his horse. One of our earlier family horses was an ex-show jumper called Blaze. He was a wonderful ride for the experienced, but was wary and unpredictable, liable to panic if things went awry, and far from being a suitable mount for a nervous, moderate rider aged twelve. However, to our surprise and relief, despite some fraught moments in the beginning, the horse and his young rider came to terms and established a rapport that was good to see. Eventually they were well known in the hunting field for their confident ability to give a lead to some large Thoroughbred, looking askance at anything from a five-barred gate downward. Yet a few years later when Blaze was handed down to an equally competent younger sister, the combination was a complete failure.

Again, the difference in temperament between a mare and a gelding means that some people get on better with the one, some with the other. In the Middle East, where geldings are the exception, it was a rewarding experience to ride stallions, but in England and other countries where, except for breeding purposes, the entire horse is usually an unsuitable proposition, a good gelding is hard to beat. Mares are often highly intelligent, but they can also be very unpredictable, as Smith I taught me. Most mares are affectionate and become very attached to their owners. At one of the big show-jumping competitions where the winning four riders were then required to exchange horses, the single mare in the jump-off made it very plain how much she resented the three strange riders. The relief on her face and improvement in her performance when reunited with her owner were unmistakable. A highly sexed, very ''marey'' mare can, like her human counterpart, cause a lot of trouble in an otherwise equable establishment. Our Devon contingent was forced to part with an excellent pony because of the trouble she caused among the geldings, all former friends who became over-protective would-be swains, so jealous that they attacked each other on sight.

A farmer who works his land with horses cites as one good reason for his preference the indisputable fact that tractors cannot reproduce themselves, and his Shire mares can. This ability is another advantage in owning a mare, and of all young creatures a foal is one of the most delightful. But sentiment alone is not always the best of reasons for breeding from some old favorite. Queen Elizabeth is an acknowledged world expert on Thoroughbred bloodlines and always works out the mating program for her own blood

mares, but she gave her stud manager food for thought when she decided to breed from Betsy. This black mare had been the favorite royal riding horse for years, and since she possessed considerably more character than pretensions to blue blood, the Queen's determination was based entirely on affection. But for all her lack of breeding, Betsy was a good type, she was sound, and with the right stallion could have been expected to produce a useful stamp of foal—a supposition never proved one way or the other, because Betsy declined to cooperate.

There are many people who decide similarly to breed from a favored mare when she gets too old to ride, or is redundant or outgrown. As long as the parentage is such that a reasonable foal can be expected, and there are the facilities and experience to cope with it, no one can cavil at the idea.

The facilities depend largely on the breed of horse and the climate of the country concerned. More often than not Australian mares foal in their own pleasant, dry paddock. The offspring of a British Thoroughbred first sees the light of day in an aseptic foaling box, under the unceasing if unsuspected vigil of the stud groom. Ponies often take charge themselves. There was some doubt as to when Russ, a granddaughter's Connemara, was due to foal, but each night she was called to the gate to receive a late supper and assurance that all was well. One night she was fed early and the final ritual was somehow omitted. The next morning there was Aprilli cavorting about the field on her absurdly long, new-born foal legs—after a birth that took place under the natural conditions most pony mares prefer.

This was the first foal in the family and her handling was largely a matter of experiment. At first, Aprilli was very timid and no one could lay a hand on her. Then the sight of a human, not all that much bigger than herself, lying in the grass and reading a book, was too much for the foal's inquisitiveness. Before long, Aprilli was whiffling human hair with her soft lips and snuffing at the strange smell of printer's ink.

After that experience her confidence in humans grew so quickly that she became overbold and cheeky, and that was the stage, with the future in mind, when amusing little tricks like rearing up or kicking out with a miniature hoof had to be firmly discouraged. At six months she

was a well-grown, friendly creature that made no fuss about such things as wearing a foal slip, being led in hand, and holding up her feet as required. Weaning and separation from her dam presented no difficulties because she went to a neighboring farm, where she could spend each day eating, playing, and sleeping in the company of another foal. With equally suitable facilities and good parentage, adding a foal to the establishment is both easy and fun, and one of the joys of the horseman's world.

Quite another matter is that difficult moment when the horseman realizes that a well-loved animal has lived out its days. Affection and sentiment are sometimes closely allied and difficult to differentiate. It was affection that made me conclude Smith's days when age and her teeth prevented her from enjoying life any more. It was affection that made my husband talk to her and feed her carrots in her paddock up to the last moment so that she died unaware. Unless an old favorite adapts happily to a life of retirement, is free from pain, and continues to receive proper care and attention, it is not even sentimental but cruel to keep the animal alive.

At twenty-six Twala remains in such excellent spirits that the display of bucking and showing-

off he puts on at our approach would do credit to a two-year-old. He is still the apple of this family's eye, but as soon as his life loses its savor or his health fails, we shall fulfill the last obligation people owe to the animals in their care. From our point of view that will not be an easy day.

I am still not sure whether sentiment did not outweigh common sense when we took the decision to have Jobiska partially denerved. The X-ray showed that she has both navicular and pedal ostitis, but when the vet blocked out the nerves experimentally, the old girl stepped out as good as new. And although the operation can do nothing in the way of a cure, it has been successful in removing all pain, and it has given her a lease of life that should last at lease one year and could extend to several, and . . . she is Jobiska. But when the time does come, as it must, that the pain returns, she will not be allowed to suffer.

When Smith ended her days the farm hands dug her grave and buried her in her own paddock. Nowadays such an idea is scarcely practical or possible for the average owner, but there are other ways of having a horse's life ended peacefully, in unfrightening surroundings and with someone it trusts to hand.

Horses
of the
East

Some two hundred or more different breeds and types of modern horse have stemmed from *equus caballus,* the domestic horse. *Equus* itself is the product of millions of years of evolution from a fox-sized creature known as Eohippus. Through the ages such factors as climate, altitude, and food have all had a hand in fashioning an animal that can vary from more than 18 hands in height and a ton-plus in weight, to less than 30 inches from ground to top of withers. Chance has had a finger in the pie as well, but man himself has been the chief architect in producing the many different breeds of horse and, to a lesser degree, pony. He has done it by cross and selective breeding, originally for purely functional purposes—some of them since modified and changed to fit new ways of life—and occasionally at the dictates of fashion. The breed considered to be the oldest and purest of all is the Arabian, a perfect product of the combined influence of man and environment.

The Arabian's origins and antiquity are both disputed, but it is accepted that from at least the seventh century A.D. the tribes of central Arabia were breeding and keeping truly *asil* (pure) several strains of the most beautiful and prepotent horse the world has ever seen.

The way of the Bedouin is the way of the desert, and that is not the natural way of the horse. The tribes acknowledge no man-made boundaries, but follow narrow, seasonal grazing trails. Their lives and those of the animals on which they depend are a constant battle against starvation, water shortage, and the elements. Arabian horses have short periodic opportunities for grazing, but otherwise they are hand-fed on anything available—locusts, dried dates, occasional uncrushed barley, meat, and camel's milk (which, as we discovered in Iran, is a strong brew). It was the Bedouin custom to water horses only once every twenty-four-hour period, not a practice to be recommended but one that fitted the animals for desert survival. There were, in addition, the desert environment's arduous extremes of heat and cold to further the process of survival of the fittest. The Bedouin themselves culled horses whose stamina was suspect, or which lacked the requisite beauty, speed, or other distinctions. Weaklings were allowed to perish. Thus, to anyone who has experienced the bitter cold of night in the desert, it comes as

no surprise that there should be a thriving stud of Arabian horses in Minnesota, close by the Canadian border, where the snows are deep and lasting and the temperature hovers near zero for weeks on end.

By evolving in a rigorous climate, on a diet not much different from that of its human keepers, the Arabian horse became a hard, thrifty animal, able to survive on a minimum of food and drink. Moreover, the centuries of close contact with man (not only were horses hand-fed, but a sheik's favorite mare often shared his goat's-hair tent) fostered the breed's high intelligence and liking for human companionship.

The Bedouin's horse was the embodiment of tribal honor. The very best colts were kept for stud, while the others, left entire according to Bedouin custom, were mostly sold to horse dealers to become throughout the centuries the source of most of the Arabian blood in the background of almost every other modern breed. It was the cherished mares that were kept for riding, hunting, and the continual tribal raiding that ranked almost as sport in Bedouin life.

Prestige, honor, and a man's safety were entrusted to the Bedouin's horse. It had to be hardy, of outstanding stamina, sound, fertile, and long-lived. It needed round, hard hooves to withstand the yielding sand and stony surfaces of the desert, with legs of flat, dense bone. It had to be sure-footed, fleet, and balanced, adaptable to all requirements. It had to combine fire with calmness, alertness with patience, energy with good manners. Invested with the honor of its owner and his tribe, this horse had also to be an animal of beauty and noble bearing.

The breed was fixed as near as possible to this ideal by interbreeding within the strains, substrains, and families, all of which stemmed without blemish from the original, ancient pure stock. Its overall qualities were consolidated, yet the characteristics of the different bloodlines were retained.

The head of the pure-bred Arabian is unmistakable—comparatively small, lean and chiseled, with tapering muzzle, deep, wide jowls, profile straight or preferably dished, and with the characteristic broad, prominent forehead called the *jibbah.* It has a long neck, typically arched at the top of the crest, and a clean-cut throat. Its body is muscular, with well-sprung ribs and a

To Bedouin, horses
were source of pride and
tribal honor. Camels
provided food and drink,
fuel, wool for clothing,
leather for ropes,
freedom to roam the desert.

Opposite: Biblical
Abraham's goat's-hair tent
was made like this
at Bedouin encampment
near Ma'an, Jordan. Walls
"breathe" in and out to
onslaughts of desert gales,
but exclude drafts.
At night it may shelter
a favorite mare.

short, level back usually of one less vertebra than
in other breeds. The elegant, plumed tail had to
be strong enough to carry the weight of a Bedouin rider's heavy cloak.

Mares and stallions were selected for breeding
on the basis of performance and purity of blood,
and the offspring was known by the strain of the
dam. No horse of either sex with even the faint-
est question about its ancestry was tolerated as a
mate, however perfect in appearance, and all the
matings of *asil* mares were officially witnessed.
Like the Bedouin's own ancestry, a horse's
pedigree was handed down by word of mouth,
and though either might be colored by legend,
the desert code of honor held it unthinkable for
a man to lie about the genealogies of himself or

his horse.

Today tribal warfare has ceased, mechanization has penetrated the desert's isolation, and in
this new world the Bedouin's fanatical adher-
ence to breeding only from *asil* animals has
largely ended. Even at the turn of the twentieth
century, the original desert-type animals had become so scarce that an English couple, Lady
Anne Blunt and her husband Wilfred Scawen
Blunt, were inspired to start breeding them outside the country of their origin. This decision led
to the founding of the Crabbet Stud, made famous and influential throughout the world by
the Blunts' daughter, Lady Wentworth. Today
there are many studs of beautiful, if not *asil*,
Arabians—including many built upon Crabbet

Preceding pages:
**Turkoman mares run
semiwild on steppes
southeast of Caspian
Sea, dependent only on
man for water.
Each day they gallop to
the infrequent wells,
cued by rising
dust of well-keeper's Jeep.**

stock—in Britain, Spain, Poland, Hungary, as well as in other European countries and in Australia and New Zealand.

No animal, two- or four-legged, bred in or out of the desert, is perfect in every way, but the best of these horses—varying somewhat from each other in type, according to the ideas of the country concerned—embody the physical and mental virtues of the classic Arabian. On the lush feeding that is alien to their hereditary environment, they have tended to grow larger, sometimes a little coarser, and there is an inclination to produce them for the show ring carrying fat that hides the lean, fine symmetry of the desert beauties. The true desert Arabian is a horse of only about 14 hands, or even less, but strong enough to carry its rider far and fast all day. The requirements of modern life call mostly for a larger animal, but until Lady Wentworth succeeded in breeding an Arabian of 15.2 hands that was a true replica of the smaller horse, breeding for comparable size was too often achieved at the expense of classic Arabian characteristics.

Outside its native land, the Arabian breed went through a period earlier in this century when it was looked upon as little more than a beautiful showpiece, to be exhibited in hand. Fortunately, this absurd outlook has changed and the breed has come into its own as the riding horse *par excellence* with a willingness to have a go at almost anything.

Arabians are becoming appreciated for dressage and in the hunting field. Contrary to popular belief, they will jump well—if they are trained like any other horse and carefully introduced to the water that is not a part of their race memory. Their innate intelligence and interest in all that goes on make them easy, willing pupils.

In general, even the larger Arabian is too small to compete in open jumping and eventing classes, but the shows and trials now being organized in England or elsewhere for pure and part-bred Arab horses give them a sporting chance to demonstrate their versatility.

The horse of the desert was first seen in the United States as part of a show at the 1893 Columbian Exposition in Chicago. In 1908 the Arabian Horse Club was founded with a membership of 76. Now there are more than 70,000 registered purebreds, their owners mostly

amateurs, the type of private man who treasures what he knows to be the pleasure horse without equal.

A horse that learns quickly and is intrigued with working cattle, that can spin and turn almost as fast as a Quarter Horse, and has the stamina to go all day without effort, is of obvious use as a range horse. This is appreciated in Australia and even more in the United States, where Arab horses have been used for years in general range and cattle work on a number of western ranches.

For years Arabians or part-breds have been heading the winner lists of competitive trail rides, be it the fifty-mile Golden Horseshoe in Britain, Australia's Gawler Endurance, or that famous tough nut, America's one-hundred-miler, the Tevis Cup. But apart from this sport which might have been specially tailored for Arabians, the U.S. show calendar offers innumerable shows with every kind of class. The Arabian is not just a specialist. He excels at anything he is asked to do. His willing obedience helps the young rider perform well in an Equitation class, and he will compete as a Hunter or Jumper. His controlled fire, natural balance, and muscular flexibility add panache to the refined techniques of Dressage. He will carry a sidesaddle with aplomb, wear English tack to demonstrate the requirements of an English Pleasure class, and be equally at home carrying western saddle and bridle, expertly neck-reining at walk, jog, lope, and in navigating obstacles, in the Western Pleasure and trail-riding classes. He shows with elegance in Fine Driving; there are few speedier, quicker-turning merchants for barrel racing and other gymkhana events. And if he lacks something of the weight of the Quarter Horse, his handiness makes him a joy to ride in cutting and roping competitions.

The Arab horse is extraordinarily prepotent and transmits his quality to improve almost every other breed. The definition of a part-bred Arab varies according to country. In the British Isles there must be a minimum of twenty-five percent Arabian blood, the remainder any breed other than Thoroughbred, and often this is supplied by a Welsh or Dartmoor pony to produce high-class show ponies. In the United States fifty percent is required, which entails sire or dam being purebred Arabian. The cross is then called the half-bred Arabian.

The Anglo-Arab is a cross between Arabian and Thoroughbred blood without any other strain. In Britain the percentage of either blood is irrelevant. This means that a magnificent type of horse, now appreciated as hack or hunter, show jumper or event horse, can be bred to a formula in which the characteristics of either breed can be emphasized according to taste. There is no standard type, but most breeders are now aiming for an elegant animal of Thoroughbred size, additional speed and substance, combined with the good bone, stamina, natural balance, and lovely temperament of the Arabian. In America the Anglo-Arab is again a straight 50/50 percent cross. In France, where this type has long been established as a breed, and is renowned for its prowess as cavalry charger, jumper, eventer,

and dressage horse (indeed it is the chosen mount of the elite Cadre Noir instructors at Saumur), there are Anglo-Arab sires standing at many of the national studs.

The French race the lighter type of their Anglo-Arab, but only in contests reserved for the breed. For if there is one place where you cannot expect to find an Arabian horse—purebred, Anglo-Arab, part- or half-bred, it is on the racetracks of the world, where the word "racehorse" is synonymous with "Thoroughbred." Although Arabians founded the Thoroughbred breed, they cannot compete with the big blood horse that has been carefully and selectively bred for more than two hundred years as a racing machine.

Arabians race in Athens, on the tracks at

Winner of 100-mile Tevis Cup for four successive years from 1970 to 1973, Arabian gelding Witezarif negotiates near 45-degree incline carrying owner-trainer Donna Fitzgerald. At 14.2 hands and 850 pounds, Witezarif is legendary exponent of Arabian stamina.

Cairo, Beirut, and other centers throughout the Middle East, though many of these horses must also own to a trace of Thoroughbred blood.

To see the original type of desert-racing Arabian, you must seek out the stud of some five hundred horses kept by the ruler of Bahrein, or those others that are still cherished, still kept strictly *asil*, by the royal family of Saudi Arabia. Or—as I did—you might go to Amman, Jordan, and find your way outside the town to the Moorish style stabling, dazzling white in the hot sun, that now houses the horses of the Royal Jordanian Stud. The first time I encountered them they were in their winter quarters near the shores of the Dead Sea. We had just driven the steep descent from the heights around Amman, making for Shune, nearly a thousand feet below sea level and not far from Jericho. This was

where King Hussein had a cool, attractive villa, a refuge in which to relax close by the stud where his horses come in wintertime.

Here, circling the sanded exercise track or accompanying Bedouin royal grooms on treks into the mountains, I could revel in the springy, long walk and untiring canter, the gaiety and manners, the high intelligence and courage that are the perquisites in excess of the Arabian horse.

I was riding animals descended from a tiny nucleus of mares, all of the purest and most treasured strains, that once belonged to the Emir Abdullah, and were inherited by his grandson Hussein when he acceded to the Jordanian throne. The stud is relatively young, and since Jordan has no wealth to spare, the breeding stock has been augmented with animals of equal

Lean, chiseled beauty of the Arabian head—short from poll to elegant muzzle, with large keen-edged nostrils and deep jowls, small ears, and eyes expressive of courage and dignity.

Above: Arabian's walk is a long, free gait, and his easy, balanced gallop is untiring. In the desert he is not asked to trot, but his pace, seen here running out in hand, is smart and swinging.

73

purity that have been acquired either by chance or in ways that surround the enterprise with an aura of romance.

I was invited to try the qualities of a stallion that had come off the Beirut racetrack, a handsome chestnut, typical of his breed, but only used for stud after months of patient research revealed his ancestry to be unsullied. There was a mare, of impeccable bloodlines, discovered plowing one of the crazily sloped pockets of earth that checker the mountainsides. Her head was that of a Dorcas gazelle, but her legs bore witness to the Bedouin belief in the efficacy of the firing iron to cure most equine ills. There was a stallion which had been sent as a present to the king by a sheik who still pitches his black goat's-hair tents far out in the desert and counts a horse of the ancient blood his dearest possession.

My visit to the stud took place before the Seven-Day Arab-Israeli War of 1967. In that year the swift advance of the Israeli tanks to the banks of the Jordan River made it imperative for the horses to be moved back to Amman without delay. They left before dawn, as many as possible being ridden or led, the rest following loose. They avoided the potential dangers of the road, going up through the first of the wadis and clambering over the shaley sides of the mountains in darkness, but much of the twelve-hour trek was done in the blazing heat of the day. They arrived at their destination—mares, stallions, colts, and young stock alike—apparently as fresh as when they left, the gamboling of the loose animals a tribute to the matchless endurance of their breed.

History has dictated that King Hussein's horses now remain all year round in their quarters near Amman, but despite all the subsequent horrors of war and near-war in the Middle East, the stud has kept going and its stock is known in all countries where the Arabian horse is prized.

In our horseman's world of today there are more high-class, if not *asil,* Arabian horses bred outside the Middle East than in it. Years of soft living and luxuriant grazing inevitably change the type to a degree, so it is good to know that a few studs remain where the stamp of the original "drinkers of the wind" is preserved.

Outside of the national studs it is possible occasionally to find animals of impeccable ancestry belonging to fortunate individuals. Such a one, a

Jussor, seen here at exercise with Bedouin groom, is a Beirut stallion of the Royal Jordanian stud and one-time favorite saddle horse of King Hussein's second wife, the English-born Princess Muna.

75

Above: Persian Arab, taller, lacking concave profile of desert breed, has history going back hundreds of years.

Right: Atesh (Fire) was presented to Princess Anne when she attended 2,500th anniversary celebration of Persian Empire. Chestnut Pahlavan colt is part Thoroughbred, part Plateau Persian, part imported Arab stock.

little Yemeni stallion named Nsr, belonged to the Italian ambassador in Amman.

Nsr was of the ancient and irreproachable Hamdani strain. History does not say whether "Hamdani" means actual kinship with the legendary mare Baz and the stallion Hoshaba, which were caught up from the wild horses of the Yemen, tamed, and bred by Noah's great-great-great-grandson, but the implication is there. Blue blood apart, it was a privilege to see the quality of trust and understanding between Nsr and his owner. While planes thundered in and out of Amman airport on one side, and Arabian racehorses sped wildly by in training

gallops on the other, horse and man played in undistracted harmony and then schooled together, displaying a mutual rapport as rare as it was fascinating, the horse responding without the aid of a bit.

The Nsrs of the Middle East, are a small elite. Much more numerous are the sturdy country-breds of Arabian type still working in the same ways they have for centuries. They are likely to remain indispensable in some Middle Eastern regions for many years to come. For while community tractors, trucks, a motorbike or two are now everyday adjuncts to Bedouin life, they have not entirely displaced horses, which are

kids, golden eyed and hairy legged, leaping high onto my tent's sloping roof and striating the canvas with their black, pointed hooves as they tobogganed down. A passing pi-dog had a dirty sidelong look for me, a hobbled camel browsed on clumps of kefi, a goggle-eyed colt peered and blew in distaste at my alien smell, a donkey brayed its rasping noise cut off in midnote as though strangled. Between me and the horizon, where the orange-red rim of the sun was just surfacing, was a vast, soul-satisfying expanse of nothing but the sand and scrub and gray stones that make up the *suwwan,* the stony desert of Jordan.

Close by—tethered by the multicolored rope and the bitless, embroidered headstall that comprise a Bedouin bridle, and wearing the treeless Bedouin saddle—was the mare that awaited my pleasure.

First, though, came breakfast, eaten in the shelter of a propped-out wall of the tent with the early rays of the sun to warm us. It was a satisfying meal of curdled butter, Arab bread, ground almonds, cheese, "bully beef" (in deference to me), and a welcome drink of hot, sweet sheep's milk to wash it all down. Then to horse, and the usual dilemma due to immovable leathers and the fact that my legs are longer than those of the Bedouin. Perched like a monkey I set off for the ride's objective, the Hejaz railway, originally constructed by an Ottoman Turkish sultan —who denuded the surrounding countryside of trees for the purpose—and destroyed for the first time in 1918 by T. E. Lawrence and the Emir Feisal's guerrillas.

After some thought and—due to the language difficulty—no advice, steerage with a single rope "rein" was achieved by a tug one way, a kind of neck-rein the other. The mare was willing and lively, and the half-lope, half-jog with which she covered the appallingly rough ground was both quick and comfortable.

There was much about that little horse to advertise her claim to at least part-Arabian blood, but she bore little resemblance to that other type of elegant Arab horse subsequently encountered in Iran.

This was a day that took us on horseback into the peaks of the Elburz range, north of Tehran. There was a tortoise sunning itself on the rocky track at the 6,000-foot summit of a gorge. In

often kept for prestige. Usually there are countrybreds about, like those I encountered near Ma'an, where Bedouin hospitality permitted me to experience briefly the life of a desert tent dweller.

The night of my arrival there was peaceful, except for the thin, distant wail of a new-born child and the sudden entrance of two cats that raced across my face and up the pole of my ex-Army bell tent. My rest was again disrupted toward morning by an unidentifiable noise, as if a giant were ripping calico just over my head. I groped my way outside into the pristine half-light of predawn to find a bunch of impudent goat

surroundings where the winter temperatures can plummet to chilling depths, a tortoise seemed incongruous, but no one else found it so. As our horses wound their way on down, there were clumps of wild fig and pampas grass clothing the rockface on one side. Above the ravine, high above timberline, one caught a momentary glimpse of the curving horns of an ibex, while far below the Jajroud river tumbled toward red and gold groves of aspen and poplar in autumn leaf. Our way was enlivened by being informed that Iranian tortoises catch and eat snakes. Maybe.

I had begun the trek on Saab, a splendid Anglo-Persian stallion, one of the excellent Thoroughbred-Persian crosses that the Iranian royal stables has been breeding for some years. (The latest cross, equally successful and initiated by the father of the present Royal Master of Horse, is the Pahlavan, now established as a breed and named after the country's ruling dynasty. It was evolved from constant proportions of Thoroughbred, Plateau Persian, and imported Arabian stock.)

Later on the trek I changed to Saar—the Starling—colored to merit his name. He was a Plateau Persian, the composite title given to all the strains of Persian horse that vary only through geographical and climatic conditions, plus the selective breeding of the different tribes that raise them. Like all the horses of Persia, they have fire and elegance.

Saar was a superlative mountain horse, negotiating the trickiest terrain with contemptuous ease, although he alarmed me at first on the steeper slopes with serpentine waggings of his head and neck, evidently threats to buck which, in fact, he never implemented.

On another day I was to see Saar galloped down a steep, rock-strewn hillside by his owner, the Master of Horse, in pursuit of a wounded mouflon—the local wild sheep—a feat that placed horse and rider in a category of their own. My own mount that day was an ebullient, elegant Darashouri named Shabrang, with slender ears incurved like scimitars and a silky mane that swung from his arched chest with each dancing step. "Do not let Shabrang out, Mrs. Campbell," I had been told. "He is the fifth fastest horse in the stables."

Let him out? They must have been joking. Yet before the day ended the coal-black Shabrang

Colts and fillies of this Turkoman mare will race, like so many of their breed, in autumn tribal contests and on the more sophisticated track outside Tehran. These racers from Iran evolved partly from tough ponies of marauding Tartars, refined to slim elegance by selective breeding and desert diet.

has his way. Left briefly in charge of the grooms, they converged upon me with hisses of encouragement and gestures to go faster. Shabrang needed no urging. He sprang forward and we passed the leaders within seconds, the echo of a number of words not usually heard on the lips of females of my generation floating behind us as my horse strove to live up to his reputation. The ten miles of rocky track and shale-covered descent that yet lay between us and Shabrang's stable were no place for speed, but eventually self-preservation prevailed and he obligingly consented to slow down, then to prance and dance for a mile or so, saying as clearly as speech: "I have shown you what I can do, and now you ask me to *walk?!*"

According to the design of the Shah of Iran's "white" revolution, mechanization is rapidly engulfing many of the work horses that have been an integral part of Persian life for thousands of years. Even so, the country is so vast that it must be a long time to come before motorized trucks entirely replace horses. Some will persist, like those with beaded headstalls we saw trundling high-wheeled carts past the glistening blue and gold mosaics of the mosques in Isfahan; or those teams, almost invisible beneath the bulging sacks of rice that we met on our way to the Caspian littoral. And though Japanese minitractors are now indispensable in many regions, wherever irrigation ditches surround small plots, horses still pull the cultivators. All of which ensures there will be work for a few more generations of harness makers, men who sit cross-legged in their booths in the bazaars, surrounded by mounds of saddles, embroidered nose bags, ornamented bridles, high wooden cart collars all beaded and belled, and the strings of neck beads worn by all Persian working horses as a potent bringer of good luck.

With few exceptions, the new ideas have turned the nomad Turkoman—his forebears a leftover from Genghis Khan and for long the scourge of Persia's northeast corner—into a prosperous, settled farmer. More often than not he has forsaken his beautiful, reed-constructed yurt for the solid comforts of a concrete house, his wealth obtained from sheep and camels and cereal crops, rather than from the traditional herds of horses. The once inevitable breeding stallion that was tethered outside the home from the age of eighteen months, hand-fed and swathed in the customary seven layers of heat-and-cold-insulating felt, is now seldom seen. The Turkomans come in from their steppeland for the seasonal tribal races by car and truck, instead of astride the horses that carried them through the dust in former days. But in those same trucks they transport their greyhound-shaped animals of characteristic high head carriage—the Turkoman horse that is the predominant racehorse of Iran. They come hundreds of miles south to the sophisticated track outside Tehran, and they do not return empty-handed. Come what may, wherever there is a Turkoman with his high-cheekboned face and black lamb's wool hat, there will be a horse—typically a lean, frugal-living animal of iron constitution and incredible endurance—somewhere close by.

There are two races of Turkoman (or Turkmen) horse. It was a Jomud, the smaller and—if possible—tougher of the two, that set off from our Turkoman encampment carrying me with what seemed relentless purpose toward the Russian border only five miles distant. Maybe he had an assignation with an Akhal-Teké mare, the other race of Turkoman, bred in those regions but primarily in the U.S.S.R., a breed of ancient ancestry and such speed that, known as Turkoman Atti, they were always the assigned mounts of the bodyguard of the caliphs of Baghdad. Fortunately that Jomud horse and I came to terms before I was forced to find out his intentions, and the only Akhal-Teké of my acquaintance remains the stallion Mele-Kush, which Nikita Khrushchev gave to Prince Philip in 1956. Taller, speedier, and altogether a more elegant animal than my friend of the Turkoman steppe, Mele-Kush had the thin tail and sparse mane of his breed and the wonderful, iridescent golden coloring that is also characteristic.

Pleasure riding, even show jumping, is now a growing part of the sporting scene around Tehran, and the recently formed Royal Horse Society—its chief and gigantic task the preservation and registration of all the Plateau Persian and other recognized Persian breeds—is helping materially to maintain a heritage that goes back four thousand or more years.

Not long ago a surprising discovery was made in Persia when a chunk of its most ancient history, thought to have been extinct for a thousand

years or so, was found to be still alive and, occasionally, kicking. This is the almost confirmed outcome of an interest taken by the American-born wife of a Persian in a little 11-hand stallion—thin, covered with lice and sores but appearing to be of a specific breed—that she saw in 1965 pulling a cart through the narrow alleys of the bazaar in Amol, close by the shores of the Caspian Sea.

There were very few other such "Persian miniatures" to be found in the Caspian region, not more than fifty at most, with another one or two located on the summer grazing grounds of the north face of the Elburz range. It took Louise Firouz two years to discover sufficient animals —in the paddy fields, pulling cotton planters, or toting loads of faggots down from the mountains—to establish a small breeding herd.

We saw one of these elegant little creatures, bred at her stud outside Tehran, in the royal stables at Farahabad. Although little larger than its stock Shetland companions, the Caspian —with its fine head, slender legs, and graceful body—stood out like the miniature horse it is.

We could see for ourselves the truth of all that is said about the Caspian's innately charming disposition—willing and spirited, but kind and safe for a young child, with excellent jumping ability when required. Proof was the stallion we saw, ridden by Mrs. Firouz' small son, walking quietly in a miscellaneous crowd of racehorses and ponies with which it had just been competing in a children's race.

What we could not then know was that years of meticulous research would eventually reveal the Caspian to be almost surely the last remaining example of Iran's native wild horse, a direct descendant of the pony-sized animal thought to have existed from about the Second Millennium B.C. to the Islamic conquests of the seventh century A.D.

This little horse is also the only one in the world to share some of the physical characteristics—especially the wedge-shaped head structure—of the Arabian. It is now considered feasible that the Caspian comes from root-stock from which the Arabian horse also evolved.

4.

The World's Favorite Breeds

Grace, beauty, the symmetry of speed, the heart of a lion, the blood of Arabian ancestors—this is the Thoroughbred, evolved through two centuries of breeding "best to best." This is Hyperion mare Libra and her foal, running on the bluegrass of Kentucky.

Opposite: Kentucky-bred foals play "You take mine and I'll take yours."

Bluegrass country in the month of May is a time when beauty matches beauty. The sun is warm without being hot, and spikelets in flower add a shimmering blue tinge to the paddocks. Comely Thoroughbred matrons graze contentedly while their long-legged, irresistible offspring leap and race about or lie flat soaking up the sunshine. Looking at it all I wonder if the Thoroughbred has come so far from England after all. The green parkland and stately trees seem familiar, and the dry-stone walls bordering the roads might be in Devon or Yorkshire. Yet that robin perched on a nearby branch is twice the size and half the ruddiness of its British cousin, and that fine low house with its white-pillared portico is of an architecture uniquely "old South."

Bluegrass country is the loosely defined area around Lexington, Kentucky, traditionally the stronghold of the American Thoroughbred. It is dotted with breeding farms, some old with traditions reaching back many generations, some new, the lucrative if also expensive hobbies of businessmen from "outside." Wherever two or three are gathered together in the Bluegrass—be they breeders or trainers, buyers or sellers, husbands or wives—the conversation is of horses. Bloodlines, mating programs, purchases, prices, performances are talked about everywhere—in the barns, in the dining rooms over tables laden with rich Kentucky cuisine.

Unmistakable in the atmosphere is the equine snobbism that has always surrounded the Thoroughbred. For this is the horse that spoils one for other breeds, as a Rolls-Royce spoils one for other makes of car. And as with the Rolls, the Thoroughbred—by price, constitution, and disposition—is rarely successful as a poor man's property, just as he is seldom a novice ride. Basically the breed was evolved to produce the perfect racing machine. Racing is the *raison d'être* for almost all the Thoroughbred breeding studs in the world and it is the taproot of the wealth that circulates around these horses.

The Thoroughbred is the masterpiece of all the numerous other types and breeds of horse in the world today that owe many of their qualities to Arabian blood. It is a comparatively young breed, with all modern Thoroughbreds tracing their descent in the direct male line to Matchem, Herod, and Eclipse, and through them to three

potent Arabian sires imported into England during a period spanning the end of the seventeenth century and the early part of the eighteenth century. The origins of the foundation mares is more obscure, but they are believed by many to have been oriental types such as the "royal mares" that once graced King Charles II's royal mews.

While the original breed was an English creation, all modern English Thoroughbreds are now produced jointly with Ireland through a linked breeding industry and common stud book. In that true country of the horse, the limestone in pasture and water combined with a mild climate constitute ideal conditions for breeding first-class Thoroughbreds. Ireland's many famous studs are a constant source of superb racers on the flat, and of stallions that have enormous influence on the racing stock of the world. (It is amazing, for example, to see how many times the name of the great Irish-bred Nasrullah crops up in the pedigrees of blood horses bred in Kentucky.) Wherever racing over the sticks is practiced—in America it is a less popular sport than in England and Ireland—the Irish steeplechaser, a type of big stayer that is allowed to mature slowly to embody stamina and jumping power, is supreme. There is no more legendary name in steeplechasing than that of the Irish-bred Arkle.

Since the early nineteenth century, many other countries have carried on bloodstock industries, based mainly on imported English stock. Only recently have breeders in England and Ireland realized that they were exporting too many of their best blood horses for their own good. The latest big buyer in the Thoroughbred market is Japan.

Basically Thoroughbreds breed true and are not "improved" by the introduction of any other breed, but bloodlines developed in countries as far removed as, say, Argentina and Italy, Australia and Russia, South Africa and Hungary, are affected by the varying climates and geographical regions, as well as by the different racing requirements. France, where the lush pastures and good climate of Normandy tend to produce slow-maturing stayers of great stamina, was the first country to breed racehorses capable of successfully taking on their English counterparts on their own turf. North America, where the Thoroughbred breeding industry is now the largest in the world, is mostly geared to create

Principally show-ring
animals, American Saddle
Horses have no
European equivalent. Bred
for brilliance and
animation of action, their
background includes the
Morgan, Narragansett Pacer,
Standardbred, and
Thoroughbred in good
measure. Rider's seat and
legs must encourage and
cope with strong
impulsion from
hindquarters, while
hands maintain high
head carriage and
extreme leg action.

speed at the earliest age possible, and therefore produces the majority of the famous sprinters.

But the Thoroughbred, whatever its country of birth, is really an international product, the outcome of generations of breeding best to best to achieve the ultimate capabilities of speed over varying distances. All typical Thoroughbreds share the common factors of a wonderfully smooth action plus the conformation, strength, and grace that make them the finest athletes of the animal kingdom. Except over very short distances they are undoubtedly the fastest, with stamina and sometimes jumping ability to match their speed. In 1945 the American sprinter, Big Racket, set the record for the quarter mile with the 20⁴/₅ seconds, which meant a top acceleration of 43.3 mph; it was calculated that, unimpeded by the weight of a rider, he would have clocked up 55.4 mph. The cheetah is faster, but cannot sustain its speed for distances equal to the Thoroughbred's.

For any Thoroughbred that cannot show sufficient speed on the track there are plenty of other jobs where his innate class and ability can be used to the full. In the English shires, over the formidable walls of Virginia or the five-strand barbed-wire fences of New Zealand, wherever there is still room to gallop and to jump taking your own line, fox hunters mostly swear by Thoroughbreds. You can find blood animals working as stock horses in Australia and the United States. In America, too, the horse preferred for hunter-class competition is the Thoroughbred; indeed, all the show jumpers the American team brought to Hickstead for the World Cup in 1974 were Thoroughbreds. And while the British show jumper is more likely to be a Thoroughbred-cross, most of the leading show hacks are blood horses.

In the United States Thoroughbred breeding and racing is not only one of the largest industries but also one of the wealthiest. Except for Alaska, these horses are bred in all the states, with California, Florida, and Virginia (where the incomparable Mill Reef was bred on the Paul Mellon estate) increasingly important. But the biggest business, the most money, the largest number of fine Thoroughbreds to the acre are to be found in Kentucky, around Lexington.

There is nothing immediately apparent about Bluegrass pasture to make it different from any

dams, who seem to know instinctively that a Thoroughbred's destiny is to run, run fast, and run again. But how is an old "heavy" to appreciate that?)

Normally Thoroughbred mares are sent away to be bred. Unlike some that fly in from all parts of the world, those Kentucky matrons rarely have far to go. Most of the top-flight American stallions have always been kept in this region, a practice dictated almost by necessity in a country where distances are so vast.

Many top-class Thoroughbred stallions, proven on racetrack and at stud, are so valuable that ownership is possible only through syndication. The most noteworthy recent example was Secretariat, whose $6 million price as a stud horse was made up by the sale of thirty-two shares at $190,000 each.

It is awe-inspiring to view in Lexington neighboring paddocks occupied by great sires or retired heroes of the track whose success as progenitors is in process of being proven. At one establishment the redoubtable American sire Graustark is neighbor to Roberto, winner of the 1972 Epsom Derby, while a short space away is the elaborate resting place of the very great Italian-bred Ribot, who ruled the stud until his death in 1972. Such is the heady and international atmosphere of the Bluegrass.

They do have other makes of horse in Kentucky, and more than one farm is involved in breeding Standardbred harness horses.

In the early part of the nineteenth century trotting was a sport of amateurs—neighbors who raced their buggies against each other en route for town, and young bloods who bought the fastest steppers they could find precisely to race against each other, in harness or under saddle, on broad avenues of the newly laid out cities of New York, Boston, and Philadelphia. Horses qualified not by their breeding, but by their ability to trot a fast mile.

As the sport became more organized a specialized type of horse was bred for its ability to trot within a standard time for the mile, hence "Standardbred." (The standard time for the mile now stands at 2:20, but in 1845 a 2:30 mile in harness was proclaimed as phenomenal.) It was noted that the progeny of Rysdyk's Hambletonian, a great-grandson of the English stallion Messenger who was imported to Philadelphia in

other good grazing. Its fame lies with its nutritive value, due partly to the limestone soil in which it grows, which, as all Irish horse breeders will appreciate, makes for quality of bone and good sound stock.

The aristocrats that graze these white-fenced pastures get treatment fully in accord with their value. Everything possible is done to keep the mares functioning as breeding units, and to ensure that foals and young stock get the best possible start in life. Beauty is served as well as efficiency. On one farm, where the white and red buildings stand amid fine trees upon a sea of green grass, the mares and foals can evade the heat of the day in the cool luxury of their stalls. Here geraniums grow in hanging baskets, the flycatchers are electrically operated, and the centerpiece is an oval of turf with a fountain and the cool tinkling of water to set it off.

(Among the bluebloods on that farm, there is one animal who looks as though she feels a little out of place, an honest nurse mare, hairy and of relatively ponderous Percheron dimensions and patchwork coloring. She is, they say, meticulous in nursing her blue-blooded suckling, but sadly neglectful about chivvying her charge to take exercise, a duty always observed by the other

1788, had speed and the innate propensity to trot or pace. Various other strains came into the picture, both before and after Hambletonian, including the Narragansett Pacer, Norfolk Trotter, Arabian, Morgan, Barb, Cleveland Bay, and Hackney, but the predominant blood remains that of the Thoroughbred, originally supplied by Messenger.

Different strains of Standardbred either trot or pace, although the pacer, the slightly faster of the two, is now the favored performer in such countries as the United States, Canada, Australia, and New Zealand. On the Continent the trotter has held his own over the pacer, and while most countries have their own breeds, the Standardbred has made important contributions. This is particularly true of the Russian Trotter, known up to 1949 as the Orlov-American Crossbred. Trotting has been going on in France since 1836, and in that country the French Trotter is in a class of its own, its prowess due to a mixed ancestry, including Thoroughbred, Norfolk Trotter, and Anglo-Norman blood.

In the place where the trotting sport originated, the north of England, it is still very much in its infancy, being limited until recent years to the northern counties and Scottish lowlands. Now there are a few permanent tracks in addition to the unofficial grass ones, and the signs point to a continued gain in popularity.

Wales has a high-class Standardbred stud —one of the few studs in Britain where many horses in transit from the United States to Australia stay out their quarantine. It also races its own horses, and often exports animals to America and to Australia and New Zealand, a surprising reversal of the usual procedure, and an indication of the worldwide vigor of the harness-horse breeding industry. It was at this stud that I made my first close acquaintance with a Standardbred. While speed and performance are more important than looks in judging this breed, here was an individual with presence and the look of quality. Typically longer in the body and shorter in the leg than a Thoroughbred, he had powerful sloping quarters and long pasterns for propelling. Though an entire and only three years old, he had the equable temperament that is characteristic Standardbred make-up.

It may come as something of a surprise—if not a scandal to traditionalists—to hear that the tal-

ents of this rugged little horse did not stop with harness racing. When his owner, who also trains him, was short of a hunter, she spent a while in teaching her trotter how to cope with a moderate-sized fence, and then took him to a local meet of fox hounds. His behavior was exemplary, but there was some consternation when the Field, galloping on after hounds, was caught up by a horse bowling along at a trot. Astonishment followed when this racing Standardbred popped neatly over a fence, and continued on his speedy way with scarcely a pause in the rhythm of his gait.

In the days when the small and gentle palfrey was in fashion, its main attraction was its innate propensity to amble or pace, since the lateral motion of the legs ensured a smooth ride. Were it required, most of the native British pony breeds could show inherent talent for the pacing gait. But over the last two hundred years ambling or pacing has been bred out of most horses in favor of trotting ability. There are a few breeds that produce their own variation of either one or the other gait, which becomes even more stylized due to the disciplines imposed by man.

The United States has at least two such breeds, the American Saddle Horse and the Tennessee Walking Horse. One southerner courteously gave me a demonstration of what his highly trained Walker could do.

It was a horse of substance, level-backed and short-coupled, with high head carriage and a set tail. The eye was intelligent, the overall impression one of proud compliance. Its feet were abnormally and to my mind appallingly long, their appearance, and the apparent strain on the pasterns, accentuated by the thick pads under weighted shoes.

This animal was evolved originally for the old-time planters' convenience and ease, a horse that could tote them around their vast properties—covering up to fifty miles in a day —at a running-gliding walk of 6 to 8 mph, kept up without distress for hours on end. A true American cocktail of a horse, it owes much of its substance and the basis of its gait to the Canadian Pacer and the Standardbred, its elegance to the Saddle Horse, its characteristic cooperation to the Morgan, its quality to Thoroughbred infusions.

The stallion's owner was happy to oblige

Tennessee Walking Horses are short-backed, deep-chested, sturdier than Saddlers. Their gaits— a flat-footed walk, running walk, and "rocking chair" canter—are unique.

Overleaf: Normandy raises the French Trotter and French Saddle Horse (Selle Français), both stemming from Anglo-Norman stock. Trotter also has strains of Russian and American blood. This is French Trotting stallion Cotentin, at Haras du Pin.

when I asked to see his Tennessee Walker under saddle. Within minutes they re-emerged from the barn, the horse tacked up with the traditional gear of straight-panelled saddle, the same as used with American Saddle Horses, and long-cheeked bit with a single rein. The rider was a professional trainer, as are ninety percent of those who show Walking Horses in other than Pleasure Classes. He appeared to sit on the back end of the saddle, with knees slightly bent and heels thrust down to bring his lower leg behind the girth, and he held his hands high. Away they went in a spectacular running walk, the stallion nodding his head with each beat, grinding his teeth and flopping his ears in time, covering the ground with a fast, smooth glide that left the rider completely unjarred and brought the animal's hind feet overstriding the front by inches. When they changed gear to canter, the horse elevated his front end in a slow ''rocking chair'' move-

ment while his quarters remained level, an action that must be seen to be appreciated.

This was a brilliant, highly-schooled show horse, but there are Pleasure Horse versions of this breed which provide comfort and excellent temperament without extreme exaggeration of the gaits, without the set tail and the excessive length of hoof that in show horses sometimes raises the heel to an angle approaching ninety degrees. Were the pleasure Walkers the only examples of the breed there would be neither reason nor foundation for the stories of unpleasant methods being used to train Tennessee Walking Horses to show standard.

Spokesmen for the breed maintain that former excesses have been stamped out, that judges are now meticulous, and that if or where cruelty still exists, it is carried on only by a few evil and ignorant people trying to do a training job for which they are not qualified. Even so, it is not pleasant to think that the unique canter I watched could have been induced by so weighting the animal's overlong hind feet that a normal canter is impossible, and that he might have been literally forced to walk behind and pump in front, or that the over-reach boots he was wearing could have covered a sore or abrasion, the result of caustic applied to promote more brilliance of action.

They say that many foals of this breed "run-walk" beside their dams from birth, that no other type of horse can be taught to move in this fashion, and that seventy-five percent of the Walker's show gait is natural. If that is so, it seems to me an unnecessary pursuit of fashion to induce the other twenty-five percent at all.

Another product of the South, virtually unknown outside America, is the American Saddle Horse, a breed of somewhat similar if more refined antecedents than the Tennessee Walker, with a good dash of Thoroughbred blood. Actually the situation is changing. The breed is popular in South Africa both for pleasure and show, and Australia had its first sale of the American Saddle Horse in 1973.

Few who have not seen an individual of this breed can really believe in the existence of the animals as they are shown in photographs. For how could one imagine a flesh-and-blood horse with such a long and graceful neck? With such an exaggeratedly lofty head carriage epitomizing so much pride and spirit? With eyes so very large and lustrous, and with such incredible animation of action? My first sight of these horses at show made me a believer.

The ring filled suddenly with teen-age competitors all wearing drain-pipe trousers, long-skirted jackets, and Derby hats perched atop their neatly tied-back hair. Their hands were held apart and roughly waist-high, their torsos were erect with chests lifted and tilted forward slightly to promote correct position of the lower leg, with heels rammed down to keep grip at the knee but not at the thigh. This is the classic saddle seat, unlike any other style. It produces a constant but sensitive restraint, which, coupled with steady leg pressure engaging the animal's hindquarters, ensures the balance and action, the brilliance, bearing, and supreme animation of the show type of American Saddle Horse. These performances require skill, concentration, and cooperation, and the constant schooling of both horses and riders.

"Up . . . down, Up . . . down, Up . . . down," went the young equestrians as the prancing walk changed to a high-actioned trot, its rhythm accented by the beat of the music. "Up . . . down, Up . . . down," rising for an appreciable time to allow for a stride as long as it is lofty, and being moved by the energetic thrust of the horse's propulsion, not by anticipation of a jolt.

This was an equitation class and the horses were Three-Gaited, their status proclaimed by tails shaved down the base. Their third gait is a relatively slow yet animated and very smooth canter.

In the Five-Gaited classes, the horse alone is judged and he must be a showy, thrilling creature, with flowing mane and full, set tail, supremely fiery and elegant. Except for amateur/owner classes, the riders here are professionals, guiding their horses at two man-made gaits, in addition to walk, trot, and canter. The first of these is the stepping pace, not more than 10 mph with a slight break in cadence that gives a fluent ride. Then the ringmaster calls "Rack on! Rack on!" and the trainers yell "Shake it! Shake it!" as the beat of the music quickens. The riders, sitting immobile to steady their horses, but jiggling their hands from side to side, come dashing by. The horses strike the ground with each foot separately in a fast, exhausting gait that is said to be exhibited correctly only by the American Saddle Horse.

These horses are natural exhibitionists, giving all they have the moment they enter the ring, and they are also very intelligent. In a test designed by Arabian breeders to show which type of horse relates best to humans, to everyone's surprise the American Saddle Horse came out on top. (Which, as was pointed out, had to be due to the Arabian blood in its make-up.) They are well-named the peacocks of the horse world, but it is a pity that up to a short while ago all the emphasis was put on their supremacy as show animals. They do make excellent pleasure horses, they can jump and hunt and are sure-footed and comfortable for trail riding, and many show good cow sense. But until these qualities are given proper weight and fully appreciated, the Saddle Horse will remain chiefly the province of the relatively few show people who can

Opposite: Well-bred Quarter Horses of obvious quality—short heads, small muzzles, "foxy" ears, strong jaws, eyes wide-set and kind. They have "riding" (i.e., sloping) shoulders, powerful muscles in quarters and thighs.

Above: Morgans on
trail in Virginia woods
belong to one of America's
most versatile breeds.
They are strong yet light,
ideal general-purpose
saddle horses, powerful in
draft, and excellent
fast-stepping roadsters.

Opposite: Mustang
stallion warns off a rival.
Mustangs that survive
from huge bands that once
roamed the West
are endowed with extreme
hardiness, thriftiness,
and intelligence.

afford to keep them and have them profession-
ally trained and ridden.

There is another side to the picture, however.
It is easy to blunder where angels are treading
delicately, and the right to criticize should be
reserved to those who know every aspect of a
question. Though the Saddle Horse show people are known to have put much of their house in
order, there remain things that I find hard to
understand. One was the animal I saw with the
underside of its dock rubbed raw by the tail-set.
(This is the metal contraption that American
Saddle Horses are fitted with to support and train
their tails at an unnaturally high angle, and which
they wear, except in the show ring, for the
duration of their show careers.) It is easy to contend that this particular set was insufficiently
padded, and certainly the horses I visited in their
stalls behind the scenes appeared contented and
kind. But why should a beautiful horse provided
by nature with an elegant tail carriage—as

demonstrated by the pleasure-horse type—have
to spend its showing life wearing not only the
tail-set itself, but the variety of straps that hold it
in place? Why, when off duty, should these
horses be encumbered with wide straps around
the top of their necks, that sweat off the dimensions of throats already refined by nature and by
their resemblance to the Thoroughbred Denmark, foundation sire of the breed. Why should
the same feet that serve the pleasure horses so
well over the roughest of ground, in show animals be grown to such a length that often wires
or other devices are needed to hold on the pads
and weighted shoes, simply in order to enhance
an action that is already so highly distinctive?
Apart from these dictates of fashion, it could not
seem that comfort was envisaged for those animals I saw limbering up with the use of "fetters"
strapped round their fetlocks and joined by a
short length of chain to make them snatch their
feet in action. Nor can I imagine ever wishing to

ride a horse that had been induced to hold his tail even higher by the practice known as gingering.

Easy enough to criticize, and these horses are not the only ones to be subjected to extreme measures. I prefer to remember the Saddle Horse colt I saw, being schooled up and down the passageway between the stalls of a big breeding barn. True, his tail had been set, but its carriage owed nothing to a wad of ginger, and his feet though longer than normal were not in any way extravagant or overweighted; his elevation of head—which encourages high-stepping—was the result of knowledgeable training. He was being driven on long lines, his trainer running behind and to one side, and later he flashed by drawing a four-wheeled show buggy. Either way, he presented such a picture of fire and spirit, of such perfect physical beauty and overall brilliance that I shall not forget him.

So here is a breed so lovely in looks and disposition, and so worthy of being better known, that surely any practice that might detract from it should best be discontinued.

The American Saddle Horse is such a versatile animal that he is also distinctive in Fine Harness classes, showing his paces at walk, animated park trot, and the exciting "show your horse" event, a display of speed and judgement wisely reserved for professional drivers. The fact that he goes well in harness could be due to the Morgan blood that runs in his veins.

America's Morgan Horse traces back to the one prepotent foundation sire, foaled in Massachusetts around 1793 and called Justin Morgan after his breeder. Morgans—black, bay, or black-bay in color—are smallish animals, low and powerful, with distinctive good looks that may stem from a cross of Arabian on Dutch light draft horse—as some believe—or from the siring of Justin Morgan by a famous imported racing stallion that became the charger of a Tory officer.

Before being superseded by the Standardbred, the Morgan was important as a racing trotter. But his primary work was that of an all-rounder—indispensable as a saddle horse, roadster, and farm worker. There was a time when the Morgan was the mainstay of the U.S. Cavalry, and a time when the breed was threatened by crossing with the Standardbred for the sake of speed.

Mechanization hit the Morgan as hard as it did any other horse used then in harness, but the breed has made a striking comeback. Today the Morgan is valued as a perfect family horse, of the right size and temperament for both young and adult riders and drivers. Friendly and generous by nature, these horses compete pretty much across the board—as roadsters, park horses, hunters, jumpers, and saddle horses. By reason of their stamina and character, they are suitable for trail riding, endurance rides, and for use by the mounted police.

The Cleveland Bay is England's version of an all-purpose horse. It is a notable leaper, and in addition to its qualities as a harness horse it makes a first-class—if not very fast—up-to-weight hunter. The Cleveland's origins are ancient and somewhat obscure. The breed stems from the pack horses known for centuries in the Yorkshire dales and is considered to be without trace of cold blood. The modern Cleveland has an elegance not unlike that of the notable and now extinct Yorkshire Coach Horse, which was Cleveland Bay with a good mingling of Thoroughbred.

The breed itself was at one time in danger of dying out, but in the years since World War II its quality has been rediscovered and it is widely used for crossing with other breeds. There are pure and cross-bred Clevelands in Canada, Australia, South Africa, and Japan. The United States has its own Cleveland Bay Society, and the blood figures in several American breeds. Once again, carriage horses are being bred up with infusions of Cleveland blood, which was a common practice before World War I, and the same blood has helped build up the all-round sporting type of horse that has largely superseded the heavier Continental harness horse.

The Cleveland's equable temperament was demonstrated to me the day I rode a newly-broken three-year-old stallion on the edge of the Home Park at Windsor, a horse that has since become one of the leading sires of his breed. Although not then at full strength, he was of a height and scope that would have been beyond my strength had he chosen to play up. In fact he behaved like a perfect gentleman—a sedate trot was the most that was asked of him—and since our performance was within range of the castle windows and under the impassive gaze of one of the sentries, this is something for which I remain

96

most grateful.

The German Holstein of saddle-horse type owes some of its jumping prowess to the Cleveland Bay. The German Oldenburg, a breed popular also in Denmark, was largely resuscitated by use of the Cleveland. And currently gray Oldenburgs predominate among the royal Windsor Greys (horses that are not a specific breed but owe their title to Queen Victoria's preference for driving gray "ponies" around the grounds of Windsor Castle). On days when the royal mews at Buckingham Palace are open to the public, these horses together with purebred Clevelands and others with the popular Thoroughbred cross are brought from their roomy boxes to stand tied in the company of other state animals, all with their names inscribed above their heads, in the graceful stalls originally designed for King George III by the architect Nash. Some of the cross-bred royal teams, which are faster than the pure Clevelands, get an exciting change to their more decorous ceremonial duties when Prince Philip takes off with one of them on a competitive cross-country driving marathon.

Hackney horses, those spectacular highsteppers long considered the specialists of the show ring, are sometimes also to be seen competing successfully in the same sport in England. Elsewhere, these alert, spirited creatures, with an action that is truly breathtaking, remain essentially show animals. The United States is their main supporter outside of England.

The Hackney horse was evolved from the Norfolk Trotter, with the pony being developed within the past eighty years. Apart from size, some typical pony characteristics, and added brilliance of action, there is little to separate the two. Although they share the same stud book in England, horse and pony are now regarded almost as separate breeds. Although classes for American Hackney Horses are becoming rarer, the pony continues to gain in popularity in the United States, Canada, Holland, and Australia. It's still possible to see the smaller Hackney Ponies, those classified as roadsters and shown more for speed and action than looks, highstepping it round an American show ring without long tails. The docking of tails has been illegal in Britain since 1948 and the practice is also illegal now in many of the states, but there is no law against showing animals that have been docked elsewhere.

The particolored breeds, for some reason, seem to attract the most partisan supporters. The golden-coated Palomino, whose salad days were in the fifties, has been overtaken by the Paint and the Appaloosa in capturing the enthusiasm of western horsemen.

The Appaloosa has had to be resurrected several times over. It is believed to have originated with a type of spotted horse that appealed to both King Xerxes of Persia and the Chinese Emperor Wu Ti, and that it has descendants in the Austrian Pinzgauer and in the dark-red spotted variety once known in England as Bloody Buttocks.

The forebears of this animal would have had to reach the Americas on the ships of the conquistadors. By 1870 the spotted horses were known as "Palouse horses" from the herds of them found grazing in the vicinity of the Palouse River in the Northwest. History is vague about how they became associated particularly with the Nez Percé Indians or how this high-country tribe learned the principles of breed development. From early in the eighteenth century, the Nez Percé were breeding up and culling their horses in a painstaking manner, quite different from the careless approach of most of the Plains tribes. They achieved a very fine type for war and for hunting and running the dangerous bison, their chief source of food. Conditioned for their work by grueling races, the Appaloosa's stamina and courage was tested to the limit when the Nez Percé, defeated in 1877, were given an impossibly short time to cross the rapids of the Snake River on their return to the Lapwai Reservation in Idaho. The horses, ridden by braves and hitched to buffalo-skin rafts for transporting the women, the old, the young, and the sick, plunged to and fro through the swirling, rockstrewn waters until all the tribe were safely ferried across—at the cost of several hundred animals, including young stock and pregnant mares, drowned in the effort.

With the tribe banished to a reservation, the Appaloosas were dispersed, mostly to people who abandoned the Indians' selective breeding program. Thus was debased a breed of horse that had been the admiration of all. It remained neglected until 1920, when an interested

Dartmoor foal, one of pony breeds native to Britain, lives at a stud on its native territory. Type makes a fine 12.2-hand child's riding pony.

Right: Welsh ponies are among the world's most beautiful. This mare and her (uncommon) twins are Section B, Welsh Riding Ponies.

horseman decided to try to bring back the spotted breed. The Appaloosa Horse Club was started up in 1938, and in three years succeeded in registering only 113 horses. Then came World War II, and it was not until 1947 that the first stud registry could be put together.

I met a particularly fine Appaloosa in Kentucky, on a Thoroughbred breeding farm. He had the symmetrical, well-muscled physique, the deep chest and short back of his breed. He was blanket-spotted on his pasterns, sparse of mane and tail, with striped hooves and the white sclera round the eye that resembles a human's. This horse's mission in life was that of a teaser of mares. It is said that the best teaser is a dumb horse—because a smart one would realize it is an unproductive job and quit. I wouldn't know about that particular Appaloosa, but lack of brain is certainly not characteristic of the breed. They

are essentially versatile, as proven down the centuries, and take kindly to most equine pursuits. After the Quarter Horse, the Appaloosa is perhaps the most popular American breed.

Not that the popularity of Quarter Horses is now confined to the States. These muscular, handsome, quick-off-the-mark all-rounders come in types for racing or cutting, as cow ponies, pleasure horses, Western or English equitation exponents, or what you will. They are now proving they can jump. They go back in part to the Chickasaw Horse, a superior type developed by the Indians of the Southeast from captured Spanish horses, which was bred up with European animals, principally the progeny of the famed blood sire Janus.

The prototype of the Quarter Horse was known as the Quarter-Pather or the Colonial Quarter-of-a-Mile Running Horse, and was used

on the race streets of villages and towns, or on even shorter straightaways hewn from the forest to satisfy the sporting instincts of the old-time colonists. The Quarter Horse was the first breed developed in America, although not officially recognized until 1941, and there are now more of them in the United States than any other breed. There are also about 20,000 in Canada, and although Australia was slow to react after the first imports in 1954, a register of 2,000 plus a growing demand suggests that interest is picking up there too. In England these horses are now being bred pure and used for crossing, with the annual increase in numbers in ratio to the expanding interest in western riding.

Though these horses originated in the East, you must go to the West to find real Quarter Horse country. They moved that way with the wagons and the cattle, and were kept and prized

and bred as the finest cattle horses, with the fastest turns and starting speed and the best cow sense of any stock horse in the world. But they have such varied talents that it has been useful to differentiate and to develop types strong in one quality or another—but at all times retaining the frontal weight that makes possible the Quarter Horse's famous get-off burst of speed. Oklahomans chiefly breed the racer, infused with more Thoroughbred blood to give a rangier conformation than the short, muscular build admirable for holding a half-ton of wild steer on the end of a lariat. But the working type is ubiquitous in the West and I particularly remember Buck, an amiable, if not overenergetic horse employed on a ranch where former sprinters of the caliber of Kid Meyers, the First Supreme Champion, and the legendary Go Man Go have been at stud.

The breeding of racing Quarter Horses is a

comparatively new and profitable industry, especially when combined with raising cattle. Those who race the animals they breed can watch them run by flying through the mountains to Ruidoso Downs, the exclusive racetrack in New Mexico built for Quarter-Horse racing, and especially for the world's richest horse race, bar none, the All-American Futurity.

They say it was the railroads plus barbed wire—the Arrow Plate and Buckthorn, the Lazy Plate and Thorny Fence, or the other patterns of equally wicked efficiency—that killed off the Old West. Whatever the fate of the railroads in Oklahoma, there certainly are no signs of barbed wire near any of the numerous Quarter Horse breeding farms there. Those thousands of acres of Bermuda grass—full of vitamins and green all year round—are enclosed and divided by white wooden rails.

Maybe in some ways and for some people, life in those parts has not altered all that much since the turn of the century. The tempo is as drawn out as the southern drawl, beautiful houses and gardens spell luxury and comfort. And if the seasonal cyclones have altered course to include Oklahoma more frequently than before, it is still a good climate for those that like it. The wild turkeys are gone, but there are as many doves as cottontail rabbits, and pairs of quail that explode up out of the grass.

Honest Buck was my escort for an exploratory ride into Oklahoma country. It had rained in the night, but the sun was shining, the air balmy when I hoisted myself into his western saddle. Round the barn where he had been cross-tied to await me were paddocks with open shelters where groups of breedy, good-looking Quarter Horse mares and foals—the "bab-ies" beloved of all—were enjoying the increasing heat. It is said a Quarter Horse needs the sun on his back, and certainly the healthy stock of the region seldom avail themselves of any shade. One of the fine studs, sighting a mare being led into the barn, was loping round and round his enclosure. On the open ranch, herds of cattle moved across the skyline or lay in clusters chewing the cud. Otherwise it seemed that Buck and I had the world to ourselves.

The buckskin was in a lethargic mood. As we came to cross the flat bridge spanning the narrow end of a lake he suggested that, as he thought

little of water anyway, maybe half a mile on a hot morning was far enough. Heels and the ends of the long divided reins persuaded him to the contrary, we crossed, dealt with the cattle-proof catch on the gate beside a grid, and were out on the expanses of springy pasture.

There were flowers, blue and pink and yellow, the sudden flame of Indian sage brush, willow trees, cottonwood, and groves of low, spreading oaks. When we came to a series of miniature water-filled canyons where the soil is as red as in Devon, there were unfamiliar soup-plate imprints down by the waterside. Buck stood still

and silent and after a while a long, wrinkled neck pushed a reptilian head slowly above the surface, and I gazed into the unwinking, expressionless eye of a snapper turtle.

We went on our way, reveling in the quietness and wide open spaces, and I understood the westerner's lyricism about his land and his horses.

Hidden out there in the West, in remote places and glimpsed only by a lucky few, are remnants of the great bands of free-running mustangs that figured so strongly in the background of the Quarter Horse. Near Ruidoso one day I got my

chance to see them.

Ray the cowboy had collected me from the town's comfortable horsemen's inn while the moon was still up and a huge moth was fluttering in the cool, windless air outside my window. We began a long drive into the Apache reservation, beginning on a winding, narrow road that took us up through mile upon mile of pine forest, where trees and undergrowth—tinder-dry —seemed to be waiting helplessly for the carelessly dropped match or the lightning that strikes and cleaves a pine as though hammered by Thor himself. Whole mountainsides were still blackened by the terrible forest fires of years before. We came out of the trees onto those vast expanses where once the herds of bison roamed and saw mile upon mile lying sere and yellow and dried, where in that season of the year it should have been green and flower-studded.

The Indians were feeding their hundreds of fine Hereford cattle—called Her'fords or Whiteface in those parts—throwing them concentrates from the back ends of slowly moving trucks; they were experiencing real hardship at a time of year when the steers should have been self-supporting. We left them, and even the faintly defined trails, driving straight through the scrub, for Ray was seeking mustangs. Occasionally a whitetail or mule deer bounded across the forest tracks in front of the truck, and we disturbed a few herds of antelope, but most of the game were banished from their usual haunts by the drought. Then suddenly Ray braked and stopped the engine, and my eyes followed the line of his pointing finger.

Not so very far away there was a moving cloud of dust with half a dozen vague shapes galloping within it. Then they stopped, the dust cleared, and a horse—the stallion—circled his mares with head high, alert to danger. Then he stood, eyes fixed on its possible source, nostrils flared to catch our scent, mane blowing in the wind. For a minute or two he remained—the first and possibly the last untamed mustang I shall ever see. Then he gathered his mares and drove them before him, while the dust swirled again behind their galloping hooves.

Later that day, but still so early that the sun was not yet showing over the mountains, we came to an Apache village. And as the sun appeared at last and the sky turned red and gold, a hundred-horse remuda took off in the corral, thundering away from us so that the different sizes and shapes and types were thrown into relief against the dawn.

There were mustangs in that lot, captured by the Apache in their horse traps. These are fenced-off areas of valley between the forest trees, which are sited around water holes. The entrance is an innocent-looking pole gate that closes behind the horses and only opens one way. The Indians do not hunt for fun however —they only catch what they need—and the majority of their horses are Quarter Horses or Appaloosas or crosses bred by themselves.

Yet by 1972, of the several million mustangs that roamed the West during the eighteenth century, only an estimated 17,000 head remained. Their demise began with the western pioneers who established ranches on mustang country, and either captured the wild horses for work or killed them off to conserve the pasture. Those that escaped made for regions where domesticated animals could not thrive, but even so they were not left in peace. Today they are in the middle of a conflict of wills between the national government, which has held it illegal to hunt unbranded horses with the use of aircraft and motor vehicles, and the states, many of which feel that the horses must be under local control.

The laws, in any case, have been flouted for years. The broomtails have been called inbred, worthless scrub that endanger the food supply of target species and spoil pasture that might conceivably be put to financial gain. There have been "sportsmen" who went their unrestricted way, bragging of the large bag of horseflesh they potted from a jeep or helicopter. Professional mustangers have thought nothing of blinding the leader of a band with buckshot fired from aircraft so that the horses could be driven into open ground for easy destruction. The practice brought them considerable income from tons of horseflesh sold to make canned pet food.

Public opinion seems to be swinging toward enlightened conservation, however. Research has revealed that the scrubbiness—the small stature of the mustang—is nature's economical method of ensuring survival on minimum nutrition; that the wild horse has his place in the natural balance because he grazes among game species that mostly browse and in the past lived in harmony with the great herds of buffalo, deer, antelope, and elk. It is known that horses in the wild do not inbreed, since the dominant stallion expels from his band all yearling colts and fillies,

Preceding pages:
Strong, quiet, willing,
these are the
qualities of the Highland
pony, second-largest
of Britain's native ponies.
They are chiefly
seen in Scotland carrying
trekkers and, as here,
at work for deer stalkers.

the former to gather bands of their own, the latter to be claimed by other leaders. And where horses have free range, they automatically regenerate the pastures, by voiding in their dung seeds that in time grow into new grass.

Since the settlement of the West, domesticated horses of various types have escaped or been loosed to join the feral mustang bands, and with rare exceptions the modern mustang differs materially from the animals captured and bred by Indian and settler. Forged by survival in the wild, those mustangs of the Apache remuda also bore small resemblance to the noble horses from Spain and Portugal that carried the conquistadors on their adventures of exploration, yet they are the inheritors of the proud blood of Barb and oriental that went into the making of their ancestor, the Andalusian horse.

The Andalusian, a powerful, majestic horse with an extravagant high and airy action, is still bred pure in the Spanish province for which it is named, particularly in the Jerez de la Frontera area, where the two famed sherry families of Domecq and Terry maintain large studs. They are peerless parade horses and their aptitude for haute école can be seen in displays given by the recently founded Andalusian School of Equestrian Art. El Caballo Español is also a notable working horse, doing its share of general range and utility work on Spanish farms, and working the herds of fighting bulls on the ranches where they are raised. Ridden *a la gineta,* (that is, with the legs virtually straight), and often without use of the reins so that the hands are left free, the Andalusian is also the highly trained, courageous mount of the *rejoneador* who fights the bull on horseback.

Even before the Renaissance dawned, the Andalusian, founded on Barb but not Arabian blood, was the foremost horse in Europe, providing chargers for war, prestige for kings, mounts for carousels, and later the ideal conformation, bearing, and temperament for the art of classical riding. The Lipizzaners, the white stallions that still perform this same art within the baroque beauty of the Spanish Riding School in Vienna, are directly descended from the Spanish Horse.

The classical equitation of the manège, emanating from Versailles and at first practiced only by the scions of the reigning houses, was nearly ended by the impact of the French Rev-

olution and the Napoleonic wars. Soon Vienna was the only remaining refuge of this rarefied art of horsemanship. Centuries later, World War II brought a new threat. The Lipizzaner breeding farm at Piber was moved by the Germans, then the irreplaceable trained stallions had to be hurriedly evacuated yet again. When war ended, their fate hung in the balance until, at the instigation of the American General George Patton, the School was placed under the protection of the U.S. Army. Thus a form of horsemanship still of supreme beauty, skill, and historical interest was assured for posterity.

Lipizzaners have the physical strength, particularly of back and quarters, the springy action, and great endurance required for the demanding movements of classical haute école. Their noble beauty enhances the spectacular performances put on at the Spanish Riding School. In character they are spirited and courageous, but they combine these traits with patience and an innate willingness to cooperate and learn, virtues essential for haute école.

These horses are used in Yugoslavia, Hungary, and other countries as harness and saddle horses, and for work on the land. The gray stallions—all of six different and distinctive lines—that are used exclusively in the Spanish Riding School, are bred at the stud at Piber. When proved as performers the most talented eventually return there for stud duty, and so guarantee the continuing excellence of this branch of the breed.

The Barbs that through the Andalusian are part-ancestors of those Lipizzan stallions, are seldom found purebred today outside Morocco, but in parts of Africa and some Middle Eastern countries there are numerous types of country-breds with the concave profiles and sloping croups indicative of the breed.

We have seen horses like this in Greece, little animals with deceptively slender and delicate-looking limbs, padding along under big loads like those toted by the ubiquitous donkeys, or tethered and dozing among the olive trees. The larger specimen the old man was riding along the sea track to Ermioni was a fine type. When its rider stopped at the wine shop where we were drinking retsina—that pine-impregnated brew of Greece that is an acquired taste—there was opportunity to study it.

Behind the old man was the sea, with Mercouri's red boat drawn up on the foreshore. Georgios and Kostulla were sorting lengths of lime-green fishing net to dry, five rangy cats gazed expectantly seawards, awaiting the next caique and the remnants of the catch. The old man did not dismount but remained seated sideways on the arrangement of wooden slats lying over a pad that goes for a saddle in Greece (only to be used astride with imminent risk to the libido). Occasionally he leaned to thwack an inquisitive donkey on the nose with his stick, or to accept our offerings of wine, downed with companionable salutations of "Yassus!" In addition to its rider, the horse was strung around with an assortment of heavy bags, containing apparently all the man's household chattels and secured by a double rope tightly hitched round the inside of one front leg. As usual, the rein consisted of a single line but was attached untypically to a bit in the form of a twisted length of chain. Yet for all the apparent discomfort of its appurtenances, this horse's chestnut coat carried a shine due more to good health than grooming, the fine-tipped ears above the long head were pricked, the eyes alert, the skin over its sloping quarters taut with muscle. He was obviously the prize possession of his owner, and a fine example of the paradox of size versus capability in the matter of horses. Whether to speak of him as a "pony" or a "horse" is debatable.

The general understanding of a pony is a small horse of about 14.2 hands or less, but the definition is oversimplified. You cannot go by height alone. The show and jumping standard for ponies gives a top limit of 14.2 hands, with a half-inch allowance for shoes. There is no height limit to a polo "pony"; a Hackney pony may not exceed 14 hands; an Arabian horse can be 13.3, the Caspian miniature horse two or more hands smaller yet; and some Lipizzaners are no more than 14.2. Both horses and ponies belong to the one species and interbreed to produce fertile young, but the two are divided by elements of conformation, and by characteristics of personality and overall expression that are all too apparent to people who have experience with both.

The confusion is not helped by those cases in which the same breed is sometimes classified as both small horses and as ponies. This is true of the Haflinger, the hardy short-legged equine in-

dispensable for every kind of work in the Austrian Alps, and now being used for both riding and driving in England and as a most suitable mount for disabled riders.

We met a pair of Haflingers in Switzerland, on the ice-covered nursery slopes at St. Moritz where they provided me with a heaven-sent excuse for a rest from trying to ski. They were a perfectly matched pair of chestnuts with flaxen manes and tails, with scarlet harness attaching them to a sleigh. Their bridles were decorated with plumes that nodded with each shake of the head and they wore the bells without which no self-respecting Swiss horse could be expected to give of its best. They were delightful to look at, friendly to talk to, and to my eye appeared to be a pair of charming, sturdy, hard-working ponies of about 14 hands.

The nine pony breeds that are indigenous to Britain are interrelated with European and Nordic ponies and have ingredients dating back to antiquity. The great popularity they now enjoy is comparatively recent. They had no registries until after World War I, and it was only after World War II, when the "Ponies of Britain" shows were staged, that this national heritage was put on the map in its country of origin. The publicizing of the native breeds was done as a rescue operation. After the war Europe was desperately short of meat, and there were many boats being loaded openly with shipments of British ponies bound for the Continent and an obvious fate. The attention brought to this situation by the Ponies of Britain and other organizations, combined with the new and growing sport of trekking, proved the salvation of the animals, particularly the larger breeds that were most endangered.

Up to then, few people outside the northern counties had heard of the up-to-14.2-hands, strong, compact Dales pony that had been the maid-of-all work of the hill farmers until ousted by mechanization. The less massive Fell, more numerous to the west of the Pennine range, is of similar origins, and was produced by selective breeding for slightly different work. Both the Dales and Fells provided the traction power at the turn of the century for the strings of pack ponies that transported lead ore over high, rough trails from mines at Allendale and Weardale to the northeast ports for shipment abroad.

**Above: At Haras d'Angers,
where both heavyweight
Bretons and Normandy Cobs
(seen here) are bred,
horses exercise in pleasant
outdoor ring.**

Now from trekking centers in some of the wildest
and most beautiful country in the British Isles
both types of pony tote even the heaviest of
trekkers safely over the treacherous slopes and
bogs of their native regions. And as with all the
native breeds, they are coming into their own
both for riding and for general driving; the Dales
is especially suited for harness work.

It was a Fell pony, one of those bred at Bal-
moral, that took me to explore the heather-clad
Scottish hillside. Though these ponies are no
larger than 14 hands, this black mare carried me
with willing ease, marching out sure-footed as a
goat over loose scree. On the homeward stretch
she demonstrated the excellent trot that also
helps make a Fell a good saddle horse.

The other large native pony breed—the
Highland—comes in two sizes and types: the
fine-limbed Western Isles Highland pony, and
the larger Mainland (sometimes wrongly called

the Garron), which originally was bred up for size
and strength in the cause of Scottish forestry.
Until the advent of trekking, mostly only those
few who shot grouse or stalked the wild red deer
on Scottish moors were familiar with the handsome looks and benign temperament of a breed
that is now widely acclaimed. Many years ago we
had one in the family, bought mainly to be the
imperturbable, completely bomb-proof mount
for a very old man, but we found her happy to
stir herself and participate in all Pony Club activities, including jumping.

Nowadays it is not only an Irishman who will
tell you that a Connemara has few, if any,
equals. We owned one once, and discovered for
ourselves that inside his handsome head he carried all the kindness and courage, the ability and
friendliness for which the breed is famous. We
discovered for ourselves, too, that a Connemara
rides like a horse, will hunt and compete and go

all day without effort, and is born with a jumping ability that makes him leap over this and that just for the hell of it. The register allows sizes from 12.2 to 14.2 hands, but like our Irish gentleman, the best types seldom exceed 13.2 hands. A lot of good Spanish blood, including Andalusian and later additions of Arabian, went into the making of the Connemara, and their attractive looks advertise the fact. Not so long ago these ponies were scarcely known outside the Emerald Isle. Now you can find them strung out across the world from Holland to New Zealand, with the satisfied exporters breeding them at their own studs or coming back for more.

The spirited, good-looking ride-and-drive Welsh Cob also has Andalusian blood running in his veins, a twelfth-century introduction. The Welsh stud book registers four types of Welsh cob and pony. The Section C animals, the least common and with attractive deer-like heads, are miniatures of the larger cob. The Twala Club's Spotty—registered as Tiger Tim—is a lovely example of the up-to-13.2-hands riding type of Welsh Pony, with an excellent front, and a long stride; he rides like a horse and has the oft quoted "look of eagles." All these types derive wholly or in part from the little Welsh Mountain pony, of Section A, which was one of those that owing to their remote habitats survived Henry VII's edict against small stallions. Its Arabian ancestry is obvious in its looks.

The Dartmoor we know only to well. For years our local hunt liked to remind me of the embarrassing moment when I threw my own child into a muddy ditch, but at the time there was little option. Our youngest daughter and her indomitable Dartmoor, The Gent, were out with hounds, I running alongside on my feet attached by a lunge rope to the bridle, to act as an emergency hand brake. There we were pounding along the tow path, canal on one side, ditch on the other, congratulating ourselves on keeping up so well with hounds, when the fox doubled back, straight through The Gent's legs. Within minutes hounds followed suit, and there were we committing one of the ultimate sins —completely blocking the path of Huntsman, Whip, Master, and a large proportion of the field, as The Gent plunged around in a frenzy of excitement. So I plucked his rider from the saddle and lobbed her into the comparative safety of the muddy ditch, thus leaving myself free to try to control each erupting end of her pony and so clear the way.

In fact it was only hounds and hunting that ever gave our splendid Dartmoor ideas beyond the capabilities of his rider. Otherwise, like all of this elegant little breed, when correctly broken The Gent proved the best possible pony for a younger child; he gave ours a confidence she never lost.

Before the introduction, now long discontinued, of alien, mostly Shetland, stallions to produce pit ponies, and before two World Wars disrupted its moorland home, the Dartmoor was somewhat larger than its Exmoor neighbors. Now, bred up with fresh blood from Wales, this attractive pony has a maximum height of 12 hands for mares. The correct type is bred in studs, although it is hoped that Dartmoor can eventually be restocked exclusively with registered ponies. Fine show ponies have resulted from the cross of Dartmoor or Welsh Mountain with Thoroughbred and/or Arabian blood.

True-blue Exmoor ponies are bred on the moor that has been their habitat since the Bronze Age, and even breeders with studs elsewhere have recourse at intervals to genuine "Moor" blood to maintain the type and characteristics. The remoteness of the parts of Exmoor where the ponies wander and breed has been instrumental in keeping them free of outside influence, but two very similar strains do exist. They are the hardiest of all the native ponies, and are unmistakable with their coloring of solid bay, brown, or brownish dun, all with black points, mealy nose, toad eyes, and the springy, waterproof winter coat that is unique. More independent in character than the Dartmoor, and a couple of inches larger, Exmoors make first-class second ponies, the perfect working-hunter type for a keen child rider.

There have been ponies roaming wild in the New Forest area for more than nine hundred years. In 1891 the Association for the Improvement of the Breed of New Forest Ponies was set up, but it was not until the formation of the New Forest Pony Breeding and Cattle Society in 1938 that any real attempt was made to establish a standard. Up to then stallions of several different breeds had been loosed in the forest; now only registered, licensed sires are allowed to

breed. Somehow, out of the previous mixing of blood, a type on which to build did emerge, produced largely by the harsh climate and sparse grazing of its environment. Only the best-adapted could survive, and care is taken that with more plentiful food the ponies do not deviate too far from that original. In the forest the herds are inspected every three weeks, and at appointed times during the autumn the mares and foals are rounded up and brought into solidly built pounds—which calls for some hard galloping and a lot of fun on a forest pony that knows his ground. Foals are caught and branded with their owner's mark and the mares are—with difficulty—wormed. Some are sent to the autumn sales, and any pony in poor condition is either sold or taken onto a holding to be fed and cared for through the winter.

The Forest is administered by ten Verderers, and they employ Agisters to collect the grazing fees. Each Agister tail-marks the ponies for which he is responsible, cutting the hair to his own recognizable shape.

At up to 14.2 hands and narrow, noticeably free of nervousness, particularly with traffic, a sparse feeder, a good jumper, and a versatile, good-tempered all-rounder, the New Forest pony makes an admirable family animal, as suitable for a lightweight parent as for a child.

There have been two Shetlands in my life: Daphne, a little half-wild mare bought out of a drove at Ashford market and loaned me for our mutual not always academic, instruction; and Twink, a splendid piebald—also loaned—on whose saddleless, hairy back our youngest managed to remain glued to tag along with her sisters on their considerably larger mounts.

These diminutive ponies, said to trace back to the Ice Age, were for centuries essential for toting peat and seaweed on the treeless, windswept Orkney and Shetland Islands. Although the Shetland for its size is the strongest of all the native ponies, its lack of inches and attractive appearance make it an obvious choice as a fun pony for a small child. But Shetlands do have a mind of their own and need to be under the kindly but firm supervision of an adult.

All these breeds of pony are now being bred and imported in large numbers in most European countries, both for their own qualities and the excellent results of cross-breeding

them (Shetlands excepted). America, too, is becoming pony-minded. Now that riding is such a burgeoning pastime with all age and income groups, the larger breeds—versatile, hardy, long-lived, and comparatively cheap to keep—are in growing demand for adults. A cross-bred can be a small horse embodying pony virtues, and in a jumper or eventer pony blood gives it the cleverness it needs to extricate itself from trouble. The picture that the word "pony" conjured up for many—that of a Shetland-sized hairy mat—is rapidly fading, to be replaced by an appreciation of the possibilities of ponies. The United States particularly favors the Welsh and the Connemara, the New Forest, and its own

Opposite: Tiny Shetland is often choice for small children. Although their stature evolved from harsh climate and short rations of their native northern isles, purebreds grow no larger under any conditions. Above: Very large contrast to minute Shetland foal is this white-faced Clydesdale colt. This is Scotland's heavy horse, handsome, powerful, and active.

Horse of the Year
Show, held each autumn
in London, centers
on horse as personality.
"Heavies'" big moment
comes during musical drive
with chain harrows.
Here a much bedecked
participant awaits entry.

refined version of the Shetland. And there is, of course, America's own invention, the Pony of the Americas, originating with an Appaloosa-Shetland cross. It is a shapely, strong, amenable mount for the younger generation, with a talent for doing anything required of it.

During the year when Daphne the Shetland was teaching me many things, including the art of falling off, my childhood was dominated by the two extremes in equine size, the diminutive pony and the giant heavies that worked ours and our neighbors' farms. One man worked his fields with teams of Shires. We never failed to go and watch these magnificent beasts during harvest, when—hitched three abreast, with their muscles rippling across their powerful bodies—they pulled the reaper round and round the diminishing area of ripened wheat.

The Shire has all the draft-horse requirements of strength, constitution, and stamina allied to docile temperament. It is thought to be the largest and heaviest purebred horse in the world, and descends in part from the Flemish animals that were ancestors of the Old English Black. Whether its forbears were indeed the "Great Horses" asserted to have carried medieval knights into battle—or if such a horse even existed—is more open to question. None of the war harness of those times fits the dimensions of a modern Shire or any other of the heavies of today. And though the average knight was a small man, as judged by his armor, he was depicted with his feet hanging below the belly line of his horse. Also, it is difficult to visualize how anyone wearing heavy armor could hoist himself aboard a 17-hand animal, so perhaps the theory holds water that the knights' warhorse was no more than a stout-hearted, stout-limbed cob.

The standards of conformation laid down by The Shire Horse Council have been revised, and judging from photographs the Shires of today do differ materially from those of the twenties and thirties. Some critics say this is to the detriment of the breed; some hint darkly at infusions of Clydesdale blood. That heavy horse of Scotland is longer in the leg, and more active than a Shire: it was once the most popular breed for heavy urban haulage.

The short-legged, feather-free, Suffolk Horses, those strong, economical, powerful "Punches" mentioned way back in 1506, have never been as well known as the two largest draft breeds. Belonging traditionally to East Anglia, they are always colored in some variation of chestnut, and are noted for their good trot. The Suffolk's ability to thrive under poor feeding conditions and heat has ensured imports by Argentina and other hot countries for some years, and the United States now has its own breed association.

That other clean-legged heavy, the Percheron, is getting back some of the enormous popularity it once enjoyed. Always colored gray or black, its handsome, active appearance owes something to a past infusion of Arabian blood. Percherons, named after their native La Perche region of France, are more widely dispersed throughout the world than any of the other heavy-horse breeds.

France pays due attention to her superb heavy-horse breeds, with the Ardennais, the light and heavy types of Percheron, the Boulonnais, the Breton, and other varieties all recognized by the State Stud Administration. The stallions are bred at big stud farms (haras) and rigorously tested before traveling the different regions during the breeding months.

Our eldest daughter became well acquainted with a compact, short-legged Ardennais, one of the most ancient and popular breeds, when at seventeen she worked for a family living in the Ardenne country, close by the Luxemburg border. Her duties included most things from looking after five children to driving the tractor—a requested chore M'sieur regretted after helper and machine made an unscheduled exit through the back of the barn. Inevitably, part of her off-time was devoted to riding, even if the only mount available was one of the farm horses, and despite her employers' scandalized protests, most summer evenings found their au pair girl clumping around the nearby countryside.

In the France of that time—not very many years ago—few ladies, young or otherwise, rode at all, let alone jean-clad and bareback on a rotund, hairy legged, strawberry-pink cart horse. The sight shocked that conservative neighborhood as much as the unfortunate episode of M'sieur's Spanish gardener, a young romantic given the sack when spied by Madame stealing a kiss from the English au pair, as she dozed decoratively beneath a rose arbor.

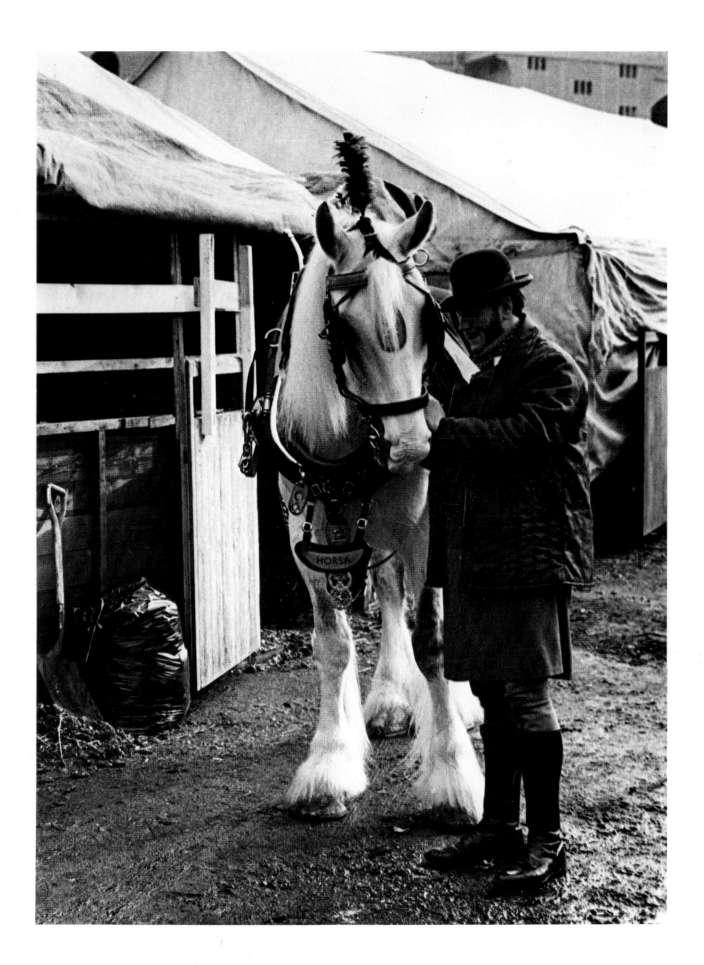

5.

Showing and Competing

Preceding pages:
Competition is booming in
the horseman's world,
with jumping specialists—
horses and riders—
earning top rank as
international athletes.

Opposite: Basic dressage
can be good systematic
training for any horse. At
top levels, the lightness
and harmony achieved are a
fine art, fascinating
to all beholders.
Victorious German team
are seen at World
Championships of 1974 at
Christianborg, Denmark.

"Keep him moving!" we urge. "Don't let him go to sleep." Twala's rider squeezes him on and they set off again around the collecting ring. "Mind that one . . . it's going to kick!" "'Scuse me, can I come through?" "You going to walk the course?"

I pull Twala's reins over his head and take him on while our daughter joins a bunch of other young competitors dismounted in the ring. Despite the growing tension that leaves the mouth dry, the mind numb, she tries to be intelligent about such vital matters as the number of strides needed between both parts of the combination, how wide to come at the corner so as to get straight at the oxer, how much extra push Twala is going to need to make those spreads.

Round and round I walk with a Twala bereft of much of his normal bulk and with a satisfactory sheen to his coat. He steps out beside me, swinging his head with interest toward the ring, gazing beningly at spectators and other ponies alike, mumbling my arm with his lips. His rider returns more tense, more terse. "It looks awful," she says as she remounts. We smile brightly, full of mendacious reassurance. "Oh, those fences only looked big because you were on your feet."

The first to go has two down—eight faults. Then there's the rakish bay. Rightly we feel he'll go clear first round, but he jumps with a flat back, head in air. Could be chancy when the fences go up. Someone has two refusals for six faults, now another clear. Someone else fails to make the grade at all and is eliminated at the in-and-out. It must be catching. Two more have followed suit but come out at the oxer. Does Twala mind oxers? Someone says Twala doesn't actually mind anything, it's just a question of whether he can get over it! There's another with four faults, and now, oh lord, it's them!

Twala trots into the ring, breaks into a canter as requested. As usual his ears are pricked, as usual he is obviously enjoying himself. His rider slaps him lightly behind the girth just to make him attentive and know she is carrying a whip. The pony drops his head and kicks back to show what he thinks about that, and we heave a sigh of relief. It's a sure sign that Twala is feeling good.

The whistle blows and they canter through the start to the first fence, a simple brush with a pole on top. No checking, no trouble, but not much dash about it either, and certainly no more than

the proverbial inch between Twala's girth and that pole. "Leg him on a bit! Wake him up!" we groan under our breath. Obedient and well used to our wingless practice jumps, there's no question of him running out at the stile, but heavens! how he rattled that gate! Never mind, it's still there, but now he's much too close to the triple. An awful heave, but he makes it somehow, and he's jumped that dreaded oxer really well.

Suddenly it dawns on us: they're halfway round and clear so far—even if our pony's indolent approach and close-shave style of jumping do have the judges raising a leg in the air in an unconscious effort to boost him over the top. The course looks encouragingly solid and only the rustic poles appear a little flimsy. (If we could see into the future we'd know that one day Twala would misjudge a rustic parallel like this and get a dangerously lightweight pole between his front legs to give him his only fall in the ring—a real purler—and smash up his rider's collarbone.)

It's unbelievable, but they're still clear and coming up to the combination fence. He'll never make it. He's got his stride all wrong. But he's put in a quick one—now there's only the wall. "Come on you two!" And they're clear, one of the four for the jump-off! A clear round? It's marvelous!

Twala is blowing a bit, but isn't he pleased with himself? His rider is out of the saddle, stirrups run up, girth loosened, arms around the pony's neck. "Good boy, Twala . . . good boy . . . good boy." She is flushed and ecstatic as we crowd around. "What a pony!" and "Well done, both of you . . . you really used your legs but you'll have to wake him up a bit more for the jump-off." Tension returns, nervous irritation in the rejoinder: "I know—just tell me how?"

The classes are running very late, the officials want no more than one jump-off if they can help it, and on the shortened course the fences go up accordingly. They look huge.

Our rider makes sure she knows the course and falls even more silent. Check the girth, leg up into the saddle, round and round the collecting ring again. Three to go, then Twala.

There's that flashy bay galloping already, fighting for his head through the start and gathering speed. He steeplechases the first two and his luck holds. No, he's flattened even more at the

gate and it's gone. The next one, too, and that one—twelve faults. Oh, we can do better than that. Now it's that nice gray mare. We've noticed how careful she is and she's got that extra pop, too. See how beautifully she jumped the double? Must be a clear, but no . . . she's clipped a brick out of the wall with a hind hoof—four faults. One to go, then us.

This one looks a real professional, doesn't he? Been winning quite a lot, so they say. See what he cleared that by? That pony could jump a house, but looks a bit green, doesn't it? Only a four-year-old . . . a bit immature for this sort of thing, isn't it? Not that it'll actually hit anything, jumping like that! We resort to our terrible, unsportsmanlike family witchcraft: You say *Bang!* under your breath as a rival competitor comes into one or another of the fences. It works so often that we feel guilty and superstitious about it, but it's not working for us today. This chestnut continues to clear his fences by feet. Nothing can stop that clear round now. There's only the wall

to go. But the course builders have really gone to town on that wall. It shouldn't be as high as that, not for a competition like this. Not that it's going to stop this particular pony . . . but it has. He's ducked out at it. Over the second time, all right. But, Twala, you've three faults to beat.

One of his braids has come undone. There are dreadful raggedy ends of gamgee hanging out under his bandages—why can't this family sew?—but Twala is looking . . . different. He's always been a show-off, loves a gallery. See how he's shaking his silly head? Kicking back for fun? She's riding with a bit more contact now, and using her back. There's some impulsion bottled up there, you know.

There is something different about both of them as they come into the first fence, more concentration, more mutual determination, pony and rider rising to the occasion. Twala is truly on the bit, even pulling a little. And if he's too clever, or too idle, ever to clear his fences by more than the absolute minimum, this time he's

Wide open spaces of Hickstead Jumping Course, plus size and scope of permanent fences, often undo the best-laid plans of newcomers.

Bottom: True horsemen adjust to strange horses, and it adds thrills to Show Jumping World Cup Championships when finalists change mounts. Here Ireland's Eddie Macken takes on Hickstead balustrade with Austrian jumper Lavendel.

119

even against long odds, a demonstration of how far these generous animals will go in their endeavor to cooperate.

Originally show jumping was merely an extention into the show ring of the leaping that became essential to the fox-hunting fraternity in England and Ireland after the enclosure of commons and open fields during the eighteenth century. The show jumps of today, whether uprights or spreads, are merely sophisticated and stylized variations of the hunter's "natural" obstacles.

In those first leaping contests, featured as a novelty in a few shows, there was only one fence, with the height or spread increased after each round until horse, or rider, had reached his not very imposing limit. Run under local rules, with no time limit, these forerunners of show jumping then developed into equally dull competitions over three or four upright fences, including one spread. There were no changes of direction. The fences were topped with slats that fell almost with a breath and exacted a different penalty for being knocked by fore or hind legs. In many respects the competitions were early versions of the Open Jumper classes long popular in the United States. In both America and Canada this type of competition has now been almost entirely superseded by those that, at all levels, conform more to the international pattern at both indoor and outdoor shows, and are often run under Fédération Equestre Internationale rules.

Until cavalry finally became obsolete as a weapon of war, it was the mounted soldier who received the benefit of equestrian training and facilities, and it was universal practice for international show-jumping teams to be drawn from the armed forces. This outlook persisted until the late 1930's, and even longer in a few countries such as Ireland. By then the majority of competitions on the Continent were being run under international rules, with much of the emphasis on speed, while British show jumpers persisted with the old British Show Jumping Association rules, which omitted this accent. Not surprisingly, British riders found themselves at a disadvantage in the international field, where they also met unfamiliar spread and combination fences. Their successes were so few that by the time war brought most sports to a standstill, show jumping had moved into the doldrums.

The change, whereby show jumping, next to

In most things you have to start at the bottom, and that goes for show jumping. And maybe no win is ever as wonderful as the first, the day a game pony carted you around a small course of flimsy poles to put you both in the ribbons.

standing back where it's necessary, jumping with a real bascule, tucking his feet up out of the way.

So they are clear at the first and the second, clear all the way to the double, there to judge their stride just right for jumping both elements admirably. Then there is only the wall, that stupid, impossible wall. And as they come into it, all we can see from the other side of the ring are the black tips of Twala's ears, and the black velvet crown of his rider's hat.

It is not the most elegant of leaps. Someone suggests that the pony has climbed a ladder on the near side, hauled it up, and used it to descend the other. But they clear that wall, and the course, without fault.

That was Twala's first, but not last show-jumping victory, one of those occasions that bring home so forcefully what mutual understanding between horse and rider can achieve, football, has become the biggest sporting draw on British television, began with a small group of ex-prisoners of war, all former show jumpers and inherent horsemen, who had wiled away their captivity by dreaming up new concepts of the sport. By 1945 their ideas had materialized with courses that were more challenging to competitors and more exciting material for spectators. The Victory Championship Show at the White City in 1945—a triumph of presentation that culminated in a dramatic win by an ex-prisoner of war—caught the imagination of press and public alike. It was much the same throughout the postwar world, with national teams moving into a period of greater sophistication in course design and jumping technique, and more civilian riders in competition.

The latest impetus to show jumping has come from color television. Here the obstacles appear higher and broader still, glistening in red and black, yellow and white. Now it's possible to see that some particular jumping hero has blue eyes and is wearing a hunting pink coat. The horses, loved and recognized for years by outline and personality, now show as gleaming chestnut or bay, black or brown. The phenomenon has brought more people than ever out to see show jumping in the flesh.

Each big horse show has its own individuality, presents its own particular challenge in the competitions. Like any entertainment that has to be eminently spectacular and crowd-pulling as well as competitive, its success depends mainly on planning and behind-the-scenes administration. For a jumping show, the competitions must be sufficiently varied—some for speed, some for height, some for the international "names" —both to hold public interest and to attract top competitors. It must all be attractively and colorfully staged, and run on time, with a commentary that is both knowledgeable and effective. It is no small accomplishment in these times, when professionals fly or entrain their horses here and there, may have to drive them the long dusty haul from Madrid to compete within a day or so back in England, or manage an equally long leg of the American circuit.

Junior events are primarily training grounds for adult competition. Many young riders find that the transition from ponies to horses takes time. In theory, ponies—defined as animals 14.2

hands and under—can be registered as horses and jumped in adult competitions, including adult Foxhunter classes, but they cannot revert to being "ponies" again in the same season. Only the exceptional pony can compete on adult courses, which are designed for full-size horses, with heights and spreads beyond the scope of most top-rank pony jumpers. Such an exception was the immortal Stroller, the pony that took his owner to the top in junior competitions, then combined with her at adult level to win—among innumerable other successes—the Women's World Championship and a silver medal at the Olympics in Mexico.

Even the front-rank shows for ponies are now run to very difficult standards, both as to courses and riders. The skill, judgment, and courage displayed is usually all that one could want, especially among young people with a grounding in Pony Club competition or who have been brought along by a knowledgeable horseman. The rough riding that occasionally mars junior show-jumping competition is more often a case of too good a pony for an inexperienced child. There are many parents who possess more money than horse sense, and who invest heavily in a top-class show-jumping pony with the expectation of seeing their child immediately in the money at important shows.

Then as the old hands know, there are those brilliant youngsters who come into adult competition at age fifteen and sixteen and ride Thoroughbred or part-bred jumpers with prize-winning form. There is never any lack of fresh blood in the realms of international show jumping. Similarly, most young riders competing in the Junior European Three-Day-Event championship come straight into adult eventing (combined training) often with marked success.

Education and show jumping are not very good mixers, however. School must come first, and in term time even getting sufficient practice presents a problem. Worse is the problem of attending the big shows that take place during the week, possible only if understanding school officials are willing to grant leave. The difficulties are compounded when a young rider is out to qualify several ponies of different heights for the National Championship. There must be many like the dedicated father we know who used to collect his daughter from school on Friday eve-

Elizabethan towers of Burghley House are formidable backdrop to effort of cross-country rider during World Championship Three-Day Event. This is the crunch, when rider and horse go it alone, success or failure dependent on their talent, training, and resources.

nings, tuck her up on the back seat to sleep, then drive through the night trailering a couple of ponies to some Saturday show miles away, returning in the same manner the next day.

Now that the height and width of fences at top and international levels has reached the limit that can or should be asked of a horse, the task of the course builder is even more important than before. From both competitor and spectator point of view, all the fences should be solid and inviting to encourage good jumping and to provide a real test of ability for the class of horse and rider. But the effect now has to be obtained by a mixture of size with other means. In the restricted space of indoor shows—particularly difficult for highly strung, impetuous, or big, long-striding horses, and where the imprisoned excitement and suspense build to almost tangible proportions—the course builder cannot use jumps of maximum size—unless the competition happens to be a puissance. He has to take into careful account such things as the effect of the number of strides required between the elements of combination fences, changes of direction, and the exact placing of uprights and spreads in relation to each other.

Outdoor shows present the course builder with additional problems, such as the state of the ground, and he has to bear in mind factors like the shortened stride of a horse on very wet ground and be prepared to adjust his fences accordingly.

In the show-jumping world, Hickstead, Britain's permanent open-air jumping course, designed on the concept of La Baule and the Hamburg Jumping Derby, is a name to conjure with on its own. There is an engagingly informal air about the place, yet when someone said that in England Hickstead does for show jumping what Glyndebourne does for opera, he knew what he was talking about. It has its own brand of contrived exclusiveness, like the famous "Hooonk!" of the old motor klaxon that is used to start, stop, or finish a round, that punctuates the drone of the big jets flying overhead. There is the imposing space of its immense arena, something which often overwhelms even champions from overseas, both horses and men, on first acquaintance. There are the undulations of the ground that, taken into account and used with skill by the course builder, can help provide a

medium-hard task for competitors of medium ability, or make the most exacting demands on an occasion like the World Show Jumping Championships.

Always there are the permanent obstacles for which the course is famous—or infamous, according to your success in negotiating them. At the annual Wills' Show Jumping Derby, they are the main ingredients of a course that for this competition remains virtually the same each year, yet has been jumped clear only by a handful of exceptional horses and horsemen.

There is ample space for galloping between obstacles on the three-quarter-mile Derby course—too much space if you're not sufficiently expert at judging pace to remain within the tight time limit without tiring your horse unduly. And each of those eighteen fences has to be met just right, pinpointing the essential art of being able to "see a stride," of lengthening or shortening your horse's stride so that he is the right distance from the jump at the moment of take-off.

Hickstead may be the least stereotyped and most enterprising course in the world, partly because even a conventional fence can be made twice as formidable if it has to be jumped up or downhill—and they know how to utilize the inclines there. When it comes to the permanent fixtures, then you have such hazards as an oxer where the main ingredient is a wide, growing hedge that some horses attempt to "bank" with disastrous results. There are those big water ditches, one after the other and spanned by poles, that demand the utmost in skill and courage from rider and horse. And there is the notorious bank. Come too fast over the top of that precipitous slide and it's odds-on the outcome will be calamitous. Allow your horse to hesitate too long, or take even one step back on the brink of what he reckons to be the edge of the Grand Canyon, and you'll be penalized. If he wavers too long he is unlikely to go at all. Come just right with a courageous horse that is both obedient and trusting and it can be a pushover; you take off two-thirds of the way down to land safely and then, with the space, the will, and the impulsion, tackle those tricky white poles that loom so close ahead. But even if the bank is securely behind you, there is still the Devil's Dyke, the dreaded "rogue" combination that to the uninitiated can look comparatively innocu-

Sheer guts are a necessity in eventing, and water obstacles always take their toll. Those who came too fast downhill to the Trout Hatchery at Burghley came in for a wetting—as M. Kubiak of Polish team discovered for himself.

ous, but usually justifies its claim to be the most decisive obstacle of all. You come in downhill to the first part, go on down to the bottom where your horse is suddenly faced with the sunken middle element over eight feet of water. The majority of competitors are in trouble even before the moment comes to gather impulsion for the third element, jumped uphill.

Only the best come to the Hickstead highlights. Only the top-flight riders and exceptional horses win there or are consistent over the course, and even they need the modicum of luck that every show jumper appreciates. A horse,

after all, is not a machine but a sentient creature. It is as subject to moods and off days as we are, may have a liking for one course and not another. Such factors can upset the most stable of applecarts.

The majority of horses and ponies can jump, even if some jump better than others. A horse with a natural jumping ability may have it either properly exploited or spoiled by ignorant, hasty schooling. We had this brought home to us by Julie, a long-backed, rakish-looking mare, with a wild eye and temperament to match, bought to be shared with our eldest child, who was at the time a small and nervous thirteen-year-old. As I had discovered from the number of horrific obstacles over which Julie had hurled herself while out hunting, she combined a really big "pop" with being virtually unstoppable. We were given one opportunity of assessing "the might-have-been" of this mare had she not been flawed before coming to us. Piloted by a strong seventeen-year-old with nerves of steel, Julie was entered for an advanced class where, given her head and allowed to career around more or less out of control, she won with ease. Her jumping was phenomenal and no doubt had been exploited in her youth, with no one taking time or trouble to school what must always have been a difficult character. By the time we acquired her, Julie's mouth was hard and no suggested remedy succeeded in keeping her tongue under the bit. Failure to match her manners to her ability in her youth had wrecked the possibilities of a really brilliant jumping career.

Among horses born with jumping ability, some prove to be specialists either at high jumping—puissance—or jumping at speed, and all jumpers have a pace that suits them best. The exceptional show jumper is the animal whose potential is guessed and then developed slowly by patient schooling. Teamed with a sensitive rider such a horse can achieve great things.

Watching the American former Olympic rider, Neal Shapiro, schooling his hopes for the future at his stable on Long Island, I felt that here was something as close as possible to the ideal. He was dealing in turn with three or four young horses of different types, temperaments, and ability, all in splendid physical condition and cooperating with calmness and enjoyment. They were all past the initial weeks of schooling on the ground to instill obedience, and had been through the next stages, of walking over poles, then trotting over cavalletti to help supple their backs and muscle up their loins. Although at different stages of development, the horses— even the least advanced—were being asked to negotiate formidable obstacles. Yet from the relaxed manner in which each horse worked, it was obvious that nothing was being asked of them for which they were not ready, both physically and mentally.

The attitude of the rider was meticulous, forceful, very quiet and patient, and shared, or rather instilled his horses' relaxed attitude. Before any jumping there was a period of work on the ground, and over the fences the emphasis was on correct approach and bascule, and on retaining the animal's willing calmness. Shapiro does not believe in hurrying a horse's preparation; even the most brilliant is not put into competition until it is ready. And none is overjumped.

For this horseman, and for all who practice intelligent, humane views on the basic, unhurried schooling of jumpers or any other horse, the rewards, barring accidents, will be animals that can perform what is required of them for many seasons. The pity of it is that these views are not universal.

In the United States and Australia the horse-show business is booming, and although British shows have declined in number, the remainder have grown bigger and better. For me, the fascination of a show lies in the fact that each has its own distinctive flavor.

Dublin, the oldest of them all, boasts that huge, picturesque arena at Ballsbridge, where the jumping is famous. You can see more hunters to a class here than anywhere else, and there is a socializing-cum-horse-trading air about it that is Ireland's own particular brew. In Australia, in another enormous arena, the Sydney Royal Agricultural Show is held, in which, true to its name, innumerable horses and ponies share the honors with prize farm beasts. The Grand Parade of Livestock is something to be remembered, and will certainly not be forgotten by the daughter, who was in theory parading a ton of Hereford bull but was precipitately removed from the scene by her charge. A humiliating demonstration of brawn taking precedence over brain.

A favorite mecca of our family is the annual Horse of the Year Show, where the jumping and showing classes are of the finest, but where the emphasis of the presentation is on the horse as a character, where the equine celebrities of the past or present—anything from a steeplechaser to a pit pony—are encouraged to step out in the "personality parade" to steal the show.

At the well-named Royal Windsor, you may see Prince Philip at an early hour, strolling about in the ring, trying to work out his turns for the Obstacle Driving later in the day. Or Prince Charles with a couple of polo ponies entered in

125

the appropriate class. Or Princess Anne and her husband competing against each other in a dressage and show-jumping competition. In the afternoon the Queen attends to watch the proceedings and present prizes. And it is all staged against a backcloth of the crenellated battlements and historic towers and walls of Windsor Castle.

At the comparatively new Dunhill International Jumping Championships, held just before Christmas, Germany's Olympic jumper, Alwin Schockemöhle, told me he thought German spectators get surfeited with an unadulterated diet of show jumping. If this is the case, then German show promoters should take thought from the Dunhill, which is a highly successful if improbable mixture of the thrills and climaxes of international jumping, stirred up with a seasoning of pantomime, circus, and Christmas spirit —all horse oriented. The jumping fraternity looks on it as a chance to relax from serious competing with such diversions as demonstrating their notions of *haute couture* in a fancy-dress relay competition over fences. Well-known equestrian characters appear for a Christmas Eve meet of Mr. Jorrocks' hounds, or personalities from Dickens congregate on horseback and in coach and carriage. There is a trio jumping relay competition, in which each team is made up of an equestrian journalist, a jockey, and some well-known actor or actress. The horsemanship and/or prowess over show jumps in this event tends to be sketchy, to say the least. I can still see the expression of a journalist during one of these relays when, after he had achieved his round in one piece and was resting thankfully on his laurels, his borrowed mount set off over the fences again, hot on the heels of the next startled competitor.

Americans ride hunt seat, saddle seat, and stock seat, and demand shows and classes to accommodate them all. The bias toward the different riding styles and the horses that go with them lies usually with locality: hunt-seat classes mainly in the East, those for the Saddle Horse or Tennessee Walker fraternity mostly in the South, stock seat and Quarter Horses to the Far West, with California often providing for the lot.

The American Horse Shows Association now officially recognizes more than seven hundred annual shows; more than fifty affiliated associations hold specialized shows of their own. The only type that is becoming as rare in the United States as in the United Kingdom are those little affairs of yesterday's vintage, run for local talent, with rosettes the only prize awarded, the accent all on fun—shows like the one I witnessed where a member fell off four times in one jumping round and won a special rosette for providing "light relief."

The original horse shows were based on showing, on the classes that are still the shop windows for the prototypes of the hunters and hacks, for

High head carriage and extreme leg action of American Saddle Horses do not fit them for dressage, but in their specialty they are America's show horses without parallel. Above, a rare-colored saddler, the much-decorated Venus in Grey.

Opposite: First phase
of Horse Trial is dressage
test. Princess Anne's
Goodwill is superb across
country, but does not
always display the
calm obedience needed
for dressage.

the cobs and show ponies, and particularly for the many different breeds. Showing, in hand or under saddle, is an art in itself, and the classes retain their value in the modern horseman's world—in France the breed classes are considered sufficiently important to be backed by the state—even though, to the uninitiated, they lack the same obvious spectator appeal of, say, show jumping.

In the days just after World War II, when we first forayed into the show world, jumping had not attained its present dominance, nor had professional standards permeated the middle levels of show activity as they have today. Memory fails me as to why we decided to enter Blaze in the 12.2 show-pony class at a local affair. Built on the lines of a heavyweight hunter in miniature, he was not in any sense a "show pony."

He was neither gross fat nor overthin, but if this show had been typical of the standards of the seventies (and Blaze himself up to standard), he would have been prepared with a program of feeding and "strapping" to add or subtract flesh and muscle in the desired areas. Suitable food additives and hours of grooming would have produced a coat not merely healthy and clean, but brightly lustrous. In addition to pulled tail, braided mane, and trimmed fetlocks, his whiskers would have been trimmed and his ears shorn of hair on the insides. (As a working pony, though, Blaze would never have been denuded of the sensitive antennae with which horses "feel" the world around their muzzles, or of the natural barriers against the unpleasant situation when your horse gets a fly or worse in its ear.)

Blaze captured no rosette in his showing debut, but his behavior was exemplary and he gave his rider a good taste of the disciplines of show competition, which today are so exacting for riders of all ages.

It was at the Devon County Show, held near Philadelphia, that I finally caught up with the essential difference between American and British horse shows.

That day it was not the weather. Though warm, the early drizzle, cloudy sky, and lack of sun were depressingly familiar, and though at the food counters the usual brisk trade was in hot dogs and black coffee instead of the accustomed flabby ham sandwiches and cups of tea, the ponies offering "rides" nearby were Shetlands,

even if tacked up western. Certainly the accommodations in the horse barns were above British average standards of comfort, and it was pleasant to note how all day the music obligingly changed rhythm to match that of the horses in the ring. The helpful instructions issued by the ringmaster over an amplifier, telling competitors exactly what the judges would like them to be doing at any given moment, were distinctly more avuncular in tone than is common with British officials. Backstage there were the usual tempting displays of saddlery, riding cloths, and accessories. The big crowds, glued to their ringside seats or milling about in search of other distractions, were the familiar mixture of the dedicated and merely curious, of the seekers after knowledge and the pursuers of holiday fun. For me, the big dissimilarity between this example of an American horse show and its counterpart in the United Kingdom lay in the ring—in the overall, uniformly good riding of the competitors and the equally exemplary behavior of their horses.

This is a direct result of the American emphasis on competitive equitation at all levels—both juniors and adult—which in any class where the English seat is requisite produces the classic style

of riding. In show-jumping classes, it is the same story, although "classic" here refers to an adaptation of the method devised by Caprilli, which is required by the size and type of modern fences.

It must have been very difficult for the judges of that Devon show to pick the winners of the equitation and the innumerable working-hunter classes of all standards. Here were all the competitors riding on a long rein with a light contact, admirably precise in their movements on the flat, and keeping a quiet, even pace over the fences. Obviously some of those Thoroughbreds looked to be "more agreeable mounts to hounds" than others; some jumped in better style, a few had the odd pole down, but the good manners that the majority displayed, the unbroken tempo they kept up around the ring, the smoothness and calmness with which they jumped, meeting every fence in their stride, excited admiration and seemed a good augury for those that would graduate to show jumping.

Equitation competitions that produce results like this would be a good thing in England, where rough, stop-go tactics, particularly among junior show jumpers, are far from unknown. And with all this in mind, I found myself missing some

element of unpredictability in those classes at the Devon Show. The basics of good riding are the same everywhere, but the British interpretation of the art runs strongly to individualism. Each man to his own variation of style, particularly among the jumping fraternity, though some styles are to be deplored. Moreover, individuality is a trait the British extend to and expect in their horses. As a spectator I found myself awaiting a rider that was just a little offbeat, just one horse that kicked back, or gave a little buck, or indulged just a few exuberant leaps. No one would suggest that Lucky Strike, once the property of a neighbor of ours, could be ridden by anyone who hadn't a special brand of patience and understanding. Here was a horse with the outstanding beauty and quality to win the Ladies' Hack Championship one day and then, for no reason except that he felt like it, put on a bucking display from sheer *joie de vivre* and almost removed his rider from the ring next time out. When he came to show jumping, at the age of eleven, he showed equal brilliance in a field very different from his former one, together with the same characteristic peccadillos. When he felt like it, Lucky Strike was unbeatable; among his

Above: Impulsion, generated by active use of the hocks, is essential for dressage. The Thoroughbred, Abound, now at Advanced Level, is being schooled at extended trot by his owner, the highly skilled Mrs. Robert Hall.

victories he included the Puissance at the Horse of the Year Show, with the wall at seven feet, and the jumping championship at the same show where he had won the hack championship some years before. Whether Lucky Strike did well or fooled around—playing to the gallery to the detriment of jumping clear—depended on how he felt. You had to be philosophical to cope with such an animal, but what a character he was, and what a crowd puller!

In the knife-edge competitions up at the top of show jumping, there is maybe little place nowadays for such inconsistent creatures as the beautiful Lucky Strike, but the competitive world of the horseman is not confined to the tense limits of the show ring. There are competitions where there is more room for the individualist.

Endurance Riding, sometimes called Competitive Trail Riding, is perhaps the form of contest farthest removed from the sophistication of

the show ring. It appeals to me as a sport that can concern almost any age group from twelve upwards, and almost any kind of horse or large pony. It has evolved from the long-distance rides for chargers that were staged three hundred years ago in Europe, and from the American cavalry tests of the 1920's that were used to compare the relative qualities of Thoroughbreds and Arabians as Army remounts.

If you live in the United States, your choice ranges from the type of competitive trail rides covering several days—most common in the East—to something on the lines of the western marathons, with the one-day, 100-mile Tevis Cup the supreme and most testing of all.

In Australia, endurance riding is a growing sport, and as in the U.S. the immense tracts of suitable terrain lend themselves to it. But whether the ride is geared to suit the scale of such vast regions, or condensed in severity to fit the dimensions of the British countryside, the challenge and the opportunities of the sport are much the same. The question lies in your ability to spend several months conditioning your horse and yourself, so that you can get the mileage without "racing" within the times required, with your mount in such a state of physical fitness that he passes all the stringent veterinary tests along the way, which are devised to insure there is no equine distress or exploitation. This conditioning is a fascinating project in itself, and with it goes the opportunity to ride over new and beautiful country. By heritage, stamina, size, and courage, horses of Arabian blood are usually to be found among the winners, but Australian Walers, Thoroughbreds, and Standardbreds have all proved their suitability.

Whether they take place over the stone walls and big fences of Virginia, or across the English countryside where the sport that gave birth to them was also born, hunter trials are friendly, informal affairs, the contestants all members of the local or neighboring hunts. As far as possible the course is constructed from natural obstacles and the lay of the land, and the horses are not racehorses in embryo, but the genuine hunter article.

Hunter trials are fun and good schooling for event riding. For anyone who competes in one, there comes that awful moment waiting for the start, when the old horse, full of good food,

fitness, and a heady sense of the occasion, dances around regardless of your tautened nerves and the sinking feeling in the pit of the stomach. The starter, holding his flag at the ready, jumps back to avoid having his feet trodden on and beguiles the minutes with facetious remarks, his colleague gluing his eyes to the stopwatch, then it's "Ready . . . Go!" The flag is down, there's a hail of divots as the old horse plunges through the start. A crash and slither and you hit the first fence hard, but no matter, you're over and it's a case of "Steady . . . now" as the horse fights for his head. "Not too fast now—we've a long way to go." Twigs slap your cheek as you take off over and through a bullfinch, there's a nasty moment as you nearly turn turtle at the stile, and if you're having qualms, however natural, about that open ditch, then . . . don't. Such is the nature of the brutes that your horse will probably share them, slither to an uncoordinated stop, and there you'll be, both left staring with equal distaste into the slimy depths below.

So, it's leg him on, keep going, never mind being winded and too tired to grip, never mind if your mount is reduced to a lumbering trot up that last Everest-like slope. You can forget that you seem to have been on course for hours because suddenly you can distinguish familiar voices among the yells of encouragement, suddenly you realize that hurdle you've just walloped was the last fence, suddenly the finishing flags are actually behind you. Never mind the time, you've made it.

And if your name isn't on the winners' list, maybe next time. You've got around, proved something to yourself, showed what the old horse can do.

Despite having all the appearance of roots embedded way down in the English countryside, eventing in its present form is a relatively new sport. Given its official and most descriptive title, Concours Complet d'Equitation—Combined Training is the best interpretation—it is scarcely surprising to learn that its most prominent facet, that of endurance, embodies Xenophon's precepts to his cavalry as developed in modern times from other European military sources by the French in their "Raids Militaires." The French Army staged a Championnat du Cheval d'Armes that proved to be the real forerunner of eventing as we know it today. At Saumur, the instructors of the famous Cadre Noir continue to produce their spectacular displays and teach the principles of the *concours complet d'équitation* to civilians and to young French officers, whose character training still includes compulsory horsemanship.

Originally, British Army officers were too busy fox hunting, playing polo, or riding point-to-point to give attention to any other form of competitive riding, let alone one that appeared suspiciously "foreign." True, Britain fielded a team for "The Military," a kind of back-to-front event included in the 1912 Olympics in which the dressage phase came last, but they failed to finish. A British team competed again in a modern type Olympic Three-Day Event in 1938 and scored sixth. At the Berlin Games of 1936, when rain turned the stiff cross-country course into a battlefield, Britain was third, with only four teams finishing out of nineteen starters.

But civilians still had no part in eventing until after World War II, and there was little interest among British riders until the 1948 Olympics, held in England. Then the subsequent enthusiasm of the Duke of Beaufort induced him to offer his magnificent park for a three-day event to be held the following year—the first of the world-famous annual Badminton Horse Trials.

Even then only a small section of horsemen took interest in this "complete" equestrian sport, and the public and press had little notion of what it was all about and cared less. Princess Anne's enthusiastic participation, with the obvious publicity and prestige attached to a member of the royal family—and a girl at that—competing in what is a very arduous and sometimes hazardous pastime, helped materially to put eventing on the map. Now at least the cross-country phase of the major events is given good television coverage, and many of the national newspapers also carry full reports and photographs. The public flocks by the tens of thousands to the great Badminton and Burghley Horse Trials, presenting major traffic problems for the police and, in wet weather, a sea of mud to greet the eyes of the titled owners of these beautiful parks the next morning.

Competitors, realizing that combined training is the ultimate challenge to the all-round horseman and his horse, have stepped up their numbers each year to fill the lists of an increasing

number of horse trials taking place yearly in America and Australia, in Europe and Britain.

Whether a horse trial consists of one day or three, the traditional three phases—dressage, cross-country and show jumping—are always included. It is the first—dressage—that proved the original stumbling block to popularizing the sport.

British riders had an instinctive antipathy to the word. It smacked too much of the imagined "unnatural" disciplines and folderols indulged in by the Germans and other Europeans in their indoor manèges, the kind of "artificial" horsemanship that had been all right in the sixteenth and seventeenth centuries but was shrugged off by the British as soon as they began their gentleman's sport of pursuing foxes flat-out across country.

It was much the same frame of mind that not so long ago impeded Australian riders from taking dressage seriously. Australians rode. No one

could question their courage or that of their horses, and they saw no reason to change their way of riding or to stomach any outsiders coming from overseas to show them how. The Olympic Three-Day Events, where Australian teams saw their excellent prowess in the other phases negated by poor dressage marks, brought about a change of heart to good effect.

Dressage was slow to be accepted at grass-roots level. Young riders tended to find it dull on first encounter when compared with jumping. And it was not only the children who moaned. One ferocious, old-school Brigadier, proud father and owner of a successful daughter-cum-pony junior show-jumping outfit, actually forbade either to be taught anything of "the stuff"; he was convinced it would spoil their chances of further winning. It took time to realize that in its elemental form "dressage" covers the kind of training that any good horseman would wish to give his animal. It took time to appreciate

that all the children who learned dressage were becoming better riders, and that the ponies they rode were more obedient and cooperative than before. Gradually dressage appeared in its true guise, as an integral and beneficial training of horse and rider for all facets of equestrianism. Many riders are now succumbing to the fascination of a graduated system of horse training that, done correctly, results in "the harmonious development of the physique and ability of the horse" and in perfect harmony between horse and rider. Such horsemen are fired with ambition to possess the horse and the ability to participate in competitive dressage at higher levels than novice. Those privileged with the time and the talent to train can aspire to the Grand Prix or Reprise Olympique tests, which comprise the paces and figures of the "airs on the ground" taught in haute école, and they require a superlative horse, superlatively schooled for years.

At the Spanish Riding School in Vienna, the

133

classic equestrian art of haute école is still practiced and demonstrated in its original purity by the famous gray Lipizzaner stallions. It was my good fortune to meet one of these magnificent horses at close hand. This was Siglavy Flora II, a twelve-year-old Lipizzaner who was at the time in transit for Australia. Before being sold he was trained and worked in Vienna and then used for breeding at the Lipizzaner stud at Piber for two years. At nearly 15.3 hands, this is a big horse for the breed. He has all the beauty and noble bearing of his race, and with it the gentleness and good manners not always associated with stallions. At the Spanish Riding School all the horses are schooled in the "airs on the ground" for three or four years, then some specialize in the movement for which they show the most talent, while the select few, after further training, are used to demonstrate the spectacular "airs above the ground." This horse had been an exponent of the piaffe, the difficult movement on one spot, originating in the trot, where cadence and regularity of pace are more important than high elevation.

When he was loosed in the covered school to prance and spring and curvet, at will and with a grace and fire lovely to see, it was easy to understand that many of the stylized movements and school jumps of haute école were indeed de-

veloped from the natural paces and leaps of horses at play.

The dressage tests used in eventing's Phase I vary in difficulty according to the type of horse trial. But whatever the movements required and at whatever standard, ideally they are executed by a horse that is free-going, light, and cadenced in its paces. It does not deviate on straight lines and is correctly bent on curves. It remains motionless at "halt" with its weight evenly distributed and is so willingly obedient to its rider's lightest aids all through the test, that it gives the impression of "doing it all on its own."

Much of that is not very easy to attain with the type of high-mettled, courageous animal also capable of the endurance and jumping demands of a three-day event, a horse of necessity so fit that it is almost bursting out of its skin with well-being. But however far off such a goal of perfection may appear to the majority, there are benefits to be had from practice of the elementary movements, as the Pony Club has recognized. Its one-day events are nurseries for the three-day marathons, and come within the scope of the young rider with a good jumping horse or pony. The cross-country is the most exciting phase and the final show jumping often the decisive one. But the dressage is always interesting and demonstrates the jack-of-all-trades

Pages 134-135: Princess Anne and Doublet winning European Horse Trial Championships at Burghley in 1971. Once-difficult Argentine-bred horse was reaching full promise when he broke a leg and had to be destroyed.

Opposite: Classic advice to jumpers is "throw your heart over the fence and the horse will follow after."

Above: Captain Mark Phillips on now famous Columbus, impetuous son of Winston Churchill's racehorse, Colonist II.

137

character that event horses and riders have.

Eventing is essentially a pastime of the countryside, and with it goes a delightful informality that belies the months of planning and efficient organization essential to making these affairs the successes they are.

For the English there is the luxury of being within traveling distance of world-class events, the products of months of planning and efficient organization. Usually they are held on one of the big country estates, where sufficient space has been preserved. No settings could be more perfect than Badminton, the Cotswold home of the Dukes of Beaufort where the famous spring trials are held, or Burghley, seat of the Marquess of Exeter at Northampton, which is the site of the comparable autumn trials. While the space around any dressage arena is perforce limited, and only early application will ensure a seat for the last day's show jumping, for the cross-country phase both parks provide the acreage to completely absorb even the huge crowds that now flock to watch the sport.

If we can, we make Badminton an annual date. As with Burghley, that is where the world's top riders meet for what, bar the Olympics, are the world's most grueling equestrian competitions.

Even around the dressage arenas the atmosphere is electric, something that adds to the difficulties of Phase 1, where you are trying to demonstrate that your horse is educated and obedient, balanced and supple. With that kind of animal, conditioned for that kind of occasion, impulsion is seldom lacking, but it takes a top-quality horseman, with real understanding and tact, to coax a polished, relaxed performance out of an animal that is often a bottled-up equine volcano.

The exceptional horse is amenable to the disciplines of the dressage test, as he is bold and brilliant across country, but he is a rare bird. Princess Anne's Doublet, bred by Queen Elizabeth out of an Argentine ex-polo pony mare, proved to be such a one despite being a difficult customer in his youth, and it was a sad and terrible day for Princess Anne when Doublet broke his leg in 1974. Anne and her horse had come to terms and learned their eventing together, and their winning of the European Horse Trials Championships of 1971 was a tribute to a

The fixed barriers of the Maryland Hunt Cup course are a test to man and horse alike. Here rider A. P. Smithwick comes to grief as his mount, Moonlove, in attempting to complete the jump on the horizontal, loses control entirely.

Above: World Championship dressage competitors in the exercise arena at Christianborg. While only expert spectators can appreciate the finer points of the art, the public reacts enthusiastically to exhibitions where horses seem to be doing it on their own.

partnership based on much hard work, mutual courage, and the trust and confidence that builds between a rider and horse that are attuned.

Good marks in Phase 1 can be an excellent bonus towards the final placings, and an adequate test is a necessity, but good dressage is of little account if the horse does not go comparably well across country. In theory, the second day, comprising the speed, endurance, and cross-country sections, has four times more influence on the result than the dressage, and twelve times more than the final jumping over show fences, but technical adjustments to prevent this being arbitrary are allowed for in the rules.

However well or badly you have fared in Phase I, the second day finds you setting off on the first three and a quarter miles or so of roads and tracks. Your horse is fresh and so are you, and all that is necessary is to combine periods of fast trotting or walk and canter, so that you remain within the time limit and don't tire your animal unnecessarily by trying to undercut it. Then it's away onto the two-and-a-quarter-mile

steeplechase course, where ability to jump at speed (averaging about 26 mph overall) without taking too much out of your horse is the criterion. There are no other runners thudding alongside to boost morale and fire the blood. Your only rival is the timekeepers' stopwatch. You must use your own judgment in varying the pace at the beginning and the end, taking a cue from the way your animal is meeting his fences.

You come straight off the steeplechase knowing there are another five miles plus of roads and tracks to tackle. This time, for a start, you have a blowing, sweating horse to consider, and if it seems a good idea to jump off and run beside him for a while, you still have to bear in mind that a late arrival at the conclusion of this section carries severe penalties.

There is a ten-minute break while your horse is examined by a team of experts for fitness to continue, then it's back into the saddle for the nearly five miles of cross-country that, for many, is the summit of the whole affair.

You meet posts and rails, double oxers, and

Advanced dressage horse is the *danseur noble* of equitation. Those few riders who know horse's extreme lightness when mouth and action are in complete harmony enjoy quintessence of equestrian art. Above, Christine Stückelberger, Swiss competitor, on Smaragd.

Classical horsemen
of old noted the exuberant
leaps of stallions at
play. Medieval knights
utilized similar movements
to confuse the enemy.
From such sources grew the
astounding "airs above
the ground," leaps such as
the capriole seen here,
performed by especially
talented stallions at the
Spanish Riding School.

rock-solid wood piles. You jump genuine stone walls, with or without a ditch lurking on the far side, and take your decided line with problems provided by zigzags, or stars or intricate pens, fences that, like some others, usually have an easier but time-wasting alternative to that offered to the bold. There are varieties of the Coffin and Quarry jumps to contend with, and sometimes such agricultural items as hay-racks and pheasant feeders. You come to formidable combinations of sunken roads, ditches, banks, and rails. Recently there was one obstacle comprising a big tree trunk set over a gulley, and we were entranced to see an enterprising horse achieve the impossible. He emerged from underneath with rider still intact and no penalties incurred. There are big hedges with big drops, and ramps with bigger ones yet. At some stage at Badminton you will leap in and out of the lake, maybe to join the many who have taken an involuntary ducking there. At this hazard we watched a famous Australian rider come perforce to a stop; he had persuaded his swimming horse to rejoin him on the bank only to discover its bridle broken beyond repair. At the 1974 World Championship at Burghley, it was jumping a post-and-rails into water after an awkward downhill approach that caused most of the grief that day and not a few spectacular total immersions, fortunately without injury.

The maximum height for the cross-country fences is less than four feet, with six feet as the maximum spread, but unlike show jumps, all those thirty to thirty-five obstacles are fixed and solid. The time limit is very tight for a course designed so that speed must vary according to terrain, and even a second lost negotiating a jump or by too slow a gallop can have a bearing on the result. Each horse and rider will have completed eleven strenuous miles or more before even starting the cross-country, and a sense of pace and timing, and the sensitivity to judge how much more can be safely asked of a tiring horse, are requisites of every combined-training competitor. So, too, are the guts to take the inevitable falls, each incurring 60 penalty points, that are an accepted, if costly, hazard of the sport.

With the cross-country accomplished, only two tests remain. Early the next morning, your horse has to pass a stringent veterinary examina-

tion to show that it is physically fit to carry on, and then there remains only the final phase.

The show jumping consists of one round only, its object to prove the versatility of horse and rider over a relatively modest course of artificial show fences. By top show-jumping standards, the obstacles may appear easy, but combined with clever changes of direction, the tense excitement of the show-ring atmosphere, and the exigencies of the previous day, this phase often juggles the expected final placings out of line.

Combined training provides some of the most exciting and most exacting equestrian competitions, and the competitive aspect of the horseman's world is the facet that is now expanding the fastest. It is also the one where man can most easily abuse the horse's generous will to cooperate.

It must have been somewhere along the line of evolution, after man achieved time beyond what he needed for hunting and eating, for copulating and sleeping, for fighting and dying, that the instinct to compete was born. Now at work or play the urge to prove oneself or one's belongings that much better than the other man or his possessions permeates most sides of life, providing the spur that at best is only stimulating. At worst it can be corruptive, sometimes destructive, too often cruel.

The advent of big money often triggers off happenings that mar otherwise admirable sports, and on this score show jumping cannot be excluded. In some ways the sport has developed into show business, an entertainment where the customer demands his money's worth, where those who provide it deserve and must receive their due. By old standards the prize money is generous, but the expenses are also vast. Young horses with jumping potential can, with luck, be found going cheap, but they do not grow on trees. The normal outlay means paying high prices, and even then the exceptional horse is rare. Wages, horse feed, shoeing, veterinary bills, the traveling to the major shows at home and abroad where good money is offered during a season that lasts from April to Christmas—all this and more adds up to one result: very few of the show-jumping fraternity can afford to own and ride their own horses. The majority ride, or hope to ride, for a wealthy owner or for one of the commercial empires that either lease or own the horses and retain the riders. As a commercial proposition, the real incentive is in the advertising value that comes to firms backing top horses and riders who remain successfully in the public eye.

Without this kind of sponsoring modern show jumping could not exist, but it does contribute to the stresses of competing, it does make frequent winning more of a necessity. Perhaps it also makes more explicable, if never pardonable, some of the methods used by some people to make horses jump.

A real horseman remains one whatever the pressures. His knowledge and treatment are innate, and founded on affection and respect, plus a down-to-earth appreciation of long-term policies. There is no sentiment in this approach. When the gloves are off, the horseman will ask the utmost of his horse, but he will know exactly what the animal is capable of and whether it is physically and mentally prepared for what he demands. The tempo of modern life does not provide anyone with the leisure hours our ancestors enjoyed, but the true horseman avoids haste. He knows you cannot cut corners with the training of a young horse without damaging unattuned muscles and an immature understanding—whether the animal is destined for jumping or dressage.

The majority of show jumpers are horsemen. They appreciate this outlook and the fact that patient, unhurried schooling pays off in the end with more promise of a long, rewarding partnership. Still, there are the ignorant and the unscrupulous who will skimp and hurry the schooling in order to qualify for some competition that could spell money. If the luck holds and they get away with it, they applaud their own cleverness and try again, maybe with a more difficult youngster that should receive even more time and patience. When things go wrong they resort to gadgets, and then more gadgets to counteract the undesirable side effects of the first. By the use of two pairs of spurs, one of them electric, horses are induced to jump the heights and spreads that should come effortlessly through weeks of graduated training. Boasts are made about the invention of devices that give shocks to horses who hit practice fences. There are a few competitors who are at pains not to mention that under the concealing bandages on their horse's forelegs the skin has been split and an irritant applied so that the animal is terrified of its legs touching anything, let alone a jumping pole.

Overjumping is a big temptation, but it can result in horses so footsore that to stand they have to shift from foot to foot, and it often puts them out of the game altogether after only a season or two. The rider who looks on his horses as money-spinning, expendable machines, may become a top-line winner, but he can never consider himself a horseman.

Everything possible should be done to ensure that, by the greed and ignorance of a few, the image of such an enthralling and popular sport does not become tarnished.

Show jumping is certainly not the only medium where horses are exploited. In combined-training competitions the prize money is relatively small, and the entire concept is of a sport for the true amateur. But at the top and international levels the competition grows fiercer, the standard higher, and once again, it is tempting to some to discount the skilled and long-drawn-out process of training and conditioning of an event horse. Strong evidence suggests that at these levels an occasional competitor resorts to drugs, tranquilizing his horse for Phase I, or stimulating a tired animal for the show jumping.

Even in international competitive dressage—competitions involving the quintessence of the classical art of the horseman—the same problem exists of drugs occasionally being administered to make the rider's task that much easier.

Experienced judges can usually recognize signs of drugging and mark down accordingly, so that a morally indefensible practice, which is against the rules and entire concept of equestrianism, is of little gain. And there is talk of introducing the extremely accurate drug tests employed by the Jockey Club as a deterrent in these competitions.

Surely anyone who stoops to the use of drugs or other short-cut aids, is admitting abysmal ignorance, incompetent horsemanship, and a total disregard of the relationship possible between a rider and his horse.

Away from the disciplines of haute école, Lipizzaner stallion Siglavy Flora II plays in the freedom of the indoor school at Fulmer in England.

6.

Horses
in
Harness

Whatever the reasons—freedom from mechanical din and fumes, unconscious disenchantment with a technological world, even the possibility of driving country tracks still impassable to motorized vehicles—driving as a pastime is on the upsurge everywhere. And, ironically, with oil-based energy a universal problem, this method of transport, which Progress had consigned to the trash heap, is achieving an aura of respectable economy to add to the pure pleasure it always provided.

American highways are no places for driving horses, but in a country the size of the United States there are locations that lend themselves well to the sport of driving, with the gentle hunt country of southwestern New Jersey perhaps in the forefront. American coaching enthusiasts even have shown that this mode of highway transportation is not entirely impractical; a group of coaches recently made the trip from New York to Philadelphia in a day to prove the point. Antique carriages have very quietly become both rare and expensive in America, and there is a healthy schedule of meets where drivers can display their equipages and their skills. For the time being, the Middle Atlantic states seem to offer the most in driving and coaching activity, but the enthusiasm is spreading. The handsome Carriage Association Journal keeps up with it all.

The bulk of American driving and harness-horse interest centers round the show ring. Much the same holds for Australia, where the big Agricultural and Royal shows now provide harness classes for children as well as for adults. In Britain, too, apart from the Hackney classes held for the breed that many consider the doyen of driving animals, there is a growing number for other harness animals. Some, on the lines of their gallery-pleasing American counterparts, require competitors to negotiate small obstacles and perform various maneuvers such as backing through a simulated gateway. Also beginning to percolate in England is the excellent American idea of classes where dual-purpose breeds, such as the Saddle Horse and the Morgan, perform under saddle and in fine harness. For sheer spectator appeal the Scurry Competitions are hard to beat. This is obstacle-driving against the clock, where numerous spills add to the fun, especially for the audience, and speed dependent on length of stride is subordinate to maneuver-

ability—as was proved by the famed pair of Shetland stallions that literally scurried their way to victory after victory over more conventionally sized opponents.

In many countries—Holland, Belgium, Switzerland, Portugal, Hungary, Poland, and Scandinavia—the art of driving has remained a living skill. At some famous studs, huge teams of stallions, up to twelve at a time, are driven for display and exercise. No Spanish feria would be complete without bell-decked teams like those Andalusians and Arabians, driven sometimes as a five- or seven-in-hand, that prance proudly up and down the streets of Seville.

The British Driving Society was formed in 1955 to provide for those who drive horses in single harness, in pairs and in tandems, and less than twenty years later it was boasting a membership of around fifteen hundred. The Society has branches in those parts of the country that lend themselves to the sport, and meets are held, often at some country mansion. Sometimes this includes various classes judged on various aspects of turn-out and driving skill, but the main business of the day is to set out—with an assortment of gigs and rally carts, phaetons, dog carts, what you will, drawn by a miscellany that can range from a pair of Cleveland Bays to a Welsh Cob, through Irish hunters to New Forest ponies, Welsh ponies, Dartmoors, and even Shetlands—all trotting and jingling merrily along in company around the country lanes, sometimes with a picnic stop en route.

The driving competitions, involving the negotiation of rough ground, steep hills, river fords, and the like, that had been popular in Europe for some years and particularly successful in Germany, Hungary, and Switzerland, got added impetus when Prince Philip became involved as president of the Fédération Equestre Internationale. In 1969 his interest extended, with the help of top British drivers, into formulating a set of international rules that developed combined driving, at the top echelon, into the equivalent of a ridden three-day event. The first of these to be held in Britain was part of the Royal Windsor Horse Show a year later.

Prince Philip always said that he would give up polo when he was fifty, a milestone reached in 1971. Prompted by the Crown Equerry, himself a notable whip, he was already contemplating

Above: Prince Philip
is an exponent of
Competitive Driving,
exciting contests run along
lines of ridden
three-day events. He
learned Whip's art first
with single harness,
then, as here, with pair.

Left: Cleveland Bay
is elegant in harness.
This one, driven to
a brougham, is on mail
call to Buckingham
Palace, duty performed—
come wind, come rain—
twice each day.

driving as an alternative sport. For a man of his temperament, a relaxation such as polo—which provided excitement suitably spiced with danger as well as violent exercise—was a necessity. And if the art of park driving does not, on its own, fulfill all these requirements, the competitive form of driving does not fall far short. By the time that Prince Philip, graduating via a single harness horse to a pair and then to a team, was sufficiently competent to embark on a combined driving competition, he was finding what he had already assumed—that though for one reason and another the majority of competitors are middle-aged, this is no "old man's sport."

Originally restricted to teams of four horses, which made it a sport for at least the moderately wealthy, the competition has been extended to include pairs and single horses and is geared to different standards, bringing it all within the scope of many more enthusiastic harness-horse owners. The most suitable vehicles for teams and pairs seem to be brakes, four-wheeled dog carts and, less frequently, phaetons, but for single horses, two-wheeled vehicles such as rally and dog carts are safer and easier to maneuver.

At the outset, the British public were as mystified by this sport, and as disinterested in it, as they once had been by ridden events. But Prince Philip's enthusiasm, which in turn engendered interest from the television moguls, began to do for combined driving what his daughter had helped to achieve for combined training. And once a wide audience saw for themselves the splendor of a team of fit horses performing together in the hands of an expert whip, the sheer spectacular beauty of the affair began to catch the popular imagination. It only needed the excitement of the couple of royal capsizes, among all those looked on as the normal competitive hazards of the sport, and combined driving was well on the way to being on the map.

Like its ridden twin, a combined-driving contest at national and international level consists of three phases performed over three days by competitors who have already qualified their horses. Their vehicles have to comply with the weight stated in the rules, and in Section A of Phase 1 the presentation requires everything to be considered—from the whip's and groom's handling of the horses, to the condition and suitability of turn-out, clothes, and the "spares"

Though few American roads are suited to horse-drawn transport, Amish people of rural Pennsylvania can accommodate pleasantly to tenets of their faith by eschewing cars in favor of strong and stylish trotters.

"Putting to" a team
of Percheron stallions at
Haras du Pin, one of
the French state-owned
studs. Heavy horses
normally wear neck collars,
but these breast collars,
usual for racing and
other light-harness work,
are commonly used in
some European countries.
Drive out is good
exercise for horses that
must be fit for stud.

carried aboard. Anyone who has studied dressage knows the difficulty for beginners of such elementary movements as circling and turning at walk, or collected, working, and extended trot, and will all the better appreciate the challenge of Section B of Phase 1—where four horses under the more remote control of driving reins have to execute these and other movements correctly in an arena only 131 feet by 328 feet (40 by 100 meters). But it is a joy to see the smoothness with which the top drivers achieve their evolutions.

For the five sections of the marathon phase, supreme fitness, as in a ridden event, is of first importance. The horses have to contend with about twenty miles of "roads and tracks typical of the country." The different sections are done at walk or trot, and each one is to be performed in a set time without breaking the required pace. Hazards abound: uphill and downhill going, rough ground and smooth, grassland and woodland tracks—all interspersed with narrow gateways and scarcely an inch to spare; tight, difficult turns around trees where a team of extra-big horses can easily come to grief; fearsome-looking rivers to be forded, where you pray devoutly your leaders will not waver; horse-frightening obstacles such as piles of logs to be driven between, where a "jink" from the wheelers can catch a wheel hub and break an axle, or send the steering "boss-eyed." The coachman needs expert judgment of width to an

inch. He must know his horses and have a fine sense of when it is safe to push them on to make up for precious seconds lost. He needs also a good slice of luck, and he hopes devoutly that the pole and axles will remain intact whatever happens, that the tires stay put around the wheels and the brakes survive the ordeal—and that if they do happen to turn over everything can be righted again with the least possible delay.

There are penalties for stopping or reversing, for circling, for dismounting from the vehicle, and for horses breaking the required pace, and each vehicle carries a referee to ensure nothing is overlooked. It all has to be achieved within the time allowed, with just a couple of compulsory ten-minute stops inserted as breathing spaces, and the art is to keep the team going on to finish the course without becoming exhausted. There is still tomorrow to think about.

That last phase is equivalent to the show jumping of the ridden event, and has the same objectives—to prove the continuing fitness, suppleness, and obedience of horses subjected to the ardors of the marathon on the previous day.

The teams drive a set course between a number of narrow gaps marked by cone bollards, each topped with a rubber ball that falls with the slightest touch. There may be—as at one recent event—Trakehners from Germany, high-stepping Hackneys, an eye-catching team

of Lipizzaners, honest Dutch Gelderlanders, Welsh Cobs with their ground-covering action, bay Holsteiners from the United States, teams of Irish hunters and English coach horses matched by color, and an heraldic quartet of black Friesians. Prince Philip often drives his team of half-bred Cleveland Bays, while the Crown Equerry takes charge of the Queen's gray Oldenburgs.

Inevitably, combined driving has its few detractors, the chief criticism being that the art and dignity of driving a four-in-hand does not go along with competitive tactics suited more to the circus, or to the American West's exciting pastime of chuck-wagon racing. But the dignity of these competitions is ensured by the insistence on correct turn-out and correct dress for whips, grooms, and horses alike. And without a skilled appreciation of the coachman's art no one is going to be very successful at bending four horses in and out of obstacles where there is only just room for the wheels to pass, and where, if time penalties are to be avoided, accuracy has to be equated with sufficient speed. There are turns on the right rein and on the left, quickly followed by others to either hand. There is the difficult maneuver of driving a double, represented by poles on the ground. There are water splashes, where at least one pair of leaders have been known to hop up on the concrete sides to the

confusion of their wheelers. Here a navigator has made a mistake and only the whip's masterly turn back at speed has made up for lost time; here someone's leader has jumped an obstacle and thoroughly unsettled his teammates. That whip has crossed his tracks with consequent penalties, this one has lost his way and been eliminated. Some teams are not fast enough, some become overexcited, the majority though are a credit to their training. And if, with only seconds to spare, some competitors leave the ring at a canter, no whip enjoys that lickety-split finale more than Prince Philip, urging his horses on by voice to the encouraging cheers of an appreciative crowd.

Like all good sports, combined driving brings people together from many different countries and promotes understanding and good fellowship. It seems odd that France, with such good records in international and Olympic show jumping and ridden eventing, with such an historic tradition of excellent carriage horses and elegant conveyances, should lack drivers of the caliber requisite for combined driving. At the state studs at Haras du Pin, at Tarbes, Pompadour, and the others, there are many drivers with the skill to exercise the stallions as a six-in-hand, or to ride one and drive another in front. And when it comes to harness racing, French drivers more than hold their own, while *le trotteur,* whether

Opposite: Vincennes, near Paris, is one of the classic tracks of the harness-racing world, each February hosting Prix d'Amérique for international field of top trotters.

Left: French Trotter and groom wear owner's distinguishing color. Like Thoroughbreds, harness racers can be big moneywinners and receive every possible care and attention.

ridden or driven, takes precedence over the more conventional flat racer or steeplechaser.

My most memorable experience of four-in-hand driving followed an invitation to go on exercise with a team. There was no need for the invitation to be repeated. I found myself seated on the box, beside the whip driving the big luggage brake often used for these excursions, be hind the four dappled rumps of some of the best-known horses in Britain, those belonging to a team of the famous royal Windsor Greys.

The second coachman, who combines the important duty of brakeman with the ability to move swiftly to the horses' heads at need, was sitting up behind us, straight as a ramrod in his black coat, a cockade enlivening the side of his tall black hat. There are always a few people to stop and stare when any of the royal horses appear, and altogether, as we swung out through the high stone archway that is the entrance to the Royal Mews at Windsor Castle, the moment was a proud one.

These mews are where Queen Elizabeth keeps her private animals, the horses she and her family and guests love to ride out around the royal parks. For much of the year, the stables, run as the friendly working unit that they are, resound only to the clatter of those relatively few and more or less permanent residents, augmented by young animals in various stages of

training whose numbers fluctuate as they come and go. Only during the polo season does the noise grow in frequency and volume in proportion to the strings of polo ponies going to and fro with their girl grooms. In the days before he gave up the game, Prince Philip would have been the owner of some of those, and nowadays Prince Charles may possibly own one or two, but otherwise they are all the property of the Household Brigade Polo Club, who have the use of much of the stabling.

All the royal carriage horses are animals of state, kept in the Mews at Buckingham Palace, which also houses one of the largest and most historic collections of carriages and harness in the world. However, several teams are brought to Windsor annually in preparation for the traditional royal drive that takes place each day, weather permitting, up the course during the Royal Ascot Race Meeting. And young harness animals also do a part of their training at Windsor, on roads not quite so heavily congested with traffic as the London streets.

On the day of my drive a less experienced horse had been included as near-side wheeler. As we turned in through one of the gates giving access onto the peaceful roadways that traverse Windsor Great Park, it was fascinating to watch the expertise with which a skilled whip "converses" with his team, conveying—through deli-

155

cate adjustments of his left hand and wrist, supplemented at need with his right, through the merest controlled flicks of his bow-topped whip, through a judicious use of the voice—exactly the message he wishes to relay to any particular horse. This coachman knew exactly when that young horse was forging ahead a fraction too fast, exactly when the off-side wheeler was managing to idle with unapparent cunning and needed a reminder. He was meticulous in ensuring that the entire team remained "in draft," with each animal pulling its weight.

Needless to remark, this coachman was employing the so-called English school of driving, sometimes known as park driving, where the aim is a high degree of control of pace and direction, with presence and style taking precedence over pure speed. The horses were moving in the requisite, delightfully collected manner, with their powerful quarters swaying rhythmically, and we progressed to the regular two-time beat of eight pairs of iron-clad hooves trotting on the road. The sun was shining and the birds sang. The huge oak and beech trees were newly green, and looking much as they must have done a couple of centuries before when the dashing Prinny, one day to be King George IV, used to speed by, driving a pair or tandem to a spider phaeton, that elegant, absurdly high and dangerous vehicle to which he was addicted, with one of the beauties of the day tucked up beside him. That Prince of Wales was also a polished coachman, with an enthusiasm for the sport that inspired the young bloods about town to make it a fashionable pastime—after they had illicitly learned the art by bribing the professional drivers of the stage coaches. In 1871 the Coaching Club was founded, an exclusive affair designed to accommodate those who had failed to be accepted by the older, even more select Four-in-Hand Club. In 1894 a record thirty-nine private coaches met at the Magazine in Hyde Park, to drive off together for luncheon at the Hurlingham Club. And despite modern conditions —monetary and otherwise—not exactly favorable to private owners of coaching teams, when the Club celebrated its centenary the number of members was much the same.

We drove into the estate timber yard to give an order, and it was decided that this was an opportune moment to give the young horse a change

Peak speed of
harness racer is not
far short of Derby winner's.
Pacers, fractionally
faster than trotters, do
not race in France.

Below: The trotters race
by, drivers grim-faced
and perched on
minimal seat between
wheels, their
horses sweat-streaked,
with every muscle attuned
to maximum effort.

of position to near-side wheeler. I bethought me of a whispered warning delivered before we had set out, not to be left marooned on the box "in charge" and jumped hastily down to give a hand at ground level. And it was only when standing facing the two horses I was holding, that it dawned just how big and powerful these carriage animals are, and how necessary it is that they should possess the equable temperaments and good training for which they are famed.

On the road once more and bowling along at a steady eight miles an hour, there was the added pleasure of meeting up with another team. While the horses were brought to a standstill, the two whips were able to pass the time of day and appraise each other's teams, secretly satisfying themselves of what they believed in already, the superior quality of their own beasts.

We turned for home, trotting out of the park onto a byroad, and I had a short while of comparative peace in which to contemplate—from my position parallel to the tops of concealing hedgerows and palings—the contents and state of other people's gardens. Then we emerged onto the main road. And as cars and charabancs, motorbikes and lorries converged and roared and hooted and flashed their way past within a whisker's length, it became more than ever evident why not even a moderately busy modern road is any place for a horse, unless he is as steady and traffic-proof and obedient as any creature of flesh and blood can be, and is ridden or driven by an expert.

His three mature teammates took good care of the young Windsor Grey. Tucked in on the near side with a companion's comforting bulk between him and the traffic, held from swerving by their combined weight, and guided and cajoled and coerced along the right lines by a skilled whip, there was little way he could go astray even if he had had the mind. By the time we reached the town, the youngster was spanking along as happy and eager for stable and bait as the other three. As we came up to the T road, where, at that time at least, those for the Mews had to turn left, the green lights flicked to red, and there was a lesson for me in the limited braking power of a four-in-hand. Only confusion could have followed an abrupt attempt to clamp on the inadequate equivalent of four-wheel brakes; the answer lay in a cool head and the

quick decision to let the team go on unchecked, swinging round the corner into the face of oncoming traffic, expecting—rightly—that the drivers on the road would accommodate. In another few moments we had entered the Mews and the drive was over.

The outing was an exciting one for me and recalled my own novice efforts behind, instead of on the back of, a horse. It was shortly after the end of the war that some private demon prompted me to have the highly temperamental pony Blaze broken to harness. In fact, it was the sight of an unused governess cart we had once bought together with a wayward pony (the only horse I have ever actively disliked) that stirred my innately economical mind; it seemed such a waste not to use a cheap form of transport that was actually there to hand. Even my husband, shortly returned from three and a half years' service in the Middle East, allowed his normally cautious approach to my equine schemes to be overrun.

The good lady of great experience who cheerfully undertook Blaze's education as a trap pony also underestimated our animal. Before embarking on the enterprise a price had been agreed upon that would cover generously the time she normally allowed. But as the weeks passed her progress reports became more guarded. She knew there was no question of our being able to expend more than the agreed sum, and eventually she announced that, although Blaze needed a little more experience, she thought we could cope.

A good neighbor living higher up the hill agreed to house the cart and harness in an unused garage, and so the cobbled space outside their back door became the venue for the start of our driving enterprises. And each time we led Blaze to that spot, he made it plainer how insufferable he found the whole proceeding. Partly it had to do with our efforts to adjust a harness that had been made for a pony a good hand shorter and smaller-built all-round than Blaze. At least it was a breast harness, so we were saved having to make that would surely have been a calamitous attempt to put a neck collar on over Blaze's head. But nothing we could do, by way of smoothing the hairs and adjusting the backstrap, would mitigate his obvious loathing for having his tail doubled up and inserted through the crupper; indeed, his taut, stiffened reaction to the entire business did not help. Eventually, after a good deal of pulling in here and letting out there, we would be satisfied that the girth and belly band were pulled up just tight enough, that the shaft tugs were in the correct place and the traces correctly adjusted, that the breeching didn't rub. All the while Blaze's eyes bulged behind the blinkers. Though his trainer had somehow induced him to stand still to be harnessed, it was like dealing with a bunched-up bundle of raw nerve ends, poised for flight.

The final part of the operation, the moment when, sighing with relief, we threaded the reins through the turrets to buckle onto the bit, was the moment when Blaze's patience always snapped. If he was checked, even by someone at his head, he stood straight up on his hind legs. The odd thing was that once under way Blaze appeared to enjoy himself. So long as his driver had the nerve to let him go on, he would prick his ears and keep rattling along at a spanking ten or twelve miles per hour, trotting tirelessly uphill, downhill until we had reached an obvious destination or had returned home once more. If he was seriously checked en route he reared at once—a horrid habit he never indulged in when ridden; fortunately for our peace of mind, there was only one set of traffic lights to be finessed.

On one memorable occasion we drove Blaze to a meet of the local fox hounds. We rattled up in fine style, having taken the precaution to arrive early, and put Blaze up in the stabling at the village inn. Our leaving the scene, some hours later, was done in a less orthodox manner.

I cannot imagine why it had not occurred to me that the effect of the sound of hounds and horn on a pony long accustomed to hunting might be exciting, to say the least. As it was, after running happily with hounds on foot for a few hours, we returned to the inn—to spend the next forty nerve-wracked minutes trying to induce our sweat-soaked, madly agitated pony to remain between the shafts long enough to strap him there. Eventually we left town at full gallop, encouraged on our way by the cheers of those members of the field who were already drinking to the success of the day.

In the end Blaze solved our driving problem for himself. Through the ensuing weeks he did improve, to the extent where short journeys

could successfully be made. One morning I arrived with him at the village shop, when, with no warning whatever, the pony set to and systematically and very quickly kicked his harness to pieces. It was all over so fast that before I could do anything Blaze was standing there quietly and more or less nude, with one shaft lying across his back that kept the cart and myself in the upright position.

I took the hint and led him home. Later the governess cart was trucked off to be sold, and Blaze returned happily to his chosen role in life, that of an excellent hunter—for those who understood him.

As much as Blaze resented his work in harness, there are horses who delight in it, being so disposed by temperament, training, and heredity. Driving such a horse is one of the keen pleasures of the horseman's world. The experience of sailing down a country lane to the cadence of a sparkling trot should not be missed. It will explain why so many more horsemen are now taking up the reinsman's sport.

Drivers of harness racers are masters of yet another driving technique, one I sampled for myself while at a Standardbred stud in Wales.

This was a curious locality in which to be furthering my acquaintance with a breed that is essentially American, and with a sport that in its modern form was originated and adopted by America as her own. For although the blood of this racing breed traces back to the English horse Messenger, imported in 1790, and although the idea of the early American trotting matches (thought to be less sinful and more democratic than the ridden variety) came with the settlers from the mother country, modern harness racing has been slow to catch on in England, except in the North. Now, however, there is a National Harness Racing Club and a number of permanent tracks have appeared, particularly in Scotland. Most of the excellent products of that Welsh Standardbred stud are destined for markets overseas, however, and they have been achieving marked success in the States and Australia. But before being sold the majority of the young stock are trained and raced for a while in the land of their birth.

For my debut on the half-mile elliptical training track, a steady minded mare was chosen and I watched her being harnessed. For maximum

Crack drivers steer
their Standardbreds at
speed. Tracks from New
Zealand to Moscow
now draw crowds to this
native American sport,
though fans miss
out on the most exciting
aspect of the game,
the tremendous
exhilaration of riding
behind a trotter or pacer
at a flat-out 30 mph.
Pacers, in pictures far
right, wear hopples
to maintain lateral gait.

speed, the angle at which a harness racer holds his head is very important; it is entirely different to the collected "bend" required of an animal being park-driven. There is always the occasional perfect racer that naturally assumes the proper angle and can be driven in a simple open bridle with no attachments, but he is rare. Like this mare, most wear either an overcheck strap, or one combined with the small "extra" bit, called an overcheck bit, which is attached to the lines with the snaffle but not to the bridle. This method of keeping a horse's head where it should be is effective and comfortable when fitted and used by someone who knows what he is about. As with most gadgets, any abuses of the overcheck bit are mostly due to ignorance.

The mare was a pacer, an exponent of the camel gait where fore and hind legs on the same side move forward together, and for this reason she was fitted with hopples, or hobbles, as they are called in some localities. Galloping is a horse's natural gait at speed, and in this sense both racing trotters and pacers are artificially gaited. But ambling (pacing) is inherent in some eastern breeds, and because, in its unexaggerated form the amble is very comfortable for the rider, horses of that gait were sought as riding horses in the Middle Ages. When Americans first developed a specific breed for harness racing, however, the Standardbred that paced was very much the "poor relation" of the sport, and generally had its gait changed to the trot by corrective shoeing. In France and many other Continental countries pacers still are barred from the race track; *le trotteur* reigns supreme.

In the United States the fashion has reversed itself—the pacer, which is fractionally faster than the trotter, is now more popular. But although the gait is now so inbred that many Standardbred foals pace naturally from birth, most pacers have to be steadied on the corners and discouraged from "breaking" into a gallop when racing by the use of the hopples—the four lightweight loops that attach front and hind leg on the same side together and are adjusted so that the animal's stride just "fills" them. Some trainers consider that if harness horses started racing when they were a little older, so that more time could then be devoted to their training, a considerable number of pacers would be racing successfully without the use of hopples.

The mare was also fitted with a shadow roll, the broad sheepskin noseband that is also regarded as essential equipment for many racers, particularly for pacers. Fitted correctly, this does not impede the animal's forward vision, but it does prevent it searching the ground immediately ahead for actual or imaginary hazards that might make it shy and go off gait. The theory is that pacers are more likely to do this because they feel restricted by the hopples, and are anxious about tripping.

The mare was led onto the track and hitched to the training cart. It was a heavier and larger affair than the lightweight racing sulkies or bikes used in the United States, and the longer shafts place the driver considerably farther behind the horse's quarters. Even so, it looked a flimsy affair, with little to prevent my tipping forward off that frighteningly small seat and descending between the cart and the mare's tail. Once aboard, it was comforting to realize that the awkward-looking posture is actually a balanced one with the driver's weight behind the wheels offset by

the thrust of his feet into the "stirrups." I was shown how to hold the lines, decided to dispense with the added incitement of a whip, and was heartened by the presence of the trainer, who perched on the near-side shaft to act as an emergency handbrake.

My horse was very sensitive and immediately responsive to even the lightest pressure to right or left. At speed it took awhile to adjust to the feel of the mare's mouth so far out in front of my outstretched legs and feet; it was only too easy to realize why a ham-handed driver so quickly makes a hard-mouthed puller. We moved off left-handed round the track—the compulsory direction for all American racing, ridden or driven.

The mare was jogging and, as confidence grew and I eased my hands, she began to pick up speed, rolling into her stride, legs moving like pistons. There was a sense of gathering momentum and of sheer power that made me visualize her as an equine version of one of the famous steam locomotives of other days. When we came round the circuit again and the trainer said, "Let her go!" she slipped into top gear, legs churning to and fro, to and fro in unison, her strong body rocking and rolling in a motion quite different to that of the trotter, whose equilibrium is always balanced in the center. The sensation of imprisoned power and of speed was fantastic, the wind seemed to whip past as though we were doing 100 mph—and it was unbelievable that I should be finding this even more exhilarating than riding a galloping horse.

Possibly we topped 22 mph and as track speeds go it was nothing very great; the pacing record of an average for the mile of just over 32 mph is not far short of Mahmoud's galloping record for the Epsom Derby of just over 35 mph.

My taste of harness racing was good preparation for the American scene, where the sport has taken such a hold that almost wherever one goes there is a track somewhere within easy traveling distance. Possibly the only constant in harness racing is the Standardbred himself, an animal of impressive overall good nature and a breed not much older than 125 years. Almost everything else about harness racing in America is stamped with modernity. The sulkies are as sophisticated as can be, pared down to the minimum weight, with short shafts that bring the driver into the closest possible contact with his horse. Most

tracks are now all-weather, but the surfaces do harden with age and use, and it is necessary to recondition them periodically to regain the ideal resiliency, a process that is a science in itself.

While theories of jogging and training are much as they have been since revolutionized by Leland Stanford near the turn of the century, it was delightful to watch an enterprising trainer using his golf buggy to lead a horse on a jogging exercise. Shoeing is customized to fit the conditions of the particular track to be raced, and done skillfully it can make the difference between being a winner and being an also-ran.

Drivers are seasoned and canny men, many with decades of experience on the track. Occasionally one meets owner, trainer, and driver embodied in one man. To watch them racing is to see high professionalism at work. One of the most elaborate settings in America in which to view the action is Roosevelt Raceway, on Long Island, a short drive from New York City.

I was there on a brisk, early summer evening when the music blared and the crowds milled around, as they do every night when racing is in session. They were making bets, eating, drinking, studying the big, explicit tote board, or surging forward onto the sloping apron as horses and sulkies jogged past in prerace parades. The elliptical mile track, appearing not all that large in the surrounding vastness, stood out under the arc lights like a jewel in its setting, and it was difficult to visualize the sport as it used largely to be in the years before World War II, when the "trots" were the liveliest events of the annual state fairs. But just as it since has happened in Australia and New Zealand, it was the idea of racing at night, after work and under flood lights, that boosted the sport and caught the imagination and the bulging pockets of the postwar enthusiasts.

The program offered nine races, with a maximum of eight starters to a race. A variety of betting schemes was possible, and anyone hitting the combination of winners for the Big Triple or Exacta might leave the track considerably richer. The starters for each race filed along demurely behind a pretty girl who cantered at the head of the parade. Then the sulkies wheeled to jog off round the track, scoring down the backstretch to where the starting gate was positioned at the three-quarter pole. As the car carrying the gate moved on, the horses moved on too, gathering speed until they passed the starting line and the mobile gate sped away off the track. Now the horses were bowling along at the trot, or rolling in that devouring pacing stride I sampled in Wales. From here on it's a question of stamina and speed, of courage and good training on the part of the horse, and natural ability mixed with intelligence, good judgment, and common sense on the part of its driver. He must know when to push on, when to pass, when to seize an opening, when to hold back.

All race drivers must be licensed to race, but though that qualification can cut out the foolhardy novice who thinks it big to run before he can walk it does not guarantee a good driver. The great ones are born, not made, and light hands and horse sense are two of the ingredients. A driver must know each horse he drives—its limits, its speeds, its quirks—as well as he knows himself. And he must know too the qualities of his opponents. A driver who started in his teens is still polishing his skills in his sixties. There was a moment when two sulkies hooked wheels while in full career. It could have meant a nasty accident, at least a pile-up. Such a situation severely tests the ability of the drivers, and these put into effect the traffic rules of the game, which call for the driver on the inside to keep his horse going on straight, while the other, keeping equally straight, takes a hold of his horse and gently eases him back until the wheels part. Both trotters and pacers are likely to break their gait, but where a trotter will easily adjust himself from gallop back to trot, the pacer does sometimes go down, and if his driver is not alert to what is happening and quick to shout a warning, then the horses behind may well pile in on top.

Harness racing is horse racing after all. The tension of such moments, the excitement of the finishes, the absorption in the displays of driving expertise did not for a moment obscure the wonderful willing spirit of the Standardbreds on that oval, striving to do their best.

None of my bets came home to roost, but I could not share the despair of the drunken young man sitting on the slope in front of us, who slowly tore his ticket into shreds as tears rolled down his cheeks. I had for a while been a traveler in this colorful province of the horseman's world, where it is possible for a man, whatever his age or weight, to practice the crowning pride of racing the horse he owns . . . himself.

Driving is coming back as a pleasure hobby, and is practical wherever there are country lanes to take to with a pair in harness, or a horse or pony in single hitch.

The
Racing
Scene

The camel—folded up, snoozing and grumbling—was eventually abandoned by its irate "jockey" in the center of a sandy, Middle Eastern racing track. On the other side of the world, two fat ponies were tearing across a field where neither they nor their riders had any right to be, stretching out their necks in a desperate bid to show superior speed. This competitive spirit, embodied in the horse and conspicuously absent in the camel, has ever been a source of fascination to man, who has used it in the service of his own need to excel.

Horseracing is one of the oldest sports. Long before the Roman invaders were racing against each other in occupied Britain, the ancient Egyptians were devising contests to establish which of their horses were the most fleet of foot. In 624 B.C. the Greeks included mounted racing in their thirty-third Olympiad. During the reign of Henry II, there was racing at Smithfield, then London's largest horse market. It was the involvement of the English monarchs that gave racing its greatest impetus. After King James I discovered Newmarket as a hare-hunting base, his court found it ideally suited for the sport of the runners. Charles II could forget the ennui of politics when riding matches against his nobles on the Newmarket Heath (the Rowley Mile, scene of both The 1,000 and The 2,000 Guineas, is named after Charles' match-winning stallion).

This king's oriental mares, with others of their like, were instrumental in the production of the improved breed of horse, the "thoroughbred," a word that became synonymous with flat racing in modern times. Queen Anne, the last of the Stuarts, has come down in history as a racing enthusiast responsible for the creation of the course on Ascot Heath. By 1784, the royal passion for racing produced one of the high-society scandals of the time in the racing debts of the then Prince of Wales, so huge as to appall his father, the Hanoverian King George III.

The Thoroughbred was considered an animal fully deserving of the patronage lavished on it by the aristocracy. The Thoroughbred was itself an aristocrat in their view, without equal for speed and stamina and heart. The view still holds, though it is now shared by all lovers of the sport, of whatever station and nationality.

However, the tendency to equate "racing" with "Thoroughbred" causes many people to forget that there are other kinds of racehorses, and other forms of racing than galloping end-to-end.

There is for example the Quarter Horse, an athlete of growing popularity.

All these horses—working, show, or racing variety—carry a percentage of Thoroughbred blood, much of it traceable to studs of the United States Cavalry taken west to replace casualties and frequently bred to the local mares. The modern Quarter Horse has much more Thoroughbred about him than that, however. By the rules, the quarter-mile running horse of today need have only one registered parent. He can contain up to seven-eighths Thoroughbred blood and sometimes does, to the dismay of those who value a marvelous stamp above the acquisition of pure speed, and who visualize the eventual loss of the very characteristics that make a Quarter Horse what he is. For it is the heavy front of the Quarter Horse, its superlative muscles of thigh and quarter that contribute to its ability to sprint four or five hundred yards from a standstill at amazing speed.

The breeders who care about this aspect still use Quarter Horse sires of the characteristic type, and fortunately these remain dominant, at least for the time being.

Go Man Go, legendary on track and at stud, was by a Thoroughbred out of a pure Quarter Horse mare. He stands at Buena Suerte Ranch, near Roswell, New Mexico. When we arrived to visit Go Man Go, the sun was beating down and he had forsaken his own private paddock for the cool shadows of his barn, where his name is lettered in gold over the doorway. At the request of his trainer, the old horse, the biggest money-spinner on the track for three consecutive years during the fifties, emerged to pose as he has done so many times before. Head up, small ears pricked with interest, wide-set eyes still bright with life, he looked as full of quality as any horse could be, yet was unmistakable for what he is—a superb specimen of Quarter Horse, not a small-size near-Thoroughbred.

When spoken to and handled, Go Man Go displayed the kindness and gentleness of his breed, although as a stallion, had he shown signs of frustration or unreliability, he might have been forgiven. For, while this stud is one of the most successful sires of winners ever, with mares still

Something Else:
Quarter Horses leave gate
at California's Bay
Meadows track, San Mateo.
They will reach finish line,
strung across the track
much as they are here,
about twenty seconds later.
Though a Quarter Horse
may be as much as
seven-eighths
Thoroughbred,
its singular conformation
allows peak speed of
c. 45 mph to be reached
within two lengths of gate.

flocking to Buena Suerte from all over to be bred to him, like all of his kind Go Man Go never leads a natural life with any of the matrons or fillies we saw gracing the paddocks; the racing Quarter Horse is bred by artificial insemination.

The dream of everyone who breeds a racing Quarter Horse is to hit it big in the All-American Futurity Stakes, which offers the richest purse in the world; indeed it is the world's only million-dollar race.

The suspense of this annual event begins to build in January each year, when optimistic Quarter Horse owners—mostly Texans and Oklahomans, mostly ranchers or oil magnates, with a sprinkling of professional men and screen and stage celebrities, join with the occasional small man, of more optimism than cash, to make an act of faith. And that concerns some little colt or filly running in a paddock, a youngster scarcely weaned, but in the eyes of its owner of a lineage to turn a dream into reality.

At this moment the Quarter Horse men make the first offering on the altar of their ambition, by posting a sum of money in anticipation of running a two-year-old in the next year's All-American. Maybe two thousand names are entered at that stage, but many drop out before the next payment comes due in June. This whittling-down process continues as more due dates pass—in October, December, and the following March. Late aspirants can buy eligibility for their two-year-olds, at a price, before the first of June. They get a final chance, for perhaps double the June fee, before August 15th, the date when the final increment from the original nominees must be paid.

The All-American Futurity is run on the Labor Day holiday, observed on the first Monday in September. The place of the running is Ruidoso Downs, high up in the Sierra Blanca Mountains. It was Texans, vacationing in the fresh mountain air, who first brought Quarter Horses to Ruidoso. Hell-bent on wagering, they brought along their cow ponies to bet on in two-horse matches. There was only one spot sufficiently level for sprinting, and that is the site of the present track.

Both Quarter Horse and Thoroughbred racing go on in Ruidoso all summer from May. Since acclimatization to the altitude plays a big part in any horse's chances of winning, most entries in elimination trials for the big race are brought there weeks ahead to train and race, too, if there is room in the program. Latecomers flown in from lower elevations may well need a ration of bottled oxygen each day.

There are horses, horses everywhere, at Ruidoso — drowsing in the barns, being led around for one reason or another, getting tacked up, then receiving with nonchalance the last refinement—the squeeze of greasy menthol inhalant up each nostril as a counter to the rarefied atmosphere. Every few yards a horse-walker, electrically driven, with tie-ups for four animals, is making its slow, chunking revolutions. Sometimes a horse crazes up and injures itself on one of these contraptions, but most march around obediently for the requisite thirty minutes (forty-five for Thoroughbreds), all stopping now and again to admire the view at what appears to be a signal from the boss horse, but is in fact a scheduled pause in the machinery.

Whatever the status of the owners, the trainers (and a few are both) are almost all past or present cowboys; those that aren't dress the part —Stetson, blue jeans, buckled belt, the lot. And

since no cowboy ever walks where he can ride, these trainers get around the complex on horseback. Meanwhile there the exercise boys astride the racers' familiars, the colorful Appaloosas and Pintos that accompany them all over. Out on the track it is the same story, horses everywhere, the sprinters having the fifteen-minute workout that is all a Quarter Horse needs, the Thoroughbreds topping that with a further thirty minutes.

There is a growing warmth in the sun, spurts of dust rise from the track. The trainers sit at ease on their horses, strategically placed to issue instructions, and not to miss a trick. Bunches of two-year-olds are brought to inspect the gate, then turned to do a two-minute clip as a sharpener. Others jog or lope by, their jockeys, some of them girls, standing straight up in their stirrups, the butt end of a whip stuck conveniently into the back of their pants or hip pocket, the tip pointing heavenwards.

Suddenly there is a fracas as a black horse pulls free from an exercise rider and gallops off, scattering trainers' horses, evading the tactically placed ''runaway'' horses and riders, and gather-

ing speed as it high-tails back to the barns. Soon the sun is high, the track empty, and back there where the black was recaptured, the walkers are still turning while the horses that have been working out or having a breeze or blow, are now getting rugged up to the ears to cool off, later to be washed down, scraped off, dried, and stalled.

So the weeks go, August wanes. In a few more days the winner of the big race will be known.

Out of the many hundreds of young horses originally entered perhaps a couple of hundred remain, and of those only ten can win through to run in the All-American. Those final eligibles are decided by trial heats, run a week beforehand, with each horse timed to a hundreth of a second and qualifying on time, regardless of placings. For the also-rans, timed eleventh to fortieth, there are other races and a bite of the final stake money.

There are still Quarter Horse brush tracks in some of the states, with rail fences to set off the track, and no hint of a starting gate. There are at least a hundred of the more conventional racing plants, most of them in the West. At Ruidoso, the

oval where the Thoroughbreds race is five-eighths of a mile around. The straightaway for the short-burst specialists comes off at a divergence, wide enough to accommodate comfortably ten Quarter Horses racing abreast, in dashes of 300 yards up to the occasional 550 yards for sprinters according to age and class. The All-American is now run over 440 yards.

The mountains above the town are a backdrop to the course. The tote board is big and clear to see. And on Labor Day the grandstand where the well-heeled owners sit and the less-expensive bleacher seats all fill to capacity.

The moment the people are waiting for comes. The runners have left the cool and quiet of the long barns to be led beside their ponies to the paddock by the grandstand. Now it's saddle up, jockeys mount, and outside for the parade—with tension building up—and so down to the gate, the runners still led to conserve energy.

A Thoroughbred can be trouble enough inside "the hole," but that is nothing to what a Quarter Horse, even more tensed up, can work himself up to. And, though in any race a good start is important, it is doubly so with the sprinters, which shoot off like bullets and have to hit their rhythm right away. A good starter knows his horses, and he leaves the troublemakers till last, together with the horses that overrelax, or freeze, both types liable to be literally left standing if they have to hang around inside too long. The starter knows the ones that lead in easy, those that have to be pushed in, the few that need men linking arms behind their hocks to get them in at all.

Inside the gate, along with the jockeys and horses, are the crewmen, steel-helmeted and with the unenviable task of straightening out and containing ten 1,200-pound two-year-old colts or fillies, all high on good living and split-second training. On the ground behind the horses is a solid steel bar, the equivalent of the human sprinter's starting block.

The Quarter Horses crouch, working their hind feet up against that springboard, muscles bunched, energy pulsating, quivering until even

the gate vibrates. At last all heads and legs are approximately where they should be, the starter presses his electric button, the timing device starts up, bells jangle, the crowd's roar bounces back off the mountains, the steel gate releases the power damned up behind it, dirt flies up and wham! they're gone. They run so fast you cannot believe it—and before you can start to, it's all over, done with, runners across the track in a blanket finish, with all the places from first to last separated by no more than noses or necks. When people see their first Quarter Horse race, they can't believe horses go that fast. When they see the All-American Futurity, disbelief only grows.

For the antithesis to this kind of concentrated excitement you would have to go to the steppes where Turkoman tribesmen hold races as part of their harvest festivities. The place is near Conbad-Kavoos on the edge of the Turkoman steppeland. The autumn days sparkle, and there is dust, clouds of it, and a sky of the blue that is the traditional color of Iran.

The year we were there, we watched some of the spectators arriving by the trucks and automobiles and motorbikes that are now commonplace. But most drove in, seated on the flat, four-wheeled carts typical of the country, with the horses' collars made of wood. Others rode in on horseback, riding the lean desert-type animals they keep muffled to the ears in the customary seven layers of felt. That is how the runners arrived as well, ridden in from the steppe by their owners with the boy jockeys, aged seven to twelve, perched behind, chosen to ride not so much for their horsemanship, which is innate, but for being the lightest riding weights in their families.

As the dense crowd milled around, some spectator horsemen stood on the backs of their patient beasts to get a good view. The runners remained swathed and ground-tied to pickets, while their tails were fashioned into long thin braids. Then off came the coverings for the first race, on went the saddles and up went the jockeys—seats showing something of the con-

Turkoman horse is famed for lithe physique and long-distance ability. Horses at left are being ridden by boy jockeys during tribal meet southeast of Caspian Sea. Distance proved harder on riders than on horses.

Above: Superlative mount carries one of Iran's great riders to victory against backdrop of Elburz Mountains outside Tehran.

173

ventional short-leathered racing crouch.

There is nothing of the broad-breasted, muscled strength of the sprinting Quarter Horse about these animals. These are the Jomud race of Turkoman horse, bred for centuries to have the needed stamina for the long-distance raiding, sometimes fifty miles to plunder a village, fifty miles back again. Until recent years the raiding Turkomans were a governmental headache and the much-feared scourge of Persia's northeast. Their horses have iron-hard hooves that never know shoes, and the bellyless, spare outline of a greyhound; their sparse manes are always roached. All year round they are kept in fit, hard condition, stripped of every ounce of superfluous flesh by the Turkish-bath action of the coverings they wear. They are prepared for racing on a bulkless, high-protein diet of barley enriched with eggs and butter, and a butter-fried bread dough called *quatlame*.

These are long-distance runners. For them the start is relatively unimportant, and those that were still en route when the "Off!" was given were wheeled casually to join in where they stood. The oval track was hard and sandy and about a mile in distance. That day the two-year-olds were racing 3,000 meters (roughly two miles). For the five-year-olds and up, the distance was increased to an endurance-testing 12,000 meters (about eight miles). Round, and round, and round they went, doggedly galloping on through the clouds of dust, many of the young jockeys visibly wilting as the circuits mounted up, until they bailed out through sheer weariness, beaten but unharmed. All but one or two of the horses finished, but of the twenty-five boys who rode out for the start of that marathon, only seven came in.

In the western world, Thoroughbred racing provides a pastime on a national scale, with something for everyone—from the bloodstock breeder to the small punter who "races" on TV, gambles through the betting shop, and never sets foot on a track. It also supplies employment for the many thousands connected with the various branches, and financially is reckoned big business.

The breeding side is a fascinating, chancy enterprise, costly to run and usually demanding a large initial outlay. Yet it thrives. The combined British and Irish bloodstock industry vies with

France for pride of place in Europe; business is booming in Australia and in New Zealand, that paradise for breeding Thoroughbreds, and in America breeding is considered a major area for investment. Japan, too, is rapidly acquiring stock and expanding its industry. But there is a lot more to raising Thoroughbred racehorses than commerce.

Both parents of any bloodstock destined to race on licensed tracks must be registered in the General Stud Book, first kept in 1791, or in the American equivalent. That is where you start chasing back bloodlines, a study that, however scientifically undertaken, remains an intriguing gamble with genetics. Decisions of whether to inbreed or outcross figure largely, so does the effort to counterbalance any less desirable features in one family tree with compensatory ones in another. Good parental conformation, dispos-

ition, and racing history go into the production of good racing offspring, but a stallion's success on the track does not guarantee the equal success of his get; the mare, for her part, is at least as important as the stallion. Even when, given the necessary modicum of luck, the expert gets his equations right, the exceptional racehorse is likely to materialize only if the genes of sire and dam "nick"—that is, if their bloodlines have a happy affinity for each other.

The finest British stallions—privately owned and nowadays usually syndicated—stand, perhaps six at a time, at public studs like the beautiful National Stud at Newmarket, now housing such immortals as Never Say Die, Blakeney, and Mill Reef. There are private studs, among which Cliveden is a name to conjure with. Although for years Queen Elizabeth's Hyperion-bred stallion, Aureole, reigned in his

own quarters at Wolferton Stud, his services were not confined to the royal mares; the seasonal influx came principally from outside breeders.

The majority of the top American Thoroughbred studs are kept, as they have always been, in Kentucky, adjacent to Lexington, on famous farms like Claiborne, Darby Dan, and Calumet. Several are nurseries for their own racing stables, racing their own get, keeping their own stallions and mares, and only selling off the unwanted colts. But most of the produce of the breeding farms are intended for the bloodstock sales. The leading sires are nearly always horses that have won huge sums during their racing careers, but that is nothing compared with their worth at stud, where they command fees calculated to gain back their syndication price in five years of stud duty. (An access right to the serv-

As in all things, the
French bring elegance to
racing. Deauville
during summer meeting is
chic, serious, as
well-bred as the runners
themselves—horses in
the grand tradition of the
French Thoroughbred.

Overleaf: *Le trotteur,*
here to saddle over cinder
track at Vincennes.
The French have kept active
this form of racing,
common in America in early
1800's. Gait is
strenuous, does not require
featherweight rider.

ices of Secretariat would thus cost about $50,000.) The shares that comprise a syndicate correspond to the number of mares booked to a stallion in a single season; thirty-two is a common number.

Commercial breeders, who largely supply the market with bloodstock foals and yearlings in Britain and America, have to keep sale-ring prices in mind and are therefore obliged to breed from fashionable bloodlines. Similarly, the wealthy, privately owned breeding farms, whose interest is in producing generations of fine runners and potential classics winners, are obviously going to stay with the best blood available.

Yet history shows that there is hope for the small man unable to afford huge stud fees. That famous British runner, Brigadier Gerard, was carefully but most unfashionably bred, yet in 1972 was nominated Racehorse of the Year with a record of fifteen wins out of his sixteen notable races. Farther back in time there was Phar Lap, bred in New Zealand of low parentage and bought for Australia as an ugly yearling bargain, who galloped his way to victory in thirty-seven out of fifty-one starts to become the acclaimed darling of the Australian racing public.

Then there are horses like Hyperion, that do honor to their impeccable breeding.

In the days when it was only double-decker buses that went topless, I was with a party utilizing such a vehicle, sitting up above the hubbub and color and milling, sardine-packed crowds enjoying themselves in traditional fashion on Epsom Downs. There was an excellent view of Tattenham Corner, the notorious, demanding curve on that undulating, one-and-a-half mile Derby course that remains the world's most severe test of a three-year-old. There was an even better view of the long exacting run-in, where we cheered a little chestnut colt called Hyperion, as he flashed past the winning post in record time—and then continued on round a third of the course before he could be pulled up.

That was Derby Day 1933, and Hyperion added three other big wins to the glory of his Derby season. As a four-year-old, with a new trainer, his racing career was something of a fiasco, but at stud he became one of the greatest stallions in the history of the turf, his name appearing in the ancestry of the majority of classics horses, including Derby winners. And since he

Invincible Ribot
with groom. Embodying the
internationalism of
Thoroughbred breeding, he
was bred in Italy, raced
in Europe and England,
brought to stud in the
Bluegrass, where he died in
1972, having proved
himself a great sire of
classic horses.

remained at stud for twenty-five years, Hyperion blood has influenced racing in every country where Thoroughbreds appear.

The pattern of racing has a bearing on the type of racehorse each country breeds. In Britain and Ireland, the racing commitments cover every type. There are short, fast-run races for two-year-olds, long distances for stayers and older horses, steeplechases and hurdle races for the jumpers. Above all, are the races for the middle-distance horses, with the five "classics" run for three-year-olds: The 2,000 Guineas and The 1,000 Guineas, both for the mile (1.6 km) and the latter for fillies only; The Derby and (for fillies) The Oaks, both one-and-a-half miles (2.4 km); and The St. Leger, at one mile, six furlongs, and 127 yards (2.9 km).

In France, the Normandy region is ideal for raising Thoroughbreds that mature more slowly, gaining in stamina what they lack in precocious speed, and much of the racing is geared to middle-distance horses. It also provides a racing program for all stages of a racehorse's development, and the prize money is rightly renowned. The famous Prix de l'Arc de Triomphe at Longchamps, over one-and-a-half miles for three-year-olds and up, is the richest plum in

European racing, each year tempting the cream of the past seasons, the winners and near-winners of the classics.

America's annual crop of Thoroughbreds —based on imports from England and infused with first-class blood from other countries as well—is three times that of England and Ireland together. And it is of the highest quality. Most breeders try to follow the idealistic axiom of breeding: "best to best." Although the overall emphasis is on producing speedy juveniles, the wealthy stables can afford to breed for distance and three-year-old racing. The success of American-bred horses in the English classics is well known; recently, in the space of five years, three Epsom Derby winners hailed from the United States, and one from Canada. "The Derby" to Americans does not refer to the great race held at Epsom. It means the Kentucky Derby—huge crowds converging on Churchill Downs, the singing of "My Old Kentucky Home," a garland of red roses for the winner, and for the winning owner, bursting with pride as he leads in his colt, reason to hope that his horse can win the Triple Crown. Much the same interest and excitement grips Australia each first Tuesday in November, when they run the famous two-mile (3.2 km) handicap, the Melbourne Cup.

England's Triple Crown goes to the winner of three classics: The Epsom Derby, The 2,000 Guineas, and The St. Leger. The American counterpart consists of the Kentucky Derby, a mile-and-a-quarter race; the Preakness, over a mile-and-three-sixteenths course at Maryland's historic Pimlico; and the stamina-testing Belmont Stakes, one-and-a-half miles, held at one of New York's most famous tracks. Only fifteen horses have won the English Triple Crown. It took Secretariat, bred to win, superb to look at, winner of seven out of nine starts as a two-year-old, to take the 1973 American Triple Crown after a gap of a quarter-century, slamming the opposition in the Belmont Stakes by a record 31 lengths.

The spectrum of racing in the United States runs to extremes. While classic runners occupy the stage at such beauiful plants as Belmont and Saratoga, at the other end of the racing scale are the "gyp" tracks, the haunts of has-beens, human and equine, who will never again be anything more; they race by night as well as by day in an effort merely to exist. In between the two extremes comes the racing that occupies the most space in the American pattern—the short, fast races for the two-year-olds. Breeding and racing is the livelihood of these people. Thus they must go for precocious speed and a quick return on their investments and that means more racing for two-year-olds, more fast sprints from three furlongs up in American condition books.

Thoroughbreds do mature early, and as foals all they have to do—apart from learning to pick up their feet, and to accept handling, haltering, and being led—is to grow strong and fast as quickly as possible, a process helped along by the best of feeding and good management. But to race a horse as a two-year-old means breaking him as a yearling, when bones and tendons are even more malleable, even more at risk; the two-year-old still has three full years to go before reaching full growth. All Thoroughbreds have an official birthday on January 1st, regardless of actual date of birth, and in America, where they are backed and broken exceptionally early, a youngster born in April or May can well be carrying the admittedly light weight of an exercise man by July the following year, and be racing early in the year after that.

Compared with the time taken and the careful, patient methods used for breaking horses required in other forms of equitation, the early education of a racehorse may appear somewhat hasty and perfunctory. The yearlings learn little more than to carry a rider, to understand something of the vital relationship between the reins the rider holds and the bit in their mouths, and the essential art of galloping. The rest is up to the trainer.

There are two categories of trainer in America, those on contract to one stable, and the freelance or public trainers, which in England and Ireland are in the majority. The American trainer of this sort may be responsible for as many as forty, fifty, or sixty horses at a time, the property of nearly as many owners. To see a trainer at work, you had best get up early.

At Belmont Park you can breakfast on delicious pancakes with maple syrup. You eat, you drink coffee or Coke, you sit in the early morning sun, and just below you is the track, a flat oval of fast dirt (skinned), the type of surface preferred in America. Inside the dirt track is a grass course

(sodded) that is used on occasion. The horses —lovely, streamlined animals with gleaming coats—are doing workouts. The daily training periods on Thoroughbred tracks customarily last from daybreak until 10:30 A.M., and during that time the horses come and go. They are green youngsters learning the important routine of running straight and along the rail, runners out for a prerace sharpener, others flashing by in a longer breeze.

As is traditional on all American tracks they run counterclockwise, always leading with the inside leg and with their near sides needing to be stronger. Fortuitously, they seem to avoid becoming completely "one-sided," but it is not surprising that American runners have difficulty with the turns and gradients of English racecourses. For this reason American horses bred for the classics are sent over to English and Irish trainers when they are still yearlings. Similarly, French- and English-trained horses need six months of work before they are ready for American-style racing.

The exercise "boys"—some will never see their sixtieth birthday again, having grown old in the service of horseflesh—sing to their charges, chat to them, soothe them. There is a running commentary over the loudspeaker system to keep you in the picture, interviews with trainers and jockeys. Behind you are the beds of roses and the stately trees, the famous walking ring, the historic clubhouse, modernized without loss of charm, shops to buy souvenirs, papers, anything, everything you need, food counters, restaurants, and parking lots so extensive that buses are needed to land you plumb in the middle of it all. Of more interest to serious bettors are the complicated tote boards, the closed-circuit color TV, relaying every kind of information about runners, owners, trainers, jockeys, weights, performances, pedigrees, what you will. Except for something of the old-world charm offered by certain "medium" tracks like New York's Saratoga or Del Mar in California, Belmont lacks nothing that can entice and keep happy the vast gambling, racing public.

The public workouts of American racehorses have spectator appeal, and apart from the actual racing, this is where the experts study form, garner tips, make momentous betting decisions Things are done somewhat differently in England. There are public gallops—generally for steeplechase trainers, since most flat-race trainers have private gallops. "Public" means only that the turf is shared by several trainers; attendance by outsiders is by invitation only.

In the half-light, it is cold up on the Berkshire Downs. There is a curlew whistling, wild and high, and partridge are calling, a brace whirring up through the veils of fog swirled here and there by a bitter wind. Earlier, down by the trainer's yard, it had been darker and colder, as the trainer moved the strings of 'chasers out on the morning's work, the lads listening attentively to his clear, concise orders about each horse. The animals were a mixed lot—recent winners, maidens, three-year-olds, older animals—and the man's eyes roved knowledgeably, missing nothing.

Like most trainers he had come to the job from race riding himself, a notable winner of the Grand National, a second in the same race with the legendary Golden Miller. He knows it all from the inside. Sorting them into groups, it's "You go this way . . . walk only!" "You jog on, get up in front." "O.K., you go on the roads."

Up on the downs, the contingent arrives to stand in a circle awaiting further orders, heady turf under their feet, the horses now and again exploding like so many Chinese firecrackers, but without so much as shifting their riders who are perched seemingly precariously in the racing seat. The "Guv'nor" looks pleased. His horses are feeling good. He sends them off with strict instructions about pace. "You lot . . . canter, but stop 'em well back before coming down the hill." English horses do without the quiet, soothing presence of the American racehorse "pony," but the two due to race the next day go off with an old horse to lead them.

The horses disappear, we wait. The wind wails, the fog eddies, suddenly comes the rhythmic thud, thud of hooves on the grass, the nebulous shapes of horses loom, cantering by three behind each other, then nine more. The fog thins, the sky lightens. Another day in the life of a British 'chaser has begun.

America's racing public has never taken to steeplechasing as it has to flat racing and harness racing. Factors probably are the chanciness of a sport in which falls are part of the game, as well as the amateur tradition of the sport in America,

reflected in the general absence of grandstand facilities. Television has stepped in here, thankfully, and begun annual coverage of the difficult Colonial Cup race, relaying to an unprecedented number of Americans the excitement and beauty of 'chasing. The classic steeplechase of them all is the Maryland Hunt Cup, where amateur riders take on fences of solid timber up to 5 feet 6 inches high over a permanent course set in natural hunting country, and there is no official betting or admission charge.

Most steeplechasers start their careers—at three years old—as hurdlers, racing at speed over 3-foot 6-inch hurdles of birch or gorse set at a forty-five degree angle to the ground, with a maximum of four flights per mile. Although the 'chasing world once regarded hurdling as little more than glorified flat racing, it is now a popular part of the winter racing calendar in England.

Hurdlers resemble steeplechasers in that they fence at speed off their forehands. But they stride over the low obstacles like human hurdlers, in a way that would bring disaster to the steeplechasers. They also come into the fences at full racing pace but must tuck up their legs to avoid hitting the solid jumps, which have a minimum height of 4 feet 6 inches. In France, the hurdles are such as to allow the runners to gallop straight through the tops.

Hurdle races differ only slightly in the number of flights, the length of the race, and the quality of the runners, but steeplechasing offers much more variety.

As an amateur rider, regardless of sex or nationality, you can take your steeplechaser to Czechoslovakia to chance the yawning, lethal chasm of the Taxis ditch, the laboring stretches of plow, the plethora of open-water jumps so wide that, at first attempt, more runners descend into the element than leap over it successfully. Such are the hazards of the Grand Pardubice, a notorious race won six times to date by an intrepid Czechoslovakian lady rider.

There is some residue of steeplechasing's former status in England—that of a poor relation to flat racing. The jumping trainer's job, for example, is much less lucrative than that of his flat-racing counterpart. And few big stables can afford to concentrate on jumpers, which do not compete until they are four years old—a long time to wait for return on investment. Also,

breeding for steeplechasing is more chancy. Though many modern 'chasers have the blood of classics winners in their veins, and certain bloodlines appear frequently in the pedigrees of jumpers, the prepotency of jumping sires cannot be assessed, because so few steeplechasers are entires. Their breeding potential, so immensely valuable in the flat-racing stallion, is obviously nil.

Of the park-course races, the three-and-a-half-mile Cheltenham Gold Cup is the supreme challenge, the true-level weight championship that has stolen not a little of the Grand National's prestige. Nevertheless, for many—excepting some pundits and some owners who refuse to risk valuable horses—steeplechasing means the Grand National, thirty jumps dotted along a four-mile-856-yard course at Aintree, the world's greatest test of jumper and rider.

While the historic, unique fences—Becher's Brook, Valentine's, the dreaded "chair," and the rest—have been sloped off and modified in recent years, they still call for a superior horse. It has to be one with the physical strength and conformation to jump the succession of big

fences without tiring, and with the ability to drop its quarters to land four-square even after a mistake pitches it downward at an even more acute angle after a high jump; and it must be able to quicken and keep going on that long run-in.

There are Aintree specialists, like Red Rum, the fantastic winner two years running (1973 and 1974), and only relegated to second place in 1975 by the weight he was carrying. There are otherwise brilliant jumpers—the great Golden Miller was one—that conceive a hatred for the course or for a particular fence. Conversely, many excellent National horses fail on other courses.

Luck, too, plays a big part in a race like this. It may be good or it may be bad. Foinavon, a 100-to-1 outsider, won the National in 1967, when the other twenty-eight runners all came down or balked in a melee at fence 23. The Queen Mother's Devon Loch, a real National type, was well clear of the field with only fifty yards to go to the winning post, when he did an inexplicable slip and straddled his legs to finish up on his stomach. But barring accidents and ill winds, it is the class horse that usually wins.

Unfortunately, accidents to jockeys and horses are a frequent occurrence in steeplechasing, although the National's toll is not as bad as it once was. The very size and nature of the fences makes jumping mistakes that much more lethal. Riderless horses—running on with their companions and charging at a tangent along a fence or balking a jumper in midair—constitute a big hazard—even though they appear, without the aid of a jockey, willing to tackle the most formidable obstacles with the utmost confidence and ease. More getaway exits, where loose animals could deviate off the course, would help with this problem, but far more to the point would be a tightening of the necessary qualifications for the race, thus eliminating the proportion of runners that are started by owners more endowed with optimism than responsibility or sense.

Horses are killed steeplechasing—even sometimes hurdling—and more often in the National than in other races. When it happens, all horse lovers are saddened. But what is the logical answer? It is easy to say that horses were never intended by nature to race or jump, but neither were they intended for carrying man at all. And if horses are killed jumping fences, we have the paradox of Mill Reef, the incomparable little American-bred winner of English classics, who shattered his foreleg when being cantered at exercise over the smooth, perfectly maintained turf at the training establishment of Kingsclere.

Both steeplechasing and flat racing in England come under the jurisdiction of the Jockey Club, around which the sport has revolved for the past two hundred years. This body is responsible for upholding the rules of racing. Trainers, jockeys, officials, courses, races, infringements, complaints, and any other matters officially connected with the sport come under its scrutiny. American racing is governed by stewards, usually three to each track, of which the Jockey Club steward will be a horseman, the state steward a politician, and the racing association steward a businessman. Such diversity of outlook seldom leads to overall harmony, particularly in the difficult problem of standardizing drug rules, but by and large the notorious roguery attached to some periods of racing in the past has been eliminated. The American rule requiring every horse appearing on a Thoroughbred race track to bear an identification number tattooed on the inner surface of its upper lip has banished the hazard of ringers (horses entered under false names to procure better racing odds). In England, dope tests performed on horses that run wide of their true form, plus stringent penalties attached to the use of drugs, have brought that particular danger under control.

In the main, official racing—the sport that fills such a large space in the horseman's world—is "clean," and by the standards of today that is something remarkable. This integrity affects not only the betting public who support racing, and the owners, trainers, and jockeys at the inner circle of the sport. It concerns, too, the great army of people, male and female, young and old, who minister to and love the creatures in their charge—the stable lads, the walkers, the exercise men, even the characters like those you find haunting the environs of the racing centers, little old men well past working age who drink in the pubs where stable lads congregate, as full of racing gossip as ever they were in their heydays as jockey or head lad, speaking mostly in the mellifluous Irish brogue, with never a "th" heard between them. The honest workings of horseracing allow these people a justifiable pride in the work they do.

Many boys take on the hard work and long hours of the stable lad with the ambition of becoming jockeys. Some do make the grade, and of these some even achieve what looks from the bottom of the ladder like an impossibility—they hit the top, become great jockeys chosen to ride the horses that make history, and they make their fortunes. Whether they succeed in a big way or not, it's a life of early-morning workouts on the training gallops, of years on the sweat-box that can sap a man's health, of handling fractious two-year-olds and now and then a really difficult horse, and for steeplechase riders the almost inevitable broken bones.

An able jockey has riding ability and balance and the competence to keep his horse in balance—to swing it around the turn more with the use of body and legs than with the reins. He must be physically strong for all his small size, and have the fineness of touch called "good hands." He must have the timing to "scrub" in a close finish, moving hands forward and legs back in exact rhythm with his horse's stride. He needs to acquire the knowledge and assessment of pace, the uncanny ability to "rate" a horse that can turn a good jockey into a great one. Mentally he must have courage and intelligence. Courage, because racing is dangerous. Intelligence, because he must work with the information that trainers give him and accept their instructions on how to ride the race. But if something unforeseen occurs, he must be able to think fast and switch policy in the middle of a race. And he certainly needs a sense of humor to counteract the fact that whenever he loses it is likely to be "all his fault." Which in many ways is true. For while a good horseman will always get more out of a horse than a bad one, it is jockeys that lose races; horses win them.

Above all else, a jockey has to understand horses. Each horse is different, each has to be fed, trained, handled, raced as an individual. Some always try their hardest, some have to be pushed to show their best, some need a sharpener at the crucial moment, some sulk if the whip so much as touches them.

Arkle, the one-in-a-million racing freak that came out of Ireland, deliberately ran his opponents into the ground and then sailed ahead to break their hearts. Aureole, one of the royal stable, would go kindly only for a jockey who handled his reins as though made of silk. Colonist II, a racehorse of dogged determination and courage and the only horse I've ever met that left the swerving to you when he galloped at you in his paddock, sired a filly named Cauliflower who dashed her owner's hopes by throwing herself on the ground in a temper at the very sight of a racecourse. Yet when given away, she found the perfect combination in her new owner and his son, who rode her, and she responded by becoming an unbeatable point-to-pointer, then a champion Hunter Chaser. Mill Reef, whom I saw gamely learning to use his newly mended leg, still in plaster, plainly showed the courage and trust that made him lovable and easy to handle yet one of the great mile-and-a-half horses of all time.

All different, all adding up to the magic called racing.

One of the great riders of modern times, Braulio Baeza rode the brilliant Buckpasser in three-year career record of 32 wins and 6 losses. Third highest moneywinning American Thoroughbred, injury kept this colt on the sidelines of the 1966 Triple Crown races.

8.

The Horse at Work

The farm stable, built of flint and roofed with rough-edged Kentish slate, was long and low, the interior dim, cobwebbed, and redolent of the numberless horses accommodated there during the past century or so. The stalls were inhabited by Prince and Captain, by the giant Johnny, and the younger black mare, Topsy. I was a child then, and to my eyes Captain, an ex-Army draft horse that had served in France during the Great War, was the most romantic of the quartet. It was his broad back I demanded to brush on my sixth birthday when the wagoner lifted me onto an upturned box for a first grooming lesson.

I had least to do with Johnny. This was not entirely due to his size, although he was so big that he had bumped his head on the lintel of the stable door and thereafter had to be reversed to get through it—a proceeding that soon became so habitual that, once unhitched after work, Johnny would heave to and solemnly back himself in through the offending doorway. But although most of Johnny's reactions to life's inequities were as practical, just occasionally he would take off, usually with the water cart, and lumber down the lane with the contraption banging and rattling behind, spewing its contents to either side. Johnny was not ideal company for a small girl.

So it was in the company of old Prince and the stockman that most of those blissful days on the farm were spent. Prince was already old when we bought him, but sound as a bell and as clever and honest as they come, and the mainstay of the farm for years. His handlers always swore the old horse could count, and certainly when cultivating the loganberries with a horse-hoe it was impossible to make Prince miss any but the three requisite rows on the turn at either end of the field. When the elderly stockman, driving the wagonette eight miles home from market and liberally furnished with those extra parting pints, dozed off in the warmth of a summer's evening, Prince brought him safely back to the yard, walking and trotting soberly along on the correct side of the road, and negotiating what little motorized traffic there was in those leisurely years with no trouble at all.

Even that stocky old horse was too tall for me to be able to do much about harnessing him. And though, like each of the docile creatures, he bent his head to receive the burden, I was never of the size or strength to lift the heavy collar, broad end uppermost, over his ears, or to turn it on his neck so that the brass points of the hames could be strapped atop. But whether Prince was tacked up with breeching and saddle for carting, or with chain traces and swingletree to plow with Topsy or Captain, it was my delight to be included on the job whenever I could escape my mother's efforts to teach me the three Rs.

On even the coldest winter's day, when the wind cut like a knife across those acres that lie on the North Downs, 800 feet up from the sea, my idea of heaven was to help the stockman load a cart with roots or kale, and then plod across the fields with him and Prince, scattering the fodder for the sheep that came running and baaing at our approach. My pride was to be allowed to drive the old horse back to the yard myself, but gauging the width of those big wheels was usually beyond me when it came to turning in through the yard gate. The drunken angle of the left-hand gatepost for years bore witness to my lack of judgment.

For the last half hour of the day the plowman would also sometimes suffer my presence stumbling along beside the furrow horse, where the mold board was turning over slabs of gleaming, chocolate-colored earth. Then he would let me cadge a ride back to the stable on Captain, but would never tolerate my sitting as the true plowman does, with both legs dangling down on the same side of his horse. I was made to ride astride, with a hold on the hames for safety.

In those halcyon years my brother and I watched for two infallible signs of spring. First there was the morning when the ducks and geese suddenly took off for the distant pond on unaccustomed wings, flapping as they ran ridiculously or half-flew, quacking and honking in joyous anticipation of the spectacular aquatic mating displays to come. After that portent, we knew spring had truly arrived on the Saturday dinner time when the horses, instead of being bedded down in their stalls for the morrow's day of rest, were led to the paddock and loosed, to gallop and frisk and kick up their huge hairy heels like four inebriated, gargantuan lambs.

Around the age of eight, a friend and I were allowed the occasional treat of riding two of the cab horses that normally provided transport for the neighboring village of Wye. They were large,

Preceding pages:
For thousands of years horses were the working partners of man. Even today there are some jobs for which man has found no substitute. Here range horses muster cattle, work they have been doing ever since beef took over prairies from bison.

Opposite: French farmers have speeded up mechanization of the land, but many farms still give the heavy horse his pride of place.

raw-boned animals of uncouth appearance, and when they were saddled for us of a Sunday afternoon, our feet reached little further than the edge of the saddle flaps. But aglow with a kind of awful joy, we would set out, usually managing to persuade the horses to walk all of two miles before swinging round to make for home. The steady but determined trot that followed was as inevitable and as unstoppable as death, and clinging to the pommels we would be carried back to where the horses could resume their well-earned Sabbath rest.

We were much in awe of their owner, a portly, red-faced cabby with flaming carroty curls, who always adjured us to walk the last half mile, so as to bring his "'osses in cool." But despite manful efforts to comply we always arrived back at the same resounding trot, on a cool day the horses enveloped in a telltale cloud of steam.

It was one or another of the cabby's pairs that always doubled as fire-engine horses. One morning we were intrigued by an unpunctuated piercing whistle wafting across the farm from the northwest and set out on bicycles to investigate. It was easy enough to track the sound, growing louder every minute and soon accompanied by an intrusive, rising and falling drone, to the stack yard of a neighboring farm. And there, with fly-wheel spinning furiously and safety pressure gauge blowing its top, was a stationary traction

engine, in those days the motive power for win-
nowing the harvest. It was still attached by its
driving belt to the threshing machine and both
were surrounded by flames.

It was the old story. A spark from the engine's
funnel had set fire to the drifts of chaff covering
the yard. There was a good breeze blowing and
the fire spread with such speed there was no time
even to stop the engine. It was a fearsome scene.
A couple of the ricks were ablaze and the ear-
piercing whistle of escaping steam was growing
in volume. No one seemed to know how long
the engine could cope before blowing up, and
we were being hustled out of range when there
was a tremendous clatter of galloping hooves
and the fire brigade arrived. The engine was
drawn by Bess and Duke, two of my particular
friends, and they had been galloped most of the
four miles up from Wye. While the firemen set
about getting the situation under control, the
horses were unhitched and led around, blowing
and puffing as though they would never stop, the
sweat running off their flanks in rivulets, their
limbs trembling with the gallant effort they had
made.

The years passed, mechanization was first
creeping, then rushing onto the land, and before

you could turn round the internal combustion
engine had taken over all our lives. A few British
farmers kept on their horse teams during World
War II, but food and more food was as essential
to survival as the production of munitions. There
was little time or labor for horses. The tractor
reigned supreme.

Gone also were the two-or-more-furrow gang
plows powered by huge horse teams that had
cultivated the grain lands of Australia and
Canada and the United States. By the end of the
war it seemed that if the days of the light horse
were numbered, those of the heavies were already past and forgotten. Even when in a few
rural areas they revived the old-time plowing
matches, the traditional contestants were almost
entirely eclipsed by mechanized horsepower.

Then a brewery or two decided that the eye-
catching appeal of a magnificent pair of heavy
horses could be good advertising. Those few
dedicated breeders who, despite all difficulties,
had continued to raise a few Shires or Percherons, Clydesdales or Suffolks, began to find increased entries in the trade shows. Show or-
ganizers themselves began to find that hayrides
using pairs of heavy horses were a popular draw.
After awhile a few enthusiasts from the United

**Plowman of ages past
had company of sentient
creatures as he went
about his work, but
tractor that can turn
an ear to an urgent word
or a snatch of song
has yet to be invented.
Fine Shires opposite
work a Connecticut farm.**

**Above: There are
no heavy horses in the
Middle East. A horse is
a horse when there's
work to be done—like this
plowing on island of Crete.**

191

Turkomans are Iran's
traditional horse breeders,
now gain their wealth
from sheep, camels, and
mechanized cultivation
of the steppe. But
wherever there is
a Turkoman there is always,
too, a horse. Tribesman
and his wife, with typical
working horse and cart—
the shafts attached
directly to wooden collar.

States began to drift across the Atlantic to take note of the British heavy wares, and eventually America began to import a few British drafters to revitalize their own remaining studs, which offered little other than the big Belgian animals bred in the States since 1866. Even Australia began taking a few Clydesdales to reintroduce a breed once very popular there. None of these horses was used for working the land; they became brewery and show animals, providers of hay and picnic rides, and in America, contestants in the organized pulling matches, yoked in pairs to sledge-like weighted stoneboats or to dynamometers. Nowadays there is a steady export trade of heavies from Britain.

During the early sixties, the fortunes of the heavy horses showed a decided change in Britain. Statisticians produced figures, long apparent to those with horse sense, proving that on short haul the brewers' horse teams were not only of advertising value, but were actually more economical than the motorized transport. Today this is a fact acted on by an increasing number of firms in the United States, Canada, and on the Continent, as well as in Britain. Scientists discovered that the continual use of heavy machinery damaged soil structure as no horses had ever done. Farmers were rediscovering that horses can get on the land under conditions that immobilize tractors; that horses' soiled bedding

provides a constant source of the finest natural humus; that straw, harvested with an old-fashioned reaper and binder drawn by a team, commands a higher price than the chopped-off material produced by a combine harvester; that horses are cheaper to buy, cheaper to run, and have a longer working span than tractors.

By the spring of 1974 there was a small, incredible, but definite return to horsepower on the land. At the increasing number of plowing matches it was now the horses—in all their finery of braided manes and tails, tasseled ear caps, and breast straps hung with brasses of various designs (originally amulets to ward off the evil eye)—that outnumbered the competitors using tractors. Against all probability, it was found that there are men still willing to do the inevitable Sunday work in return for driving, caring for, and spending their working week in the company of the placid giants who are their teammates. As a quid pro quo, the modern Shire is bred cleaner-legged, to cut down on the time needed for brushing out mud-encrusted "feathers."

Except for the plowing matches, few of the farmers who combine actual and mechanized horsepower use horses for plow work, but they are finding them economical, harnessed to modern rubber-tired vehicles, for carting such materials as fodder, fertilizers, and seed corn. By copying the old American and Australian pattern

of using larger teams to draw bigger equipment, with the driver seated on the machine, instead of walking behind in the old English fashion, a productive high output of work per man can be maintained when horses are employed on such jobs as disking and harrowing. For drilling seed and working the rows between growing crops, horses like our old Prince are still hard to beat.

Just how far this limited return of the heavy horse to the land is likely to go is a matter for the future, and will be influenced perhaps by the cost and shortage of oil. What is beyond argument is that farm horses are true working animals, a distinction not always as easy to define when it comes to the increasing numbers of light horses that are taking on so many new roles in the modern horseman's world.

Smith I was just such a one. Bought and used throughout most of her life as a pleasure horse—though some who knew her well might query the adjective—she also became an indispensable working animal during the last war.

The Kent coast, where I lived, was in a military zone where private cars were taboo. Smith was my means of transport. Among other duties she was pressed into service for the family shopping, and our journey into town was sometimes enlivened by a meeting with one or another of the regiments stationed in the area out on a route march. This was a form of exercise to which Smith, who treated the advent of the occasional tank with disinterest, took the greatest exception, and the Army was quick to learn that the only method for inducing her to pass was for them to come to a halt and stand at ease. Once in town she was hitched in the forecourt of the local garage, where she proved an irresistible lure to gardeners and allotment holders, patriotically "digging for victory," who converged on my pony with shovel and bucket directly her well-known neigh of boredom echoed down the High Street.

Sometimes, despite the curfew, she was used as transport to the local movie, and collecting her after the show from the livery stable enveloped in the stygian gloom of blackout once resulted in my saddling up the wrong horse. But normally it was swiftly up into the saddle and out onto the darkened streets, where the soldiers idling the evening away only had time to exclaim incredulously, "It's a . . . horse!" before we were through and out of the built-up area. Soon we would be jogging up the stony path to the top road, where Romney Marsh and the sea beyond lay unguessed in the darkness below. And trotting along the ridge with hoofbeats scattering the silence of the

Down poplar-lined lane in rural France, a plow horse "homeward plods his weary way." As much as their size, placid nature of the giant breeds makes them suited to their work.

Above: Mare in the vicinity elicits this display from Percheron stallion.

195

night, it seemed we were the only inhabitants of a strange world where moon and stars were crisscrossed by the beams of searchlights, ceaselessly probing for marauding planes.

The threat of those weeks, when Hitler's armies were crouched just across the Channel and poised to invade, eventually passed, and Smith was never called upon—as were many horses on the Continent—to carry us in flight before advancing armies.

Horses may never again function in war, yet they continue to serve symbolically in peacetime ceremonies. Britain's Household Brigade, whose duty it is to guard the sovereign, consists principally of five regiments of Foot Guards and two of Household Cavalry. Of these last the Life Guards were drawn originally from the band of gentlemen who shared Charles II's exile and were his bodyguard. The Royal Horse Guards (The Blues), known since amalgamating with the Royal Dragoons in 1969 as the Blues and Royals, are descended from an Ironside Regiment of Heavy Horse that took up the cause of the same monarch a few months before his restoration.

The Household Cavalry consists of two armored-car regiments, and a mounted regiment of two squadrons stationed in London, with which the cavalrymen serve for only a limited time. With the Foot Guards they share the tradition of being among the best-disciplined active soldiers in the world, with feats of battle that span three centuries. Their traditions of ceremonial pageantry and splendor are unrivaled.

Royal and state occasions in London, when the Queen travels by carriage, are heightened by the presence of the Sovereign's Escort, in full-dress uniform and mounted on the customary black horses. From the ranks of the Household Cavalry come also those who provide the daily spectacle of the changing of the mounted guard at Whitehall, watched by an annual total of between nine and ten million people. Apart from this ceremony, four horses, changed every hour between 11 A.M. and 4 P.M. provide mounts for the two "boxmen," sentries on silent vigil on the Whitehall side of Horse Guards Arch. These horses appear as oblivious as their riders to the endless traffic rumbling by and the admiring crowds of sightseers who often press too close for comfort. (Nor can they know the curious historical fact that, because of Queen Victoria's

dislike of change, they are helping guard what is still the *official* entrance to the Palace—rather than the impressive access via Trafalgar Square and the Mall, in use since 1841.)

Perhaps the most notable ceremony involving the Household Cavalry is Trooping the Color, a tribute to the Queen on her official birthday. As honorary colonel of the regiment, she takes the salute—riding sidesaddle—on Horse Guards Parade. The year I attended in the company of the Chiefs of Police I had a particularly splendid view. After the Foot Guards had finished their immaculate marching and countermarching it was the turn of the cavalry. The squadrons of Life Guards and Blues and Royals—gleaming horses tossing their heads, plumes on the troop-

Percheron stallion
being trotted out at
Concours Bellême,
horse fair held in region
of La Perche for
which this breed is named.

Overleaf: Technology
never fully displaced
motive power of the heavy
horse; this French
farmer continues to plow
with one. Many
others in this ecology-
conscious age have
new understanding of
drafters' real efficiency.

ers' helmets atremble—jingled past the saluting base first at walk and then at trot, in time to the stirring lilt of the Household Cavalry band. At the rear of the column rode the sinister figure of the farrier, carrying the poleax once used to dispatch horses injured in battle; and in their turn, standing out against all the blacks and black-browns, were the gray horses of the trumpeters. And to catch the eye above all was a majestic and arresting drum horse of the Household Cavalry.

These horses are always either piebald or skewbald, 17 hands or more, and of sufficient substance to be able to support, in addition to rider and heavy ceremonial saddle, the 112 pounds that is the combined weight of two solid-silver kettledrums. Suitable animals of the

right temperament and conformation are difficult to find, and once trained they are extremely valuable. They learn to be imperturbable on parade, unflustered by the sights and sounds of huge crowds. They have the exceptional obedience and responsiveness needed by horses that have to be steered as they are, by reins attached to the stirrup irons, allowing the drummers' hands to remain free. At halt, in answer to taps behind their elbows from their riders' toes, they stretch out into the stance of a show hackney.

The 111 horses, 7 officers, and 185 soldiers that constitute the King's Troop Royal Horse Artillery contribute their own splendor on state occasions. It is they who gallop six World War I guns into action in Hyde Park to fire a royal

forty-one-gun salute. And it is their team of black horses that draws the gun carriage bearing the coffin in state and military funerals.

These are the soldiers and horses who perform the electrifying Musical Drive at the Royal Tournament, at Military Tattoos, Agricultural Shows, and similar exhibitions overseas. In these displays the six-horse gun teams draw the heavy, rattling limbers at the gallop in precise patterns, and at the climax they crisscross each other with dangerous but superb split-second timing.

The soldiers and horses of the King's Troop inhabit barracks in St. John's Wood, London, on a site that has been associated on and off with military horses, mostly those of the artillery, since 1804, when Bonaparte was threatening to invade Britain. In the dark of a winter's morning the horses, drawn up in lines on the parade ground, jingle their bits and blow in the cold air, their breath pluming in dragon's smoke, the lights throwing shadows that elongate necks and legs into grotesque, giraffe-like proportions. Orders are given, the soldiers, each riding one horse and leading one to either hand, wheel and move off in column, with outriders wearing phosphorescent orange jackets stationed at strategic points. They clatter out through the wrought-iron gateways onto the near-empty streets of St. John's Wood at a steady pace that, by some quirk of relativity, builds up to a really spanking trot at the rear. It is a matter of pride for the leaders of an exercise detachment to attempt a new route as often as possible, so for the denizens of the still-shuttered flats and houses the noise can be as unfamiliar as it is terrific. And what do they think, those people snuggled in bed behind their curtained windows as the horses, forty to fifty strong, go trotting by in the street below? Maybe the old are stirred by half-remembered dreams of childhood when the streets of London did resound day and night to the rumble of iron-clad wheels, the beat of iron-clad hooves.

The traffic starts to build, and the din of a city awakening diminishes the impact of hoofbeats. More people appear on the pavements, hurrying along to bus stops and undergrounds. The men and horses of the King's Troop continue on their way, even when the traffic lights go red. On a stretch of Rotten Row, in Hyde Park, a policeman is exercising his horse. It shows off, cantering on at the sight of them, inviting the more flighty to show off too, cantering on the road.

The detachment passes by Marble Arch (whose gates, once the entrance to the Sovereign's Palace, are opened only for the Queen and for the King's Troop entering the Park to fire a salute), and on they go to Oxford Street. Black-coated businessmen turn their heads to look. A clutch of foreign visitors appears startled. Most people hustle on to work, regardless. Wheel left into Portman Street and ride on, on, on while the traffic and pedestrians build up in density towards rush hour. At a major intersection a led mare comes to grief, slipping on the treacherous surface of a pedestrian zebra crossing in a welter of threshing legs, her big round stomach exposed to the sky. She heaves herself up with no damage but a broken rein and, being

a youngster, makes off instead of staying with the troop as an old hand would do. Some of the detachment ride in pursuit. Some have obeyed a policeman's signal to cross the converging roads, and the horses left behind fret and worry, prancing a little and trying to edge out into the streams of head-to-tail traffic.

The mare is caught. The remainder of the detachment crosses and reforms and sets off on the last stretch back to the Wood. Soon they are on their own parade ground again in the center of the barracks complex. There are blocks of stabling, each housing thirty horses in stalls, fifteen to a side, stables for the officers' chargers, a beautiful Georgian riding school, 185 by 65 feet, and a sanded manège for jumping and exercising. There is a farrier's shop, a saddler's shop where tack is made as well as repaired, a pharmacy, and hay and feed stores, including the "kitchen" where cauldrons of succulent-smelling barley bubble and simmer all day long.

The Troop, commanded by a major, is organized into Troop Headquarters and three sec-tions, each with two guns and commanded by a subaltern. Most soldiers need two to three years' training before they can drive in a gun team, but concentrated riding instruction plus days out with the Draghounds soon ensure sufficient competence to parade in detachment. The Troop holds its own point-to-point races and mounted sports competitions. It has an excellent record in show jumping, hunter trials, dressage, and combined events at all levels up to international. Three of its members have represented Great Britain in three different Olympics.

The yearly replacement rate for the horses runs about ten percent, and these arrive unbroken, usually from Ireland. The gun teams, color-matched from light bay through bay and brown to the black of the funeral team, take about two years' training before they are ready for regular parades in draft.

The biggest and strongest horses are chosen as leaders of the teams because, proportionally, they do more of the pulling. The wheelers, which act as brakes, have to be smaller, short-coupled

animals with strong and rounded rumps, to take the strain off the breeching when required to stop the one-and-a-half tons of limber and gun behind them. The drivers ride the three near-side horses and for the sake of good muscles and mouths they interchange their own two animals at intervals. They control their off horses by neck-reining and use their whips—touched lightly to the off side of the neck in front of the collar pad—for starting, keeping the animals up in the breast collar, and guiding when turning.

Between the training period of mid-January to mid-May the long Troop column frequently wends its way from the Wood to the wide-open spaces of its training ground at Wormwood Scrubs, negotiating the hazards of the traffic with growing confidence. Once on the training ground the sections are inspected, being driven by at walk and trot, and the gun teams prepare to go into action.

A bugle sounds the exciting, nerve-tingling notes of the "Charge!" Thunder of 144 galloping hooves, rattle of limbers and guns—teams wheeling, bringing the guns into position, just as they did in battle not so long ago. Halt, unhook, right-about wheel with the limbers, gallop back to the wagon lines, the mounted horse handlers —leading officers' chargers—bringing up the rear. The cannons begin to boom, white puffs of smoke melting away into the sky, then teams return to cover twenty yards to the right of their guns. When the last round is fired they rehook guns, and again hooves thunder as they gallop them away. Exercise completed.

Such drills as these are the background to the meticulous performances put on in Hyde Park, when the King's Troop fires the royal forty-one-gun salute on the sovereign's birthday. Then the drivers of the gun teams are resplendent in full dress of gold-braided jacket, breeches, highly polished boots, and busbies with upright white plumes, and their seventy-one horses are equally immaculate. Crowds flock to watch these displays and be carried back to a time when horses on parade were a natural part of the pageantry of state.

Whitbread Brewery's famous Shire horses work in stench and din of London streets. Each year, four at a time, they are sent to enjoy a month's freedom, gamboling in the fields at firm's hop farm in Kent.

Police horses, too, play a big part in ceremonial, and even in this mechanized, technological age there are still many police forces that employ horses in the actual cause of law and order. In New York City one can see mounted police patrolling the busiest sections of the city. At the training depot at Pelham Bay I watched the rookies of the New York force learning their job; the horses there already knew it. Mostly of Morgan or Quarter Horse type, the majority of the horses in the training academy have been shifted from active duty for some reason or another —age, a slight unsoundness that will not stand up under regular street patrol, maybe a distaste for heavy traffic after some run-in with a truck. Otherwise they are fully trained police horses, admirable school masters, that have themselves been schooled on much the same lines as those used at Imber Court, the well-known training establishment where all British police horses and their riders, and a number from overseas, learn the behavior and duties expected of them.

The police horse is first of all an obedient, sensitive, and enjoyable ride, but beyond that he has to prove himself equal to a tough course of "nuisance" training. With the help of infinite patience and a bowl of oats always to hand, the horses learn to disregard such hazards as fire and firearms, the clamor of bands, cheers, fire bells, and eventually the highly emotive, often menacing atmosphere generated by a large crowd. They learn to stand immobilized, hemmed in by vehicles or pressed by a crush of people, while their rider directs traffic at a busy intersection. They must not kick under any circumstances or shy at hazards that would send most horses into hysterics. They are taught to swing their quarters gently to urge people back, to straddle their legs and lean against the rowdies who try to push them over. They learn to tread over "bodies," to cope with steps, squeeze through small spaces, and if necessary carry their riders along the sidewalk to the source of a traffic jam. In police forces like the British, with no form of protective or riot gear, the horses are essential. In New York, in riot situations, one police horse is equated as worth twenty-five foot patrolmen.

Crowd control is the duty most often assigned the mounted policeman. Nowadays horses sometimes have to face retaliation in the form of steel darts thrown at them, lighted paper thrust

Barring mishap, this young farmer can expect several years of trouble-free, economical performance from pair he is showing with evident pride.

205

under their genitals, marbles strewn under their feet, hails of debris. During a few of these ugly scenes people have been hurt, often with subsequent blame on the use of horses against human beings. It is curiously twisted thinking to censure the animal that, in rearing to avoid pain, hurts someone inadvertently on coming down again.

Once, in the course of researching a book, I had the novel and exhilarating experience of riding a horse belonging to the Metropolitan Mounted Police in London. We met—that handsome chestnut called Imperial, the Superintendent who normally rode him, and I—at the indoor school, the lovely Riding House designed by John Nash in 1764 at Buckingham Palace. I had watched Imperial a week previously when, impeccably accoutred in ceremonial trappings, impeccably mannered throughout, with looks that enhanced his role of royal charger, he had carried the Queen to the Horse Guards Parade and the Trooping the Color, and back again afterward at the head of the Queen's Guard up the Mall to the Palace. Later yet there had been a glimpse of him on resuming his duties with the Superintendent, gently helping control the crowds outside the Palace.

Close to, Imperial appeared much larger than I had remembered, and with some loss of dignity a chair had to be requisitioned for me to mount. The Superintendent opened the big wooden

doors leading onto that considerable expanse of soft tan, assured himself that his horse's rider knew how to steer, and tactfully withdrew.

So, there we were—for me a really proud moment, riding round and round the school on the Queen's charger, a popular and famous animal, a police horse among police horses. Round and round at walk, first one way, then the other, finding myself rather high off the ground, finding his stride unfamiliarly long. Then into my mind came those insidious voices that would be raised on returning to the bosom of my family. "D'you mean to say you only *walked?*" Very well then, slight squeeze and into trot, Imperial taking more of a hold than expected, myself needing time to get the rhythm of that extended stride. Round and round, first on one rein then on the other, more at ease now. Again those voices. "What? Didn't you *canter,* then?"

Why not? Think how beautifully he behaved on parade and among that crowd, think how wonderfully schooled all these police horses are. Think . . . oh, heck! Let's go!

Maybe that squeeze was a bit strong for a sensitive half-bred that was a perfect parade horse but renowned for being a bit of a handful, if a highly successful one, in the competitions at the police show at Imber Court. I squeezed, and Imperial bucked, one, two, three like that, and went. Minus stirrups and reins, moving at a

Opposite: Military of some countries still train mounted units for ceremonial display. La Garde Républicaine de Paris, shown here in parade turn-out, is the French Army's last mounted unit, active in maintaining public order.

Above: Imperial Guard of Iran, under commanding officer trained by Cadre Noir.

Above: Stallions ridden by Tehran mounted police have fiery temperament, yet are trained to stand motionless while riders fire from saddle.

Opposite: There are working horses and ponies in most regions of Africa where disease and tsetse fly do not exclude their use. Lesotho tribesmen use hardy but degenerate descendants of famous Basuto pony.

speed that reduced the dimensions of the school alarmingly, I thought: "You *can't* fall off this horse, he might injure himself." Injure himself? He seemed to be gathering speed. Might he jump?

My salvation was that blessed police saddle, British-army pattern, deep-seated, and with holsters, containing nothing more lethal than first-aid kit and mackintosh, against which my knees were rammed. I managed to collect the reins and regain the stirrups, and the chestnut began to tire of his fun and slack off. By the time the Superintendent returned, rider, a little red in the face, and horse, the hint of a gleam in his eyes, were decorously walking the perimeter once more.

New equestrian pleasures of today bring new types of work for horses and ponies, and trekki,g or the more lengthy noncompetitive trail riding are sports rapidly growing in popularity. There are centers where the whole family, aged ten years upward, horse-minded or not, can be given a taste of lovely, unspoiled homeland as seen from the backs of strings of horses or ponies. There are treks for experienced horsemen that can run to days of adventure in lovely and offbeat areas of other lands. The best of them take some objective for incidental interest—to sample the inns of Provence, perhaps, or the wines of Chianti, or a typical Spanish *feria.*

For one such group, adventure on horseback was a visit to Andalusia, in Spain.

By car it is fifty or sixty miles from Jimena de la Frontera—an old walled town, Moorish-built, with streets designed only for the passage of mule trains and donkey carriers—and Jerez, the center of Spain's sherry-producing region. On horseback, navigating by compass and large-scale map, avoiding the roads and riding the *cañadas,* the ancient cattle trails that traverse the mountains, a rider will find the mileage nearer seventy and the trip taking a minimum of three days—but the journey is incomparable.

At a quarter to six, just before sunrise on a morning in May, it is pouring rain on the plain below where Jimena de la Frontera is perched on the lower slopes of the mountains. The riders collected there are buttoned into long, voluminous waterproof capes that keep them, their cowboy-style "armchair" saddles, and the comfortable sheepskins on which they sit, snug and dry. They wear chaps or, alternatively, the long Andaluz trousers with high leather boots that are the only sure protection against the dagger-like thorns encountered in the maquis.

Saddlebags, bulging with minimum necessities plus a picnic lunch, are fitted over the elevated saddle cantles, anything else slung on the horn-like pommels. They set off, feet thrust into shoe stirrups much resembling tin cans, which are admirable for cutting through the scrub. The horses, peerless for mountain work, are Andalusians—universally sweet natured, narrow in conformation, with high withers to ac-

commodate the saddles, poor hocks, and the strange, high, "dishing" Spanish action. As the party sets off towards an angry dawn, the rain eases, and the riders move over a carpet of flowers, blue anchusa, pale scabious, butter-yellow daisies, sometimes at a delightful flowing canter but mostly at the easy, ground-devouring, 6 mph jog that is a natural gait of the Andalusian.

The riding style is unequivocally western, straight-legged, one-handed—the left, and held higher than in the English mode. The horses are neck-reined only, with no pull on their mouths at all, and the entire picture is a reminder to America that the western pattern—riding, gear, and horses alike—originated in Spain a long, long time ago.

The horses go on to an encouraging *Brrrr!* They stop with a quick bump, bump from any pace, whenever the rider's hand is raised higher than normal. It is an efficient system of braking

Trekking is a
comparatively new
pastime that takes full
advantage of
the horses and ponies
indigenous to a
district. Here Dartmoor
ponies carry a string
of riders through
the heather and around
the bogs of breed's
native moorland.

that can be disconcertingly sudden to the uninitiated and painful for those who inadvertently
give the signal and then impinge onto that lethal
pommel before they realize what is happening.

The route winds upward, at first through cork
forests and outcrops of rock, where nightingales
sing continuously at that time of year. There is a
halt for lunch—bread and a hunk of goat's
cheese, fruit and chocolate—and a siesta in the
shade of the trees. At these times the horses are
hobbled with the knotted ropes that produce the
unsightly scars marring the fetlocks of almost all
Andalusian horses. But they appear unaffected
by the restraint, grazing happily and moving
about easily. The country is sere and parched.
Heat makes the climbing very thirsty work, and
the sight of a small *vanta,* where the horses can
be watered and their riders be refreshed with
wine and coffee, is welcome. Otherwise the
horses drink at the two or three rivers encountered in a day's march.

After the cork forests and olive and Spanish
chestnut groves, the riders penetrate the thick
scrub of the maquis. The track dwindles and it is
easy to get lost. Then come the pine forests,
where red squirrels chatter at intruders, and so
on above the tree line to the rocks, on trails
thousands of feet up in the High Sierras. Here
the peaks of the mountains are snow-capped,
and the saddlebags yield up their stores of warm
clothing. Winding down again there are shale-
covered precipices where the horses put their
legs together, weight back on their hocks, and
slide down to land without so much as a stumble
at the bottom. On the rock-strewn slopes they
descend very slowly and cautiously, feeling
around the boulders with each hoof in turn until
sure of the footing, and very seldom making a
mistake.

Each evening before dusk finds the trekkers
riding the narrow, tortuous street of some tiny
village to the bar, where there are many
Spaniards happy to supply needed information
as to where the horses can be stabled and fed the

Cowboy selects his horse from remuda, ropes it, saddles it, and gets to work. Roping horse below is trained to make right moves so cowboy can play his steer.

213

staple diet of barley and chopped straw. The riders eat in the bar, an omelette or spiced sausage, washed down with Fundador or coffee, amid the unbelievable din of friendly people and canned music, for only rarely anymore does one happen on a live demonstration of flamenco guitar.

After hours in the saddle, bed is early, sleeping three or four to a room—the proprieties strictly observed with men in one and women in the other—and often with the warmth and pungent smell of the animals stabled below seeping through the floor boards. They sleep in beds where the springs may be broken but the rough cotton sheets, like the room, are spotlessly clean. Washing is accomplished in a chipped enamel basin with cold water from a ewer. The local sanitation, normally a communal thunder-box used by the entire village, is best avoided. There is always the forest, or that popular spot, the dark end of the stable, where, coming in from the

sunlight and temporarily blinded, you may learn only from a rustle that the accommodation is already booked—but where etiquette then demands merely a cheery greeting and the natural acceptance of a natural situation.

They come at length to Jerez and the annual Feria del Caballo, the most splendid horse fair held in all Spain. For a whole week Old Spain comes to life. The night is given to music, the urgent rhythms of flamenco and wild Spanish singing. But the day belongs to the horses and the men who ride and drive them.

There are horses to sell and horses to buy, hundreds of them every day. There are stallions to inspect at the Depósito de Sementales, Andalusians, Carthusians, English Thoroughbreds, a hundred or more of the best the Army can produce, to travel the country during the breeding season. There are dressage competitions, displays of haute école, concurso hipico for the jumpers, ranches and bull farms to visit on

horseback. There are nostalgic events in the arena where the carriages handed down through generations of aristocratic families are drawn by teams of anything up to a 13-in-hand, the leader sometimes controlled by a single nylon thread. Above all, each day between midday and three in the afternoon, there is the *paseo*, when the entire equestrian element comes into its own.

On each side of the main street the sherry barons, Terry, Domecq, Gonzalez, hold open house in the *casetas*, the private tented booths set up where they offer to all who come snacks of this and that and the sherry, sherry, sherry that flows all through the week. During the hours of the *paseo* the horsemen parade. They wear frilly shirts and brilliant cummerbunds, enormous spurs and flat-topped Spanish hats. One has his stallion prancing and curvetting along. Others do the passage, Spanish trot, or piaffe, while in and out among the horsemen weave the red-wheeled carriages and teams.

Thus the days pass and the week comes to an end. The trekkers collect their horses from the stable outside the town where they have been tending them. Within minutes they are out of the fleshpots, back to the silence of the peaks, range upon range beneath an intensity of blue sky, to gorges where waterfalls tumble a thousand feet, to rock face and tree line. And those numberless horses, so lately parading in their finery for the *feria*, are ridden back to work in a region where the horse still plays his part in the life of everyday.

Across the ocean, in the United States, the Andalusian's New World relative, the Quarter Horse, can be found at his own brand of work, helping in the herding and branding of range cattle. It is a work for which they have a certain genius, as I learned from my cutting horse, George. He was a plain fellow with no frills. His saddle was as businesslike as the worn, grease-sodden chaps I had been loaned. We met in the middle of the prairies of New Mexico, an hour's

Left: With range horse that has never felt the hand of man, there's no time for the patient gentling accorded some horses. It's sit him and ride him until he submits— or breaks you.

Above: Round-up time on the cattle lands, where old methods can still supplement the new.

No stock horse
like the Quarter Horse—
not the streaking
sprinter of the track,
but the muscular,
chunky, turn-on-a-dime,
steer-wise working
partner of the cowboy.

drive south from Roswell, with the horizon lost to either hand and only the white, dusty road snaking on to nowhere to bring you there. It was seven o'clock in the morning and it was *hot.*

The place was a huge cattle feed lot, where the rations are worked out by computer, where the director has a hot line to the fluctuating prices of the world markets, and where the thousands and thousands of cattle that come and go all year long are worked, and tended, and cut out with the aid of a dozen cow ponies.

In the complex of metal-fenced pens, contrived with interconnecting corridors and movable sections, there were cattle to move to other units, cattle to be cut out for closer inspection, cattle to be brought back to headquarters to be physicked or dispatched. The three cowboys I was with proceeded to work as usual, each man's horse watching his steer like a lynx, flying off at tangents, twisting and turning with its movements in the ritualistic dance of the trained cutting horse. George, in his wisdom, sensed only too well my tenderfoot status, and watered down his work to suit. But after three hours that horse had given me a taste of the skills of a cow pony, and a real appreciation of why it will be a long, long time before anyone invents anything better.

The life of the cowboy may be lonely, as tradition has it, but always there is the pride of working well with horses. The partnership of man and horse tends to endure, one way or another, even after the cowboy decides to leave the work of the range to younger men.

I met a westerner who had ridden bulls for a time, then built up a business as one of the best saddle makers in the West, taking his patterns for decoration from the flowers and leaves and plants he found in the countryside, and working them into the leather with the loving skill of an artist.

He had found his heart's delight, a cabin with an overgrown orchard tucked into a mountain valley. There were four horses milling around among the trees when we arrived, but the man was alone, for his wife and daughter had no taste for rural life and had scarpered back to the city. His horses remained as his only companions. We found him surrounded by boxes; he had given up on unpacking and turned to the solace

of beer instead.

Not that he knew we were coming. But my cowboy friends said Pete's place was their own, collected beer and ice, salad materials, and huge, raw steaks from the icebox, and we set off for the valley as day lengthened toward evening.

Our host met us, swaying gently on his feet. "I sure am sorry, Ma'am," he said—his heartfelt contribution to the night's conversation, which, together with requests for more beer, was repeated at intervals and accepted in the spirit it was offered. It is not every day that a man's family takes such drastic aversion to the home of his dreams.

We sat outside in the balmy air. Crickets chirped, the steaks sizzled appetizingly on the rusty bars of the barbecue, a miscellaneous pack of dogs nosed about, the horses clumped around, knocking this, clattering on that, helping themselves with relish from a loaded truck below the steps. My guide and mentor, a noted entertainer in his day, brought out a guitar and sang in a voice no longer young, yet still true, still sweet, still resonant, the authentic cowboy songs of long ago. The darkness came, folding in the peace and solitude of the valley for the night.

"I sure am sorry, Ma'am," said our host, rising with dignity and oscillating toward the house. On his return he made the doorway all right, but missed the six-inch step down onto the patio. The result was dramatic. Not for nothing had he once ridden and been bucked off exploding, sunfishing Brahma bulls. In some inexplicable way his feet flew straight up over his head as he nosedived into the trash can.

"I sure am sorry, Ma'am," he repeated gravely, salvaged by his friends, when they could move for laughing. He had nothing worse to show for that spectacular bull rider's fall than a skinned nose, but the decision went against bringing our host inside to eat.

Old Joe sat on my left, grinning at my appreciation of the sourdough bread he had been making for the past seventy years. "Aw, c'mon, Joe," they urged, "you tell Miss Judy Ma'am all about little Isa . . . she sure was so *sweet."* But when it dawned that it was a succulent portion of little Isa's rump at that moment between my teeth, it seemed better to postpone the story of that little old heifer, however sweet, until another day.

9.

Games
and
Hunting

220

Preceding pages: To
hunters, thrill impossible
to define—the sights
and sounds of the
countryside, the feel of
a good horse going
on, of hounds working, of
speed, of danger.
It's why these Virginia
hunters are afield.

Opposite: Polo is the
fastest team game in the
world—tough, complex,
strenuous. Player
here is Prince Philip, in
Windsor Great Park.

Most equestrian games have roots embedded in the past, even if the modern version bears only small resemblance to its origins. But *buzkashi* (*buz*, a goat, *kashidan*, to pull), that favorite pastime of the Afghanistan tribesmen, is much the same as when it was allegedly introduced around seven centuries ago by the fierce horsemen of the Mongol conqueror, Genghis Khan.

In Kabul, for the sake of the tourists, they have watered down the game to a more understandable sport, playing it to rule with ten or more to a side. On the northern plains along the border with Soviet Central Asia, where the Mongols are said to have played their war game using a live prisoner of war as "ball," the rules are few and subject to local interpretation. Casualties are numerous, the speed, action, and rivalry exceptional.

Through spring and summer the Chapandaz, the top buzkashi players, pursue their normal occupations. When winter comes they ride in to the buzkashi areas, along caravan routes through the foothills of mountains where height and terrain test the stamina of horse and rider alike, and where camel drivers consider it an honor to offer hospitality to the famous Chapandaz. As they approach the center, the route is thronged with other horsemen, players, and spectators, and horse-drawn taxis crammed with passengers dashing along in the dust.

Then comes noon of the appointed day. The people forsake the food stalls to pack themselves on the slopes around the huge, stony *maidan*, crowding close to the seats of the mighty in front of the chalk-drawn circle that serves as goal.

"Goat snatching" is as good an interpretation of buzkashi as any, but in fact it is more often played with the much heavier carcass of a decapitated calf. The "ball" is placed in the circle, the signal given, 139 players converge in a football player's nightmare of a scrimmage, the heavier getting to the inside, the lightweights awaiting their chance to wrest the carcass away, when someone manages to heave it up and make a break for one of the flags at either end. Horses neigh, players shout and bawl, onlookers, experts in the sport, yell encouragement and imprecations, now and then the thunder of innumerable galloping hooves adds to the hubbub. There's skill in getting your horse well placed in the melee, in hauling that weight up

without becoming unhorsed, in fending off the press of other players who seek to tear it away, to ride you off, to encircle, and impede while striking out with their steel-tipped whips.

The Chapandaz, like jockeys, are hired by the owners of buzkashi horses. These animals are specially trained for the game for years, and they will stand beside the carcass, then try to dash off the moment they feel its weight. They are prized, valuable animals, often with a playing span of twenty years. Those owners keep their eyes glued on their horses, assessing their skill and that of the players hired to ride them. For the Chapandaz there is fame to be won, kudos for skill displayed. A successful dash around a flag earns a player one point and prize money. Getting out of the new scrum and scoring a goal in the circle earns him two points, adulation, a bigger prize.

As the game progresses horses may tire and be replaced, but the same players battle on. There is a referee who attempts to restrict the use of the whips, but as excitement grows and passions rise, the play gets rougher, rules are discarded. A knife may be slipped between a horse's belly and its girth to send saddle and rider crashing to the ground. When the game wheels, galloping up into the crowd, then it is for the spectators to get out of the way, scattering like leaves before the gale. By the time the sun dips behind the savage peaks of the Hindu Kush and the session of buzkashi ends, there will be many a broken head and bloody gash among the players, but, *insh'Allah*, no injured horses.

Many centuries ago in regions not so far from Afghanistan the game of polo was evolved, with both India and Persia claiming the initial honor. And though at Smith's Lawn and Cowdray Park they might dispute the idea, there is a hint of refined buzkashi about this mounted game.

Polo is fast and tough, calls for a good natural eye for a ball, teamwork, and the ability to ride sufficiently well to be able to concentrate on the game—although fine horsemanship does not necessarily go along with good play. Since high-goal games and those at international level call for a string of high-class ponies, at least seven-eighths English Thoroughbred or those popular specialists bred in the Argentine, it is also an expensive pastime, of necessity the province of the wealthy and such military regiments as run

polo clubs. Against long odds, the game was resurrected in England after World War II. Then the realization that any moderately handy horse can be trained to stick and ball has brought moderate-grade polo within the range of many more would-be players.

The Afghan tribesmen reckon it takes five or six years to make a fully trained buzkashi horse. A top-class polo pony—which no pony becomes without a penchant for the game—can usually learn its job in two years, yet the schooling is a skilled and costly business. And prior to each season, even trained ponies require long weeks of preparation to bring them to the required peak of fitness and ability after running out all winter at grass. The program for these hot-blooded, highly strung creatures (15.1 hands is the popular height for a polo pony) consists of an increasing ration of hard tack, linked to an extended

portion of the exercise period to be done on grass or indoors on tan, twisting and turning at the canter. For some weeks they will show occasional but uncontrollable urges to take off in any direction but the required one, or to stage their own version of an impromptu rodeo.

The more lowly candidate—handy but with no special breeding for polo—can quite quickly be brought to the stage of participating in practice games with slow chukkers, provided there is acceptance of the truth—prevailing in all forms of equitation—that the blind cannot successfully lead the blind. For while a novice rider can totally, even dangerously, confuse a highly schooled horse, a horse must at least know its job before it is a safe or sensible ride for a novice, adult or child. A novice horse always requires an experienced rider, and with polo the rule applies with especial force.

It was a revelation to watch our suspicious-minded Slingsby demonstrate the point. With no previous acquaintance with the game or its frightening-looking appurtenances, but ridden by a man who was an experienced polo player and a good horseman (the two are not necessarily synonymous), someone in whom he had complete confidence, Slingsby within one practice session was peacefully accepting a polo stick, and even allowing his rider to demonstrate the strokes, including an off-side under his neck, and a near-side back shot under his tail.

Today the United States and the Argentine are the great polo-playing centers of the world, with Australia not far behind. Out there polo is principally a game for country dwellers, where horses are still an integral part of most properties, and since polo pony types make good stock horses and vice versa, the costs are relatively low. But Australia is also the home of "poor man's polo," the game of polocrosse, in which only one horse is needed.

Polocrosse is a hard, fast, outdoor sport, a combination of polo, lacrosse, and netball played on horseback. Its popularity has grown rapidly since World War II, and a special type of horse has now evolved. This animal is usually of 14 to 15.2 hands, speedy but with some weight for riding off, and essentially amenable. Many a stock horse also fits this description, and where this is the case the animal is already used to getting quickly off the mark, stopping in its own length, and maneuvering easily, and only has to be taught to apply these virtues to a game instead of to working cattle.

Fortunately there are games on horseback that don't require the kind of physical strength needed for buzkashi or polo. For young riders there are gymkhana events, which teach a pony fitness, agility, obedience, and suppleness, and teach the rider balance and confidence. Whether curving in and out of bending poles, aiming potatoes into a bucket, or keeping gait in a trotting race, these events help discipline the competitive spirit in boys while awakening it in girls, who—at least in the era before the advent of women's liberation—were too often content with losing so long as they displayed the correct aids in doing so, while the boys, half on and half off their exhilarated ponies, went out to win at all costs.

The Afghans have their own version of polo, played with a headless calf as "ball," and a hundred or so riders in the fray. Rules of buzhashi are few and flexible, with wild surges of galloping and free use of whips a part of the action. But horses and horsemanship are superb.

There's a move to learn vaulting in the Twala Club. The requirements are simple: a surcingle with two rigid handholds and a ring on top for attaching the holding strap that permits such feats as kneeling and standing on the horse's back, and a horse that will maintain a slow canter on a lunge rein. Another requisite is an instructor, someone with the expertise and agility to instruct and demonstrate this art, which develops rhythm, balance, courage, grace, and a feeling for the movement of the horse.

In my mind's eye I see three Arab country-breds, tacked up in vaulting surcingles, belting and bucking along while their riders vaulted on and off to either side in a rough, tough, strenuous exhibition of physical training on horseback. This was on the sandy, stone-strewn parade ground of Jordan's Royal Guard. The sun beat down from the usual cloudless sky. The horses moved faster, bucked higher. One chestnut mare became so unmanageable she landed her rider, mercifully in one piece, beneath her flying hooves—to the uproarious appreciation of the spectators. The exhibition had been staged for my benefit and there were moments when I trusted that any responsibility for future gaps in the ranks of that establishment of mounted police would not be laid at my door.

None of that is quite Twala Club standard, but there is a less spectacular, and less hazardous form of vaulting popular with some Pony Clubs, particularly in the United States. And similar free-style exercises are the basis of team competitions on the Continent.

The early cowboys and vaqueros had their own games on horseback, which in time turned into the vastly popular and profitable business of rodeo. Today the riders are professionals and they travel a far-flung circuit.

Often a rodeo rider becomes one because his father was before him—though that lean, handsome man in the white Stetson, whom I met while waiting for a plane at the Dallas-Fort Worth Airport, said he would never encourage his son to follow in his own footsteps. He no longer saw much point in paying fifty or so dollars in entry fees for the right to get on a bucking horse, and after that probably getting a broken bone sooner than winning the purse. On the other hand he would not try to stop the boy if rodeo was his goal. Many a kid like his has been bitten by the rodeo bug through an ability to stay on some mean little pony.

Like a top athlete, the prime age for a bronc rider is the six years between twenty-two and twenty-eight, and that is time aplenty for him to

Horsemen of the East
have set the standards
for acrobatics on
horseback. Daredevils
of Iran's Imperial
Guard do their vaulting,
backstands, and other
feats while
galloping flat-out on fiery
oriental horses.

225

Preceding pages: Westerners have their own version of mounted games. There is danger—and fun, too—in those few seconds while a cowboy is doing his best to stay put on the loose-rolling hide of a bucking bull.

break every bone in his body. Five days in the hospital for a broken shoulder, compete again three days after coming out, but use the other hand—that's how it goes.

A few top-notch riders get rich, the majority get by. The expenses are run up in traveling to the big rodeos that start at the end of January and continue through to the National Finals at the end of December, living in hotels, maybe packing your own roping horse, or dogging team of two horses, taking the inevitable, costly time out for injuries. It all adds up to a very big sum, and for most to a financially unrewarding, crack-

ing hard kind of life. But for the man in rodeo, it is not a circus, not a spectacle. It is a dedicated sport.

He throws a lariat true to check a racing, jinking calf while his horse slithers to a stop. He launches himself off a galloping horse to clutch a steer by its horns and wrestle it and throw it in the fastest time. Above all, he waits for the big event, that moment when with or without a saddle, according to his bent, the hunk of horseflesh he straddles spills twisting, buckjumping, sunfishing out of the chute. Or if it's a Brahma bull he is astride, that ton of mean, loose-skinned strength will try to spin and "buck him off into the well," the inside, and then unlike a horse, kneel on him or step on him if it can. All that for a cowboy adds up to the most individualistic sport in the world.

The horses in top rodeo are no second fiddles. Their star quality matches that of the cowboys who ride them. Take a dogging team. There's the hazing horse, trained to gallop straight to keep the steer from swerving in a wrestling event. There's the dogging horse itself, trained to gallop alongside the steer and deviate left when the rider comes off onto the animal. It has to be a dependable, fairly high-strung creature, really able to run, and able to "rate"—to wait the moment the steer leaves the starting box. It has to be adaptable to being ridden by the different competitors to whom it will be loaned in return for a quarter of their winnings. A first-class dogging team is something of a rarity. Finding a top dogging horse is as difficult as finding a top racehorse, and owning one is about like having the Kentucky Derby winner in your barn.

There is the roping horse, trained to chase, stop fast, jerk the calf enough to daze it a little without hurting it, then keep the rope sufficiently taut so that the calf is stopped but not dragged. The owner of a good roping horse takes it around the rodeos so that cowboys who work two shows a day can borrow it, once again paying for the privilege by giving up a quarter of what they win.

There are the broncs—the bucking horses. The broncs and bulls are always allocated by a draw, so luck plays a big part in the fortunes of a rider's day. Of the maximum score, fifty percent of the marks are for riding, with disqualification if the rider fails to have his blunted spurs over the points of the horse's shoulders as its feet hit the ground on the first jump, but if he touches any part of the equipment or animal with his free hand (loses a stirrup, or changes hands on the rein in saddle-bronc events), or if he falls off. The other fifty percent of the marks are given for the way the horse bucks, and there is at least one kind with which you cannot win. He is that vastly unpopular character that comes out of the chute running until he's going real fast, then starts to buck at the same time, cutting off to the left or right, or just plumb bucking back. Even if you do manage to ride him there's half of that precious eight or ten seconds lost with no buck, so no marks, and damn sure no win. If a bronc won't buck at all, and there are a few, or if he deliberately throws himself or knocks his rider off on the chute gates, then there is a re-ride.

Most broncs have a pattern that the riders get to know. Each time they come out they go around, say, to the left, or they go straight ahead and then around to the right. The real good bronc has his rider guessing. He is going to buck all right, but each time his routine is to a different design. Some get clever, clever enough to stand still and do themselves out of a job. Broncs that have been around the rodeos for a long time sometimes get to know too much. They know when they feel the rider tense up as he's ready to go. They understand when he says "Outside!" and that "Let's look at 'em!" means "Open the chute!" That's the moment when those old hands may rear straight up and come over backwards in the chute. Otherwise very few broncs are mean. It's unusual to get bucked off over the horse's head, but if that happens he'll do his best not to step on the rider with his front feet, which is where the weight is and what hurts. Most injuries come from getting thrown up and kicked on the way down.

In Canada there are still a few "wild" horses available for bucking, but the best broncs are usually spoiled saddle horses, and they will keep right on bucking after the wild decide to quit.

Saddle-bronc riders pack their own saddles, built to certain specifications, and lacking the horn that could go into a man's chest or hook into his belt if he's thrown over the top. The saddle bronc also wears a halter and a single rope. In bareback the bronc wears nothing on his head and the rig consists of just a strap round his brisket, just behind the front legs, with a hand-

hold like a suitcase handle. And it is an odd thing about these horses that some are halter-broken and can happily be ridden bareback. But put a saddle on a saddle bronc—and, well, look out!

All broncs wear the bucking strap or flank, and this is where the controversy starts. It is alleged that this strap is often cinched tightly around the animal's genitals, and that there would be no prolonged bucking without pain as a stimulator. It is said that flanks have been used that were made of rope with sharpened rivets fixed in the vital area, that broncs are goaded with an electric prod as the chute is opened.

These pages: Bulls wear a bucking strap, bell, and braided rope with a handhold that tightens as animal bucks. A man who's bucked off but gets his hand caught in hold stakes his life on the skill of the rodeo "clown."

In the wrong hands rodeo is an easy avenue for cruelty, and unfortunately cruelty is not unknown in the horseman's world. Wherever it occurs, cruelty debases those who employ it, and all praise and power are due to those who work towards stamping out evil practices connected with horses or any other animals. On the other hand, rodeo is now a multimillion-dollar business, and, at the top levels at any rate, it seems unlikely that such big business would risk anything that might lessen the sport's popularity. The top-ranking broncs are also very valuable animals, worth some $50,000 each, and their welfare is of permanent interest to the stock contractors who supply bucking horses and bulls for rodeo. They are well fed, well looked after, "work" for a few seconds at a time, and stay around for years. Of the estimated three thousand or so rodeos held annually, about one thousand are sanctioned by the two professional leagues, the Rodeo Cowboys' Association and the International Rodeo Association. It is their standards of fairness that influence my regard for rodeo as a sport. Where those standards don't apply and real cruelty occurs, it is to be deplored.

Our daughter, who worked for a touring rodeo that made stops at various places on the Continent, affirmed that real rodeo is possible without cruelty. In every country where the outfit performed it was inspected by veterinarians and officials from each country's equivalent of the Society for the Prevention of Cruelty to Animals. Only then was it licensed. (England outlawed the bucking strap in accordance with an Act of Parliament in the twenties.) In every instance, all the animals concerned were minutely examined before and after the rodeo events, and it was conceded that horses, bulls, steers, and calves alike were completely undistressed.

The flanks were lined with sheepskin, and

Riding a bareback bronc in Yuma, Arizona. Only hold is a "suitcase" handle in that strap around Steamboat's brisket, and to make up his 8 seconds, Mark Togood will have to sit right up to his hand.

Above: Saddle bronc rider is top man in rodeo and this is his moment of truth. Chute opens, Bob Blackwood has his spurs up over Red Wing's shoulders and wham! out explodes that bronc, and does he know how to buck!

231

although tightly cinched to prevent slipping were positioned around the loins always in front of the genital area. And in all those weeks, while that bunch of authentic rodeo cowboys talked among themselves and with the grooms—endless conversation about horses, broncs, and rodeo—there was never a mention of any method that could be called cruel. They talked of horses that buck without the primer of a flank—while agreeing that most would not buck so well—but insisted that horses buck not because the strap hurts, but because it tickles, teases, exasperates if you like, causing the horse to buck and squirm to rid himself of it. They made the point that many horses, not only broncs, will buck if you put your hand down and touch it behind the ribs (a point that Twala is always delighted to demonstrate any day of the week).

What does emerge when talking to cowboys is the genuine admiration and respect they have for the broncs who provide their sport. Each animal's prowess is known and discussed heatedly and at the end of each session the riders get together and choose the bronc they consider to be the best buckjumper. That animal is then given the Bucking Horse of the Year award, and becomes a famous personality to the rodeo fraternity, as much as the rider who emerges as champion.

Bull riding, steer wrestling, chuck-wagon racing, and their like are leftovers from the days when rodeo was a part of the Wild West Shows. Steer and calf roping are part of everyday work on the range, as is the bronc riding, which evolved from methods of breaking horses that have never known the hand of man in the shortest possible time.

Both Australia and New Zealand are rodeo-oriented, and Australia also has her own related

Of all rodeo thrills, chuck-wagon racing is the wildest, craziest. Teams are Thoroughbreds, race-fit, and wagons are stripped for lightness. Drivers stand, bawling on their flat-eared, lathered horses. Collisions, calamities, and—for some—victory is the result of it all.

but individualistic and popular sport of camp-drafting. Rules for this "dressage at the gallop" were first formulated in 1928, and the event began and remains the sport of the true stockman. It grew from the necessity to separate big mobs of cattle into groups when on runs away from established yards. The drover's or stockman's horse, called the "camp" horse, was trained to cut out individual beasts and draft them off to another group, and keep them from returning. Campdrafting competitions still recruit horses and riders from the everyday world of working cattle.

The contest consists of cutting your selected beast from the mob provided in the "camp"—with twenty-six marks out of the total hundred allotted to this section—and then taking it on a marked course, something on the lines of the skier's slalom with the addition of a gate, within the time limit, usually set at fifty seconds.

Courses and times may vary according to the judge of the day. Horses may not have their heads tied down nor wear curb bits. Any abuse of horse or beast results in disqualification.

Campdrafting is a very fast, skilled, and exacting sport. Your horse must have innate cattle sense, docility, alert intelligence, the training to respond immediately to the lightest aid, and the weight to push a big bullock in the required direction by pressure on its shoulder. Many champion campdrafting horses carry Thoroughbred blood, which is true also of the Quarter Horses that are fast becoming as popular in Australia as stock and competition animals as they are in their American homeland. When it comes to the spectacular and specialized art of competitive "cutting," this is the breed that is the acknowledged king.

Cutting is another sport that is merely an extension of the everyday work of the cow pony

233

used on American ranches, and it is allied to campdrafting. I had the experience of watching it in the unlikely setting of a typical county show in England, where the Canadian Cutting Horse Team was making an appearance.

The competitor indicates his steer to the judge, one from the small mob at the end of the arena, rides quietly in among them to ease the animal out towards the center of the ring. From that moment he hands over responsibility to his horse, the rider's role being merely to make certain he does not impede it in any way. Points are deducted for reining or cueing, but since there are only two-and-a-half minutes in which to demonstrate the horse's cow sense and training, a couple of hazers do all they can to drive the beast back from the mob towards the cutting horse and so provide maximum action. When one competitor removed his horse's bridle, it

was even easier for an English crowd to appreciate the finer points of the sport.

Here was this chestnut crouched the way a border collie does when herding sheep. His head was lowered, fixing the steer almost eyeball to eyeball. He swayed on his haunches, poised to uncoil and launch himself turn for turn, twist for twist, at one with every movement of his adversary as they engaged in a kind of ritualistic dance. The cutting horse's ears were flat, he was concentrating every way he knew on keeping that bullock where he wanted it. The sudden, fantastic bursts of speed, the dead stops, abrupt changes of direction rammed home the point that however well he can "read cattle" and perform, however painstaking his training, a cutting horse will not gain winning points unless his rider is a fine horseman, able to stay with his mount's every lightning move without in any way upset-

ting its balance or distracting it.

There seems little if anything controversial about the fascinating art of competitive cutting, but talk religion, talk politics, above all mention the emotional subject of hunting, and more times than not you are slap-bang in the middle of a heated argument. And there seems no place safe from controversy, since people hunt almost everywhere.

The young girl fresh out from England and attending a meet of the Pakuranga Harriers did not realize she was having a day's sport by invitation of the oldest and best known of the twenty-six hunts affiliated with the New Zealand Hunts Association. To be truthful she was too busy at that moment trying to assess the braking efficiency of her hunter, a huge ex-steeplechaser kindly loaned by the Master, to give much thought to anything else.

When the Master, with a glance for the attention of his guest, shouted "Follow me!" they took off on a shortcut to draw covert—straight over a formidable hedge down into a sunken road. To his rider's relief, the big chaser obligingly waited while she picked herself up from the grass verge at the foot of the drop where they had landed independently and she was given a leg up onto his back once more. By the time hounds had found their hare, lost it, and then re-hit the line on a screaming scent, she was enchanted to realize that she was riding a perfect-mannered hunter, who had the added advantage of knowing all there is to know about negotiating in complete safety the five-strand barbed-wire fences they jump as a matter of course in those parts. There was nothing to do but sit tight, have faith in her horse, and enjoy the good sport and the excitements of the day.

Trick horses are products of their own intelligence allied to hours of patient and unvarying training. They are cued chiefly by imperceptible hand signals. Trick riders need agility, balance, courage, and a totally obedient, smooth-gaited horse that stays in rhythm.

235

Barrel racing, sport as popular in Australia as in U.S., is province of women riders and their specialist Quarter Horses. Racing against time, they must spin around barrels on a clover-leaf course.

In the forests of Villers and Fountainbleu, Rambouillet and the others where the French indulge *la chasse à courre*, the role of the horse is only that of the vehicle necessary to enable the hunter to go after his prey in an unathletic pursuit of stag, fallow deer, or occasionally wild boar. There is little to leap in forest hunting anyway, but certainly not for this horse is the usual requirement of the good modern hunter—to go straight, galloping on to jump all obstacles as they come. Part of the extensive ritual of French hunting is aimed at not needlessly tiring the horse or incommoding the rider, and it is de rigueur to skirt even the occasional tree trunk or ditch.

Maybe the French version of riding to hounds remains, as it has for some centuries past, more of a social than a sporting amusement. Its courtly style endures in the picturesque liveries of years ago still worn by the hunt servants, in the melodious fanfares produced on the *trompe*, the three-curled French horn, in the equally musical voice of a French pack of hounds, all set against a riot of autumnal coloring or the brilliance of sunshine on a sprinkling of snow between the trees. And if the entire hunting procedure appears to the alien to be governed by strangely archaic rules and an elaborate, equally ancient ceremonial, this is all devised by and suited to a particu-

lar form of *la chasse à courre*.

Much of the style of hunting in France, first in vogue in the fourteenth century, was adopted by the English to form the basic rules for their own sport of hunting. Even the very British hunting term "Tally-ho" is a corruption of the old French *Ty a hillaut* ("the game's afoot").

In England the deer and hare were hunted long before anyone thought of hunting the fox, and then the pace of the hunt was dictated by hounds bred more for voice than speed, and by followers who saw little reason for undue haste. To jump anything much more than a ditch was considered either the exploit of the eccentric or of the poor horseman, obviously out of control, but if there was no alternative but to leap, then it was done from a standstill. The enclosure of the land with hedges and fences, and the breeding of fast hounds specifically trained to hunt foxes, altered what had already become England's premier field sport into an approximation of fox hunting today.

By the end of the eighteenth century fox hunting was also well established in America. There are about one hundred and fifty hunts, eleven of them in Canada, listed with The Masters of Foxhounds Association of America. By invitation you may hunt the red fox, said to have been imported by the British into the Chesapeake Bay

236

In calf-roping, horse slides to haunches to hold rope taut. It's up to cowboy to rope quick, move down his rope quicker, wrestle and pig-tie his calf quickest of all.

area and now slightly smaller than the original, or the indigenous gray, with one or another of the traditional, exclusive, and very smart hunts that operate in the fair hunting countries—from Massachusetts to Virginia. If you are hunting up and down the hills and canyons of Colorado, California, or Arizona, your quarry may be a coyote. A number of hunts are drag.

Hounds vary from pure, imported British blood, through crossbreds, to the evolved American breed, longer in the leg and with narrower heads than English foxhounds. They have, and need, excellent noses for finding scent in the dry areas, equally good voices, necessary for the very extensive coverts, and they are very fast. Their qualities have been bred largely to accommodate to the hard state of the ground, and this applies as well to American hunting horses. Although in rocky, hilly districts the best hunters are often Appaloosa or Quarter Horse types, elsewhere the majority are Thoroughbreds or part-breds that can gallop easily "on top of the ground." They lack the substance of British or Irish hunters, many appearing to unaccustomed eyes to be unduly "on the leg," but this type of

Thoroughbred is admirably suited to the pace and conditions of American hunting.

The pace at which American hunts proceed can come as something of a surprise to someone just out from the old country. You find yourself zipping over everything from the stone walls and varied fences of Virginia to the solid timber typical of Maryland, and the ubiquitous wooden "chicken coops" erected over wire, and at a speed that would be undeniably stupid in England or Ireland, where the take-off is more often than not wet and soft. Americans, you might say, hunt on top of the ground; the British hunt "in" it.

Many of the old Australian families have a tradition of hunting in their blood, but nowadays the field, as in most hunting countries, contains a large proportion of the new fraternity, people who live in the suburbs but own a horse and come out for the gallop and to learn the ways of this ancient pastime. Some packs hunt a dragline. The foxes mainly descend from those that were imported around the middle of the nineteenth century to supplant dingoes and kangaroos. Wallabies, kangaroos, and deer are still the quarry with most Tasmanian hunts.

You should hunt in Ireland, where the people, the weather, and the countryside remain tuned to their age-old sport, and where most small farms can still hire you the half- or three-quarter-bred hunter that is just the horse for the job.

If it's a day out in County Wexford you have in mind, then you'll be needing a local horse, one that knows his way over those high and narrow stone-faced banks. A short-coupled, handy type, born and raised in Tipperary or Limerick, is the safest conveyance onto and over the huge, often hairy, double banks of those parts. The famous Galway Blazers that hunt in the west of Ireland are well named—they do go like blazes—and for that good, fast country with few hedges or banks but a variety of fearsome stone walls, you need one of those big, galloping horses, beautifully balanced and clever, that take their fences going on. This is the type, too, long striding and brave, to cope with those horrifying stretches of water, wide as small canals, that the Irish euphemistically call "Meath ditches." I speak, of course, of the famed Irish hunter, by a Thoroughbred sire out of something akin to a versatile Irish draft mare; she may be no beauty but she passes on grand legs and superb bone. Irish hunters are no longer easily had, being sought by Continental riders willing to pay a very big price for horses of the type that also excels in show jumping and eventing. It is big money well spent for horses with stamina inbred by the rich pastures and limestone of a country with a tradition of horse-breeding in its bones, where the youngsters thrive in the soft climate, and acquire the priceless knack of learning to look after themselves over ditches and banks at a very early age—first on the end of a lunge rope, and then quietly out with hounds.

There are many hunts in England with names famous in the annals of the sport, but the cream are generally considered to be those packs that hunt the Shires, those parts of the Midlands where it is still possible to gallop across pasture and take your own line over fences devoid of wire. If you hunt with these hounds—the Pytchley, the Quorn, the Fernie, the Belvoir, or the Cottesmore—you will need a Thoroughbred horse of speed, stamina, courage, the correct dress, an infallible knowledge of hunting etiquette, and a fat bank balance.

While still a schoolgirl, I had a day out with the Cheshire, mounted on a splendid dun gentleman called Jaundice, at 17 hands so vast after Smith I that it was difficult to adjust to his stride bucketing over ridged pasture. Fearsome high fences vanished behind us without qualm and almost without trace. Otherwise my eight or nine seasons out with hounds were spent in trappy country, where speed is of little account and the ideal hunter is small and agile, happy to crawl here, creep there, and jump anything and often, once the fox breaks covert.

In the depths of the covert something rustles, twigs snap, and a hound appears, glances briefly to where Twala and I are standing, fifty or so yards away on the edge of the rest of the Field, then plunges back into the thicket again. Twala snorts, jiggles his bit, lunges his neck forward and up, then stands, statue-like, ears cocked, listening. Comes the distant note of the horn, the huntsman's cheer to hounds, somewhere closer at hand a hound whimpers and there's the huntsman's echoing cry "Huic! Huic! to Rambler!" Twala shivers with excitement and kicks, a nervous reaction sternly repressed as another hound opens and the pack joins in with a great burst of music, smashing down the undergrowth as they rouse their fox and push him twice around through the trees.

Silence for a moment, then from far away on the down-wind side of the covert comes the shrill screech of a View-Holler, "Y . . o . . o . . i!" We can hear the Huntsman forcing his horse through the bushes. Comes the staccato, spine-shivering notes of the "Gone away!" then the cry of hounds growing fainter.

For a second we wait. Twala dances on his toes, horses plunge, then the Field Master is galloping on toward the wing of the covert, the hunt streaming along behind. We are well placed, I had kept Twala out of the rut, and though speed is not his forte he is galloping on strongly, pulling with excitement but, as always, controllable. Behind the Field Master and in front of us is a posse of the hunting fraternity well turned out, well mounted, knowing every inch of the game and always, somehow, to the fore. They are the type to choose as a pilot, less so the dashing young man on a youngster—a blood weed wearing the rogue's badge of a red ribbon

and is scrambling aboard. Somehow the seasoned hunter he hit managed to find a fifth leg and has carried on safely out of the pen, maybe encouraged by the rude names its rider is calling the thruster. Balked, Twala and I wait for the coast to clear, pop over from a trot, then out and gallop on.

Pasture—water-logged, heavy. Stick to the track and save the farmer what damage you can. Our pilots are swinging right-handed toward the covert. Wire ahead, and this the only way. It's dark under the trees beyond that little stile, but Twala does not hesitate. He canters at it slowly, taking no chances with timber. Horses converging from leafy rides—part of the Field came this way—and my pilots are lost, on ahead. Galloping on rutted tracks behind each other, ducking under branches, thwacked in the face by twigs, gobbets of mud slinging up from the horse's hooves in front. "Hold hard!" Hands are raised, gesturing to stop. We slither to a standstill in a cloud of steam. Hounds came this way all right, daylight showing the end of the covert, but in between there's the slippery, hoof-pocked track sloping down to a fence—a horrible place, a broken-down stake-and-bound, mended with barbed wire only a few inches from the top. A boggy take-off and a bit of a ditch the other side. Some veer off to either hand trying to find another way out. Some jump off their hocks and make it, ditch and all. Some make a desperate dash to no avail there are shouts, some swearing, quite a lot more refusing. If it weren't Twala I would go away, but as his turn comes and he cocks his ears to have a go, the horse in front slides to a sudden halt, chest against the obstacle, eyes peering ruefully into the distance beyond, then struggles off along the inside of the fence. We should have waited to see him over before going at it. My fault but Twala is committed and he does not falter. I shut my eyes, clutch his mane, feel him make the extra effort in midair as he sees the ditch below, then *thunk!* and I open my eyes as he gallops on. It was not exactly elegant, but this is the hunter to have for country like this.

Warning shouts, "Ware wheat!" and the Field swings to ride the headland and save the farmer's crops. A crowded gateway; pushing, shoving, here and there a horse threatening to kick. Ride him with your legs; a little opening

**Preceding pages:
Stalking the wild red deer of Scotland is sport now managed with aim of culling the herds. Familiar adjuncts are the Highland ponies used to carry heavy stags down over rough terrain.**

Opposite: What better type for fox hunting than this Irish-bred. It's all in his face—knowing, brave, dependable. He gallops on over any kind of country, goes all day, and comes out, four days later, fresh as paint.

on its tail—and most patently "in charge" now as they battle along in the rear. We round the edge of the trees. There's a hurdle with a rail on top. Nothing much to it, but take-off and landing are muddy, poached by sheep and treacherous, and the hurdles beyond turn the obstacle into a pen, an in-and-out for us.

The Field Master flips over. Four of the old hands follow suit. As the next takes off, his horse is thrown off balance by a barge from the horse behind, charging on out of control, hitting and smashing the farmer's rail and begetting its rider's own well-deserved retribution as it pecks on landing, pitching that unpopular young man over its head into the mud. No harm done to him, except to dignity. He held onto the reins

here, a little opening there, squeeze by that one, thank the gate opener, and we're through. Trot over rough ground (Twala's blowing anyway), out onto those tricky banks below the escarpment. Hounds have checked, not so far in front, one more fence — wire with a hunting rail in it — and we'll join them, but not too close. A stony approach, a little ditch before, but nothing to worry a handy hunter. Over and slow to a walk, then stop, well away from hounds, to avoid distracting them or fouling scent with the smell of sweating horse. My pilots and the twenty or so who are always there or thereabouts, have already arrived, more come straggling, children on ponies flying the fence with ease, big horses snorting, teetering about on the wrong side. On the track way below the banks stands the clutch of stalwarts who never jump, but get there in the end by gate and lane.

Huntsman sitting quietly, leaving his hounds to do their own casting for awhile. Watch them at work, sterns waving, busy trying here, there, rushing to join a babbler, a youngster falsely giving tongue, back to try another direction. But now they are discouraged, heads up, eyeing the Huntsman, foiled by a wily fox that utilized that bunch of wide-eyed bullocks to foul his scent, and by a falling barometer. Those frost-spangled cobwebs we noted as we hacked to the Meet were harbingers of a poor day for scent anyway.

Huntsman casts forward but without success, and it's "Hounds, gentlemen, please!" as he doubles back through the Field, making for the track below and another covert to draw. Switch Twala around to face hounds passing by. Normally "kick-proof," he just might be tempted to raise a hoof, and kicking a hound is the ultimate crime.

Jog off down the banks behind hounds, and now what to do? That gate, often used for access onto the track, is newly chained and padlocked. Huntsman and whips do not hesitate, and the pack spills over a dyke and the barbed wire on the other side, but a five-barred gate is one hell of a jump, and hounds are not even running. Some of the Field disperse right and left looking for a better spot, but I know there's nothing for more than a mile, and the hard core as well as my pilots are already lining up. Skylarking over fences is rightly frowned on when hounds are not running—from both the farmer's and your

horse's point of view—but it's different when there is not much of an alternative, when the Field Master has led the way and the only real deterrent is a faint heart or a bad jumper.

Own to the first, but Twala's too well known to suggest the second! Someone shouts, "Come on!" and my horse is on his toes again. It's either attempt it with determination or not at all, so we canter at it now, before there's time for further thought. Put your heels to him . . . now . . . and how could you have doubted him? Twala would never be so foolish as to clout a solid gate!

Jog on to the next covert. "Leu-in, leu-in, my beauties!" But there's no fox or no scent, and when they move on to another the moment arrives to say, "Good night, Master!" (whatever the time of day), and set off for home. For all his keenness, Twala was not living the life of a corned-up, fully fit, stabled hunter—he was trace-clipped and out at grass by day in a New Zealand rug—and after a good run, a short day was the answer.

Jog and walk the first of the six or seven miles, get off his back, loosen the girth and walk the last mile home beside your horse so that he comes in cool and relaxed. For a start Twala is overexcited, bounces around still listening for hounds, then settles and condescends to walk as required.

My thoughts are now my own, and a story comes to mind of the very Irish Irishman who taught me to ride as a child. Besides teaching he did a bit of horse dealing on the side, and always liked to get a new acquisition out with hounds before selling it on. He was on his way home from hunting and it had been a mixed kind of day, a few short runs but quite a bit of waiting about too, and the young horse he was riding had refused to settle at all, fretting, milling about, threatening to stand up, and generally being a bit of an exhausting nuisance. And by the time they had gone three miles of the ten to go home, it had still not walked a step, but tittuped and pranced and jiggled enough to drive one mad. My friend had indigestion and a quick Irish temper, and suddenly he jumped off his horse, clapped it across the bottom, and shouted, "You go on to the divil!" (or words to that effect). Away went the horse galloping down the road out of sight (in an era when motor traffic was not much of a problem), while its rider set out to walk home. Two miles farther on he caught up with his horse, held by an obliging farmer. Back into the saddle he climbed and, if he is to be believed, not only did that horse then walk quietly all the way back to its stable, but he was able to sell it a few weeks later with the recommendation of being one of the best hunters and best walkers he had ever had through his hands!

True or not, the story is not meant as a suggested remedy for a restless horse. And if either that tale, or that of my day fox hunting with Twala, had belonged to a later date, both stories would probably have ended with boxing the horse up in a trailer. It is a vastly convenient method of getting to and from meets, being able to leave home later and get back more quickly, and must in some ways be easier on your horse.

And yet . . . and yet. Were not those hunters of years gone by maybe a little fitter, a little tougher, from the benefit of those miles of slow roadwork before and after hunting? Were they not perhaps just that much more relaxed and ready for the warm mash, last feed, rubdown and deep bed, for having unwound slowly on that quiet hack home on their own four hooves? Possibly not, but I would have hated never to have known those rides home after hunting, when the smells of wet grass and rain-drenched leaves were somehow special, when the robin shrilling in the hedgerow, or the storm cock whistling his defiance of the wind that lashed his ash-tree spire, were a part of the contentment of the day, when the tingling air and brooding silence that heralds a night's frost to come were the sweetest remedies for the fatigue and stiffness of a strenuous day.

There are many different aspects of hunting as horsemen pursue it, a sport with a beauty of its own, a fascination hard to define, and the stuff of greater emotional controversy than any other.

People hunt for the sake of a day in the open air, for the sights and sounds and smells of the countryside. They hunt for companionship, for exercise, the sight of hounds and horsemen streaming along a covert side. They hunt for the interest and pleasure in watching hounds work and the skill with which a good huntsman controls his pack. They hunt for the thrill of riding across country when nothing is preplanned and you jump what comes or use your local knowledge to find another way, for the spice of danger missing from everyday life, for the joyous partnership of a good horse. The majority hunt for a mixture of these and other reasons, but tearing across country inspired by the lust to kill is not one of them, however much the idea sticks in the minds of people ignorant of the facts, or too biased to accept them.

Many fox hunters hunt for seasons and never see a fox, even fewer see a fox killed. Catching foxes is the business of the Huntsman, who is employed to hunt a pack of trained hounds to scent out and if possible kill their prey. The doing of this engenders sport, but the kill is principally at the instigation of the farmer over whose land the hunt rides, and without whose support fox hunting would cease. Foxes do kill lambs, chickens, turkeys, and any other fowl they can find, not only for food but sometimes with a seeming wantonness. Sensible and balanced control of a species is what conservation is about, and usually it means control to a point where animals can fit in with the needs of the encroaching humans, not with those of other animals. Few wild animals die of old age, because the balance of nature, left undisturbed, is a pattern of interdependency, whereby each preys on the other down the line. In Britain, man is the fox's only effective enemy, and since this is a wily animal that often evades hounds, there is no danger that hunting will do more than control the species.

During the seasons I hunted, I saw but one fox killed by hounds, or, to be correct, by the one hound that seized it by the back of the neck in the same way a terrier kills a rat—and seized for the same reason: to avoid being bitten itself. After the fox is dead it is thrown to the hounds as a reward for doing the job for which they are trained.

The views of the Royal Society for the Prevention of Cruelty to Animals and of the National Farmers' Union are that "an efficient pack of hounds is an accepted and humane method of fox control." By 1975 at any rate, they had not found a better, neither by snaring, gassing, shooting, or poisoning.

No one can tell what the future of fox hunting may be, or for that matter of any other sport. It may eventually be confined to drag hunting, a contrived sport where hounds follow an artificial scent, laid along one of several different lines over a variety of made-up fences. It may become

Be it Virginia or England, the day's hunt starts and ends the same. Hounds in cover, "Leu-in, my beauties!" Crash of a horse through undergrowth, whimper of a hound, "Huic, to Rambler!" Maybe the spine-shivering notes of the "Gone away!" At end of day, tired, muddy, content, it's "Goodnight, Master," and so home.

"clean boot" hunting, where bloodhounds are used to hunt the scent of a man running across country. Perhaps it will revert to carted stag hunting, where the quarry is unboxed at the meet and released, with a suitable start, to be recaptured eventually, unharmed by the hounds with which it is often on good terms, to run several times a season until too old.

Sometimes fox hunters are their own worst enemies. Those who suffer from that strange conceit, once they are on a horse's back, of ignoring lesser mortals, of straggling over the roads as of right and holding up traffic as they pursue their sport, do not endear themselves to sensible people. Those few who ignore the warnings of Master or Field Master to avoid crops or wet pasture, who gallop through sheep or cattle, who do not ensure there is someone behind to secure gates, who break fences and omit to report the fact, who lark over obstacles to break them when hounds are not running—they are the ones who incur the wrath of their own hunt officials, give hunting a bad name, and risk alienating the very farmers on whose good will their sport depends.

Yet despite all and everything, I still indulge a little fantasy of the future. Fifty, maybe a hundred years have passed, and some of the news media are carrying an unusual commendation for the British government of the day. "The Government are to be congratulated," so goes my imagined report, "on the success of their new measures for the necessary controlling of wild foxes. The Department responsible is providing gangs of Fox Controllers who, after exhaustive research with other means of conveyance, found to be less suitable, are now mounted on horses for the discharge of their duty, being aided by a number of specially trained dogs to find, chase, and kill the prescribed number of the growing fox population. The Controllers, in their sober black uniforms, are now becoming a familiar and welcome sight in parts of the countryside."

And of course, since neither sport nor pleasure enters into the duties of paid government officials, everyone will be happy.

Picture Credits

Photographs by George Rodger are keyed: GR

Cover: front—Jerry Cooke; **flaps**—GR. **2-3:** Horst Schäfer/Photo Trends. **8-9:** GR. **10:** Horst Schäfer/Photo Trends. **13:** Hope Ryden.

Chapter 1

14-15: GR. **17:** H. R. H. Prince Philip. **18, 19:** Norman Snyder. **20-21:** James Sugar/Rapho-Photo Researchers. **22, 23:** Bank Langmore. **24, 25:** Godfrey Argent. **26-27:** Bank Langmore. **28-29:** GR. **30, 31:** GR. **33:** Godfrey Argent.

Chapter 2

34-35: GR. **37:** Horst Schäfer/Photo Trends. **38, 39:** GR. **40-41:** GR. **42-43:** Jerry Cooke/Rapho-Photo Researchers. **44, 45:** GR. **46, 47:** GR. **48, 49:** GR. **50-51:** Y. Momatiuk/Amwest. **52:** Godfrey Argent. **53:** Jack C. Adams. **57:** Godfrey Argent. **58-59:** GR. **61:** GR.

Chapter 3

62-63: Godfrey Argent. **65:** GR. **66, 67:** Godfrey Argent. **68-69:** Godfrey Argent. **71:** Charles Barieau. **72, 73:** GR. **74:** Godfrey Argent. **76:** Godfrey Argent. **77:** GR. **78-79:** Godfrey Argent. **81:** Godfrey Argent.

Chapter 4

82-83: Jerry Cooke. **85:** Jerry Cooke/Rapho-Photo Researchers. **86, 87:** Stephen Kuni. **88:** Budd Studios. **90-91:** GR. **92:** Bank Langmore. **94:** Jerry Cooke. **95:** Hope Ryden. **98, 99:** GR. **100-101:** GR. **102:** John Keene Studio. **103:** GR. **104-105:** GR. **108:** GR. **110, 111:** GR. **113.** GR.

Chapter 5

114-115: GR. **117:** Elizabeth Weiland/Rapho-Photo Researchers. **118, 119:** GR. **120:** GR. **123:** GR. **124, 125:** GR. **126, 127:** Stephen Kuni. **128, 129:** GR. **130:** (top) GR; (bottom) Werner Müller/Peter Arnold. **132, 133:** Elizabeth Weiland/Rapho-Photo Researchers. **134-135:** Elizabeth Weiland/Rapho-Photo Researchers. **136:** Werner Müller/Peter Arnold. **137:** GR. **138-139:** Marshall P. Hawkins. **140, 141:** Elizabeth Weiland/Rapho-Photo Researchers. **142-143:** Jerry Cooke. **145:** GR.

Chapter 6

146-147: GR. **149:** (top) Clive Hiles; (bottom) GR. **150-151:** William Albert Allard. **152, 153:** GR. **154, 155:** GR. **156-157:** (top) GR; (bottom) GR. **158-159:** Jerry Cooke. **162, 163:** Melchior DiGiacomo. **165:** GR.

Chapter 7

166-167: Jerry Cooke. **169:** Horst Schäfer/Photo Trends. **170-171:** Jack Fields/Rapho-Photo Researchers. **172, 173:** Godfrey Argent. **174-175:** Jack Karpen/Photo Trends. **176, 177:** GR. **178-179:** GR. **180:** Jerry Cooke. **183:** Horst Schäfer/Photo Trends. **185:** Jerry Cooke.

Chapter 8

186-187: Bank Langmore. **189:** GR. **190:** Guy Gillette/Rapho-Photo Researchers. **191:** Tessa Papas. **192-193:** Godfrey Argent. **194, 195:** GR. **196-197:** GR. **198-199:** GR. **200, 201:** GR. **202-203:** Photo Trends. **204-205:** GR. **207:** Godfrey Argent. **208:** Godfrey Argent. **209:** Peter Shand. **210-211:** GR. **212-213:** Bank Langmore. **214-215:** Bank Langmore. **217:** Bank Langmore.

Chapter 9

218-219: Marshall P. Hawkins. **221:** *London Express.* **222-223:** H. R. H. Prince Philip. **224-225:** Godfrey Argent. **226-227:** Jay Simon/Amwest. **228, 229:** Jay Simon/Amwest. **230, 231:** James Fain/Amwest. **232-233:** Jay Simon/Amwest. **234-235:** Jay Simon/Amwest. **236:** Jay Simon/Amwest. **237:** James Fain/Amwest. **238:** Jay Simon/Amwest. **240-241:** GR. **242, 243:** GR. **246-247:** Marshall P. Hawkins.

Index

Caption references in italics